THE LAST AND LONGEST FAREWELL

The war ended for different men in different ways. Green Mountain men from Vermont who are still living gaze sadly on reminders of their comrades for whom the conflict is already done. Photographer G.H. Houghton captured the living and the dead at this temporary cemetery at Lee's Mills, Virginia, in 1862, but it is an image that could speak for men anywhere in the divided country, and at any time. For so many by 1865, the real glory, the real victory, was just to have survived.

The End of an Era

VOLUME SIX OF

The Image of War
1861-1865

EDITOR
WILLIAM C. DAVIS

SENIOR CONSULTING EDITOR
BELL I. WILEY

PHOTOGRAPHIC CONSULTANTS
WILLIAM A. FRASSANITO
MANUEL KEAN
LLOYD OSTENDORF
FREDERIC RAY

EDITORIAL ASSISTANTS
DEBORAH A. BERRIER
KAREN K. KENNEDY
DENISE MUMMERT
JAMES RIETMULDER

A Project of
The National Historical Society

Gettysburg, Pennsylvania
ROBERT H. FOWLER, Founder

EDITOR
WILLIAM C. DAVIS

SENIOR CONSULTING EDITOR
BELL I. WILEY

The End of an Era

VOLUME SIX OF

The Image of War
1861-1865

DOUBLEDAY & COMPANY, INC.
GARDEN CITY, NEW YORK
1984

OVERLEAF: The end of the long road at last. For four years the cry in blue had been "On to Richmond!" At last, in April 1865, they were there, the Stars and Stripes flying once more over the former Confederate Capitol. The Confederates themselves were gone, their cause, like much of Richmond, in ruins. (NATIONAL ARCHIVES)

Library of Congress Cataloging in Publication Data
Main entry under title:

The End of an era.

(The Image of war, 1861–1865; v. 6)
"A project of the National Historical Society"—P.
Includes index.
1. United States—History—Civil War, 1861–1865—
Campaigns—Addresses, essays, lectures.   2. United
States—History—Civil War, 1861–1865—Photography—
Addresses, essays, lectures.   3. United States—
History—Civil War, 1861–1865—Naval operations—
Addresses, essays, lectures.   I. Davis, William C., 1946–
II. National Historical Society.
III. Series.
E470.E52   1984   973.7
ISBN: 0-385-18282-1
Library of Congress Catalog Card Number 82-45884

Contents

PETERSBURG BESIEGED
AFTER THREE YEARS THE UNION FINALLY HAS LEE AT BAY,
BUT THE QUARRY GOES TO GROUND AND GRANT CAN ONLY WAIT
Richard J. Sommers
182

RICHMOND, CITY AND CAPITAL AT WAR
SYMBOL OF THE CONFEDERACY, THE VIRGINIA METROPOLIS
FIGHTS TO THE LAST
Emory M. Thomas
275

AN END AT LAST
WHEN BLOOD AND BRAVERY AND INDOMITABLE WILL COULD DO NO MORE,
THE SOUTHERN BANNERS WERE FURLED
Louis Manarin
324

THE "LATE UNPLEASANTNESS"
THE WAR DONE, THERE WAS PEACE TO WAGE, AND BATTLES ANEW
WITH THE HATREDS REMAINING, AND CHALLENGES AHEAD
FOR A NATION REUNITING
William C. Davis
363

Abbreviations
451

The Contributors
453

Index
455

A NOTE ON THE SOURCES: A credit line accompanies each photograph in this volume. Each source is written out in full when first cited, but those sources that contributed many photographs are thereafter abbreviated. A list of abbreviations is included at the end of this volume. We would especially like to acknowledge the generosity of the sources on this list.

Introduction

WILLIAM C. DAVIS

NEVER HAD AMERICA traveled a longer road than the course from Sumter to Appomattox, but as 1864 wore on into 1865 the agonizing journey seemed at last coming to a conclusion. All along the way Americans North and South had erected their own peculiar milestones marking the path—Antietam, the bloodiest day; Shiloh, the most ferocious battle; Gettysburg, the greatest and bloodiest fight. All along the way they had left their friends and comrades who could not see it through—the beloved James B. McPherson, the brilliant Stonewall Jackson, the unsung and irreplaceable private soldiers in their legions. Yet still it was not done. With the scent of victory driving them on, the men of the Union resolved that not another winter would come without peace. Defiant in the face of certain defeat, their adversaries still rallied their courage and their blood, led by the spirit of one Charlestonian who proclaimed that "we intend to die hard." Die they would. And hard.

They died at Petersburg for nearly a year. They died in Virginia's deceptively tranquil Shenandoah Valley, in the Carolinas, in the defenses of Richmond, and all along the roads that led to Appomattox. When the time came at last to yield, victor and vanquished equaled one an-

other in dignity and magnanimity. And in the long and difficult years that were to follow, while old bonds once broken did not heal without scars, yet the nation reunited grew in prosperity and power to become a world leader, made so in large measure by its adolescent years of bloody sibling rivalry.

The cost had been terrible. Nearly two thirds of a million men lay dead in the fields and roadsides and cemeteries of North and South. Half a million more embarked upon the peace carrying on their bodies the scars or maiming wounds of war. Half the nation lay in ruins, thousands of the defeated were fleeing the country, four million slaves were free with nowhere to go and nothing to do, and a great man who might have eased all the pain to come, died on a bed too short to hold his long and lanky body. The world had watched as section tore at the vitals of section. Now nations would look with equal concern to see if an America reunited could survive its convalescence. For all the certainties made clear by the outcome of the war, it created as well a host of doubts. It had, indeed, brought about the end of an era. But what did it begin? Only the generations to come could answer that.

It would also be up to generations ahead to

decide if the men who recorded that war with their cameras had been successful, if their effort and sacrifice had been worth the investment. Certainly the question remained in doubt at war's end. For all the hundreds of photographers who plied their craft during the conflict, not one made any sort of fortune out of it. Mathew Brady, the best known of the entrepreneurs, emerged with a reputation out of all proportion to his deeds, and with debts that threatened to eclipse him. He would never again enjoy his pre-war prosperity when he was the portrait photographer to the wealthy and influential. His competitors—some of them former assistants to him—like Alexander Gardner and Timothy O'Sullivan and George N. Barnard would attempt to sell their war views in portfolios and books, but with very limited success. Others like Samuel Cooley seem to have all but abandoned their trade when the war ceased and their army contracts expired. The Confederate photographers, of course, were out of business almost to a man. A few reemerged. George S. Cook continued in his portrait business in the South, and Jay D. Edwards moved from New Orleans to Atlanta and reestablished a prosperous trade. But they were few. Only the New York firm of E. & H. T. Anthony truly profited from all the effort, and even it saw its sales of war views diminish rapidly when public tastes changed. Economically, the photographing of the Civil War was on the whole a failure. At best, solely from the vantage of profit and loss, it had not been worth the effort.

Yet that seems not to have mattered to the true craftsmen, the men with more than a vision of sales receipts. Brady would spend a lifetime trying to convince the Federal government that it owed it to him to buy his views and relieve him of his indebtedness. Alexander Gardner and O'Sullivan and the others accepted their losses, softening them with at least the satisfaction of having created the finest body of work yet seen in their craft, and were anxious to move on, out to the West or out into the world, to continue their work. They knew what they had done, that it had been good work and more than worth the dangers, the hardships, and even the financial disappointments. Where Brady's eye lay chiefly on prosperity, they seem to have favored posterity the more.

And what a legacy they left! No one will ever know with certainty, but it is not outrageous to estimate that over one million photographs were made from 1861 through 1865 as a direct result of the war. After all, with over three thousand photographers in the business in 1861, each one needed to make barely seventy images a year to achieve that million. With about three million men in uniform during the war, most of them anxious to have a visual record of their service, the estimate is if anything conservative. Of course, probably 98 percent of all the images made were just that, portraits, most of them recorded by now unknown local artists in hometowns or else by itinerant cameramen who came to camps or followed the armies. Only the very smallest percentage of the scenes made are the views of men in camp and on the march, of generals and their staffs posing at headquarters, of the dead sprawled in the trenches and the wounded suffering in hospitals or languishing in prison pens. But they are all, of whatever kind, images of war. Rarely have so few left so much.

Looking backward, surveying the body of work created by these artists, we have to be impressed with the limits to which they stretched the known technology and application of their craft. The camera went to war in the mid-1840s, when an unknown daguerreotypist made a score or more of images during the war with Mexico. Englishman Roger Fenton made two or three hundred views in the Crimea during the conflict there a decade later. Yet it remained for the coming of the American Civil War for the camera itself to become a weapon and tool of war, an ever-present concomitant of the armies. The lens went to sea, on the march, perhaps up in the air in balloons, into the hospitals and prisons, into courtrooms, bombproofs, winter quarters, the testing laboratories, the ruins of cities and farms. The faces of victory and defeat were forever changed by the men who took their cameras to war.

Though all were remarkable in their way, some artists and some special portions of their work must still stand out for all time as above and apart from the rest, representing men—and women—of a special vision that transcended their time and place. R. M. Linn will always be remembered as "Linn of Lookout," the stylish man who perched his gallery atop Lookout Mountain and made his images with the great Tennessee Valley as his backdrop, making even the most ordinary soldier portrait rise above itself. Mary Reed of Quincy, Illinois, was probably the first, and maybe the only, Northern woman to ply the photographer's trade during the war, one she would follow for decades. The Confederacy, too, had a woman photographer in New Orleans at war's outset.

No one can ever forget the story of George S. Cook, perching his camera atop the rubble of Fort Sumter to photograph the enemy ironclad fleet even as those ships hurled their fire at the parapet where he stood. Georgia photographer A. J. Riddle will be forever remembered for taking his instrument to Andersonville in 1864 to record the eloquently tragic views of a Civil War prison at its squalid, horrible nadir. Though his name will never be remembered, Montgomery, Alabama, artist A. C. McIntyre earned himself a place among the great graphic historians of all time when he sensed the importance of Jefferson Davis' inauguration as Confederate President and took his camera outdoors to record the scene.

It was that special sense of the historic, exemplified by McIntyre, that set these men and women apart. Jay D. Edwards, the war's first photographer, who took one hundred or more views of Confederates at Pensacola, Florida, early in 1861, had that special sense. So did the enterprising Brownsville, Texas, artist who took his camera outdoors to record the scenes of the Southern evacuation of the town in the face of a Federal advance. So did the Cairo, Illinois, photographer who captured the scene as the great ironclad fleets were built and loosed on the Mississippi to conquer the mighty river. So did McPherson & Oliver, Armistead & White, Haas & Peale, Levy & Cohen, and the several other partnerships that left behind their trail of silvery and sepia memories. And so, of course, for all his financial motivation, did Mathew Brady.

Alas, they were all a bit too far ahead of their time, for despite the wartime fever to acquire images of events at the front or of loved ones absent in uniform, the rush to buy and own the artists' work did not sustain itself. Technology and public tastes changed too rapidly. Formats different from those of the war soon became the rage, Americans were too busy rebuilding and expanding their nation to dwell overmuch on images of the past, and there were too many wounds and hatreds to forget. Besides, the West was being won, and this was what Americans now wanted to see in their stereoscope viewers.

We will never know just how much of their invaluable work the frustrated photographers may have thrown out or destroyed when it proved not to be salable. Stories would be passed down, to later generations, of wholesale burnings, of scraping emulsion from glass plates to reuse the glass, of ambrotypes robbed of their images by being re-treated with chemicals to expose new images over the old. We will never know how many priceless scrapbooks, albums, and private collections amassed during the war have simply disappeared in attic dust, the trashman's bin, or through simple neglect. The treasures lost are probably incalculable.

But so are the treasures preserved. When Major General George G. Meade failed to pursue Lee's army vigorously and destroy it after Gettysburg, Lincoln was at first furious, but then realized that he must be grateful for what was achieved rather than remorseful over what was not. So, too, must we be thankful for what survives, not dolorous for that now lost. And besides, every now and then the "lost" has a way of being "found" again. Thus nearly a century after Lincoln's death was the only photo taken of him in his casket rediscovered. Thus only now have we found the secret images made of dreaded Confederate commerce raiders in foreign ports, taken to advise Union authorities of what they looked like. It gives us cause to hope that still lurking out there somewhere are more priceless pictures waiting to be found. So many more must have been made. Norfolk, Virginia, had its share of photographers in 1861 and 1862. Certainly, as the mighty ironclad CSS *Virginia* was being fashioned out of the old *Merrimack*, one of them at least must have taken his camera down to the dry dock to make an image of what was already the most famous ship on the continent. And perhaps, too, he took his apparatus to the nearby shore of Hampton Roads to record —admittedly at a fair distance—the *Virginia's* epic battles. So, too, is it with her arch rival. Several images were made on deck aboard the USS *Monitor,* yet how strange it is that no image has survived showing the entire ship itself. How could artist James Gibson make all those deck views without capturing the ship as a whole?

What of the CSS *Alabama?* It has never been a secret that Cherbourg photographer François Rondin made one or more views from the shore while the Confederate raider fought her last battle against the USS *Kearsarge.* Rondin's images were exhibited in shop windows and commented upon in the local press. But where are they now? Surely one print still survives, perhaps in France, perhaps in a drawer or attic of some descendant of a Yankee seaman who bought a memento of the greatest day of his life. The "lost" photos of Lincoln known to have been made are numerous, and every few years another one is at last found. Supposedly an image was made of his dead murderer, John Wilkes Booth, taken aboard a Federal monitor at Washington. Where is it? And, of course, there is always the hope that an elusive, genuine photograph of men in actual combat may have been made. It is doubtful, but just possible. The dangers would have been considerable, the technical difficulties substantial, but the photographers were accustomed to all that. Of course, if such an image had been made successfully, its artist would almost certainly have had it instantly mass produced for what would have been an enormous sale. The fact that no one did so argues persuasively against such battle scenes having been taken. But it is always possible, and that tempting possibility is all that is needed for photo historians to keep up the search.

Indeed, one of the frustrating—if happy, just the same—aspects of editing and publishing this series *The Image of War: 1861–1865* has been the fact that no sooner does a volume appear than more images that should have been included at last come to light, too late to use. As a matter of fact, even as this final volume is going through the publisher's hands, several thousand of the photographs originally published in

Francis T. Miller's ten-volume 1911 landmark *Photographic History of the Civil War,* have resurfaced. Long thought to be lost or destroyed, they have come back from oblivion, perhaps to be published again.

Meanwhile, the rest of what is known to remain is being well cared for, at least as much as understaffed and underfunded archives can manage. The grandfather of all collections, of course, is the mammoth forty-thousand-image Massachusetts Commandery of the Military Order of the Loyal Legion of the United States (MOLLUS) collection, now exquisitely housed and maintained at the U.S. Army Military History Institute at Carlisle Barracks, Pennsylvania. Rarely used and little known before it came to the institute in 1972, the collection is simply priceless, its condition near perfect, its coverage of the war and its figures more comprehensive than any other.

Not as large, yet unique in its own right, is the collection at Cleveland's Western Reserve Historical Society. Though it duplicates much of what is at the institute, still it has its specialties, most notably the several volumes of unmounted stereoscopic views made by the engaging Samuel Cooley, most of them unpublished. The New-York Historical Society has yet another collection duplicating much of the above, yet with its share of unique items. Of course, the collections of the Library of Congress in Washington, D.C., are considerable, including the Brady negatives purchased from the old photographer many years after the war. And the National Archives, also in Washington, holds a substantial body of images, many of them often overlooked.

Surely the Chicago Historical Society's thousand-image collection must be classed among the great ones, despite its relatively small size, for it contains a host of things simply not available elsewhere. Tulane University, in New Orleans, holds the largest collection of outdoor Confederate views; Louisiana State University holds the very important collection of A. D. Lytle's views of Baton Rouge and the Mississippi; and the Museum of the Confederacy and the Valentine Museum, both in Richmond, Virginia, hold between them the greatest body of Confederate portraits extant.

There are special collections all across the

country. General Meade's personal photo books rest along with several volumes of other excellent material in the Pennsylvania Commandery of the MOLLUS at its War Library and Museum in Philadelphia. The Illinois State Historical Library in Springfield holds a priceless body of cartes de visite views of Port Hudson. The Kean Archives in Philadelphia holds thousands of portraits and special views, and one of the great untapped treasuries in the nation resides at the Naval Historical Center at the Washington (D.C.) Navy Yard, where thousands of Civil War portraits of ships, men, and officers are accurately identified and filed, for public use.

The list could go on for some time. Barring calamity and the simple ravages of time, the photographic legacy of the American Civil War will be maintained and preserved for a long time to come in these storehouses of history. What is not there is largely in the hands of the small army of collectors and antiquarians who prize these treasures in their own special way. A few of the private collections number more than a thousand images, and given the specialization of subject material by some collectors, the rarities and unique items abound. A brisk trade throughout the country—indeed, throughout the world—is done in buying and selling and exchanging photographs as collections grow or disperse. So long as that interest survives, so will more and more of the old images be rescued from oblivion or destruction.

And so, too, will be the memory of the men who made them. We still know so woefully little about them. The biographies of Alexander Gardner and his brother James, of Timothy O'Sullivan, of Egbert G. Fowx, Jay D. Edwards, Osborn & Durbec, James Reekie, G. H. Houghton, and a host of others are still pathetically sparse. Indeed, for most of them the only documents we have from which to limn their lives are the photos they left behind. Mostly they went West like Alexander Gardner and O'Sullivan, returned to their studio portrait business like Lytle, or just left the trade entirely. By the time the veterans of the war were coming into their own, in the 1880s and later, the photographers had already been all but forgotten.

Perhaps in the wake of *The Image of War* they will be remembered once more. It is our earnest hope. From the beginning, more than a decade ago, a major aim of this series has been to return to prominence the men who were the first real historians of the conflict and whose work is still the most accurate. It is humbling to realize that it has taken us twice as long to produce this series as it took North and South to fight their war, yet we could take twice times twice that time and still not find everything we would want, still not correct every old error or catch every new one. As we said in introducing the first volume of this series, *Shadows of the Storm*, back in 1981, we are only part of the continuum of work in the field, not the final culmination of all of it. And we expect to do more.

It has been great fun along the way, and more enlightening than most experiences of a lifetime. The serious scholars and friendly folk encountered have been uniformly kind and helpful. What pleasure there has been in sitting back and watching William A. Frassanito, chief consultant, at his painstaking work. Truly the father of modern photographic historiography of the war, he never leaped at the easy conclusion, or let the desire that we all share to make a great "find" overcome his natural caution in identifying an image. His own work will stand for years, and we are delighted that in its own way *The Image of War* may be counted a part of it. What a joy it was working with Bell I. Wiley, friend and mentor, one of the last of the great old Southern historians, as we searched for authors and refined the editorial concept.

And always there was the search, the tantalizing possibility that under the next page or in the next dusty box might lie some treasure. Perhaps that thrill can only be felt by someone who has worked for years in the photographic record of the war. To the layman, the finding of an additional wartime portrait in uniform of Sterling Price or Joseph E. Johnston may seem of no consequence. But to someone who knows that for over a century there had been only a single existing pose of each of them, the discovery of new ones is like walking on the moon. To begin the project knowing that fewer than a hundred outdoor Confederate views were known to exist and then unexpectedly open a box to find almost fifty new ones is something that cannot be described. Columbus may have felt it when one of his sailors shouted "Land ho!" But then, unlike ours, his discovery was inevitable. It is rather difficult to accidentally overlook North America.

To be sure, there have been disappointments along the way. Hopes aroused by the promise of some image of astounding importance have been dashed upon our discovering that it was not what was supposed. We thought briefly that we had discovered a new image of Lincoln, but we did not. We thought we had one of Rondin's *Alabama* photographs, but we were wrong. More than once we crowed over the discovery of a view of some Confederate regiment drawn up for the camera, only to discover that it was a post-war militia outfit dressed in gray.

But viewed over the decade-long project, the disappointments seem very small indeed. There was never a time when we did not know in our hearts that *The Image of War* was something that would come to be and that it would be worth the time and effort invested in the project. The germ of the idea originated when the recently acquired, but not yet unpacked, vol-umes of the Massachusetts MOLLUS collection came to the Institute. Continually over a period of three or four years the concept and outline evolved, aided always by the vocal enthusiasm of everyone with whom it was discussed. It was a dream shared by thousands far beyond our little editorial walls. And now that the dream is realized, there is a certain sadness, almost a reluctance to let go this final volume, for it *is* final. As in saying a last farewell to an old and dear friend, we are loath to part. This volume represents, not just for *The Image of War,* but as well for those who conceived and produced it, truly the "end of an era."

Yet, after all, endings only make way for beginnings. There is more to do, more to find. Those first steps on the moon did not end the discovery of the heavens; they just began it. For us, as for those who explore the universe, there are whole worlds yet to find. A spirit in our feet still says "go," as it did to Mathew Brady a century and more past. A spirit in our hearts still says "seek," and we always shall.

The Modern Army

RUSSELL F. WEIGLEY

Years of war, of trial and error, produce at last
a fighting machine in the shape of things to come

WHEN Major General William Tecumseh Sherman's Union armies of the West emerged at Savannah to complete their march across Georgia from Atlanta to the sea in December 1864, a full reoutfitting of quartermaster supplies awaited the force of some 60,000 men. "Clothing, shoes, shelter tents, forage, provisions, spare parts of wagons, wagons complete, harness, leather, wax, thread, needles, and tools for all the trades which were plied on the march and in the camp were collected in the harbor of Hilton Head," reported Quartermaster General Montgomery C. Meigs. As soon as naval vessels off the coast reported Sherman's storming of Fort McAllister, a great quartermaster fleet set out for the mouth of the Savannah River with these supplies.

After seeing Sherman's soldiers warmly clothed, the fleet steamed northward again, laden with captured cotton for the Union's mills and the fabrication of more cloth. "All this," the quartermaster general added, "was done in the dead of winter. Light-draft, frail river-steamers trusted themselves, under daring Yankee captains and crews, to the storms of the stormiest coast of the world, and all arrived safely at their destination."

General Meigs considered the replenishing of

Sherman's armies the climax of the Union logistical operations of the Civil War, the proof positive that the United States Army had come of age as a finely geared yet immensely powerful machine that could exert its power across almost any distance. Meigs took equal pride in the knowledge that simultaneous with the sailing of the fleet to Sherman, quartermaster vessels were also sustaining other Union detachments all along the Southern coast from Virginia to Texas. To keep in the field the armies with which Lieutenant General Ulysses S. Grant was laying siege to Petersburg and Richmond, the Quartermaster Department had transformed City Point, Virginia, into one of the largest seaports of the world. On an average day forty steamships, seventy-five sailing vessels, and a hundred barges unloaded their cargoes at wharves there running for more than a mile along the James River and extending up the Appomattox River. Behind the wharves sprawled huge warehouses and open storage areas for all kinds of quartermaster stores —the uniforms, tents, forage, and so on that Meigs had also supplied to Sherman at Savannah —as well as the commissary, medical, and ordnance stores that were procured by departments other than Meigs's but transported by the quar-

Acting as adjutant general, one of the most important posts in the U.S. Army, responsible for communicating with and directing much of the enterprise of making war, was Brigadier General Lorenzo Thomas. Unlike Stanton, he proved sufficiently ineffective for the Secretary to order him out of Washington in 1863 and keep him on the road thereafter. (USAMHI)

Managing the U.S. War Department was the humorless but unfailingly effective Secretary of War Edwin M. Stanton. A master of organization, he oversaw the transformation of his department into a virtual war machine. (U.S. ARMY MILITARY HISTORY INSTITUTE)

termaster to the front—the army's foodstuffs, medicines, and row on row of cannon, pile on pile of rifle bullets and cannon shot and shell. From the City Point depots the United States Military Railroads, a branch of Meigs's department, operated a twenty-one-mile railroad all along the rear of Grant's lines south of the Appomattox. The trains that carried supplies to the lines returned with the wounded, who went first to a two-hundred-acre, ten-thousand-bed military hospital on a high bluff above the Appomattox.

Before the war, City Point had been the eastern terminus of Virginia's Southside Railroad,

and the military railroad used seven miles of the Southside's right of way between City Point and Petersburg. But these seven miles had had to be almost completely rebuilt (and the gauge altered from five feet to the newly standard four feet, eight and a half inches), while the bulk of the military railroad was altogether new, including all the repair facilities to keep the cars rolling. By late 1864, however, railroad operation, construction, and reconstruction were routine activities for the Quartermaster Department. In the West, during Sherman's advance from Chattanooga to Atlanta, eleven bridges were reconstructed and seventy-five miles of completely new track laid, with many more miles of track re-

An adjutant was stationed with each army as well, and every general and even colonel had an adjutant to transmit his orders, manage his paperwork, and frequently act as his amanuensis. With the Army of the Potomac, it was Brigadier General Seth Williams, who was later made a major general in recognition of his able services. (WAR LIBRARY AND MUSEUM, MOLLUS-PENNSYLVANIA)

It was to be a war far different from that known by the aged Union General-in-Chief Winfield Scott, and though he left active service in 1861, many of the old ideas that he represented lingered on in what was to be a modern war. (USAMHI)

paired. The Railroad Construction Corps typically began the rebuilding of a bridge over the Oostenaula River while the old bridge was still burning, the work being slightly delayed "because the iron rods were so hot that the men could not touch them to remove the wreck." When General John Bell Hood's Confederate army subsequently tore up twenty-seven miles of track in a spectacular raid, the Construction Corps had the break repaired in seven and a half

days. To ease such rebuilding, the Quartermaster Department took over an uncompleted Confederate mill at Chattanooga for the rolling of rails.

For the accumulating and transporting of the vast quantities of military stores depicted in the photographs of Union Army depots, the mighty industrial capacity of the North obviously underlay such improvisations near the front as the reopened Chattanooga rolling mill and the transformation of City Point into a bustling seaport. Apart from the Union Army's sheer size—probably over two million men served in it dur-

*Here in Washington, D.C., was the hub of the giant military wheel created
by the Union to ride down the rebellion. The War Department stands at left
and the Navy Department at right. Calling forth millions of men and
hundreds of millions of dollars, they brought victory through organization.*
(USAMHI)

ing the course of the war and slightly over a
million were on its muster rolls when the war
ended—the most modern dimension of the army
was the lavishness of its subsistence and equipment.

As early as December 1861 Brigadier General
Irvin McDowell testified that "a French army of
half the size of ours could be supplied with what
we waste." Meigs began the war by establishing
wagon transport beyond the railroads on a scale
based on Napoleon's allocations of wagons to
his troops. This scale proved much too limited.
It demanded too much dependence on subsisting

off the country through which the Union armies
campaigned to permit the swift mobility over
great distances needed to conquer the Confederacy. Brigadier General Rufus Ingalls, through
much of the war Chief Quartermaster of the
Army of the Potomac, led the way in developing
more generous allowances of transport wagons
and supplies for the wagons to carry. Meigs responded by investigating more current French
practice and adapting it to make further enlarge-
ments and improvements. By the time of his
marches late in the war, Sherman, though he was
famous for traveling light, was employing three

*Washington itself became a major center for army services. Massive
government repair shops like these, shown in April 1865, were established to
keep the armies moving.* (USAMHI)

times as many wagons as Napoleon had used for a similar number of men.

The Union Army could be outfitted and sustained on a scale unprecedented in world military history because behind it lay an economy well into the Industrial Revolution and rich in agriculture as well, the whole economy bound together by railroads. The industrial and transportation capacities of the North had advanced far enough for the Union Army to be the first mass army to be supplied on a scale comparable to that of the armies of the twentieth-century world wars.

Saying that about the Union Army, however, like examining the pictures of its supply depots, risks suggesting the cliché that because of the North's economic strength, the South never had a chance of winning the war. The North's industrial and agricultural wealth, and the Union

Army's becoming through that wealth the first modern mass army in the plenitude of its resources, probably did not carry quite that much importance for the outcome of the war. Notwithstanding the logistical modernity of the Union Army, the Civil War, unlike World War II, cannot be described as a "gross-national-product war," in which the decisive issue was which belligerent could outproduce the other. In World War II the productive capacity of the United States permitted the Allied coalition to bury the Axis under a sheer weight of armaments—an insurmountable tide of tanks, big guns, big ships, airplanes, shells, and bombs. The Union Army in the Civil War, for all its modernity, did not have modern arms. The weapons of the 1860s were still simple enough—mainly muzzle-loading rifles and single-shot cannon—for the Confederacy to produce or otherwise acquire enough of

Hundreds of men were employed at keeping animals shod, not least at the government horse shoeing shop. (USAMHI)

to put up a pretty equal contest on the battlefield. The material plenty of the North and of the Union Army applied less directly to the clash of arms than to the enhancement of Union morale and the gradual erosion of Confederate morale.

Nor did the North's economic strength by itself guarantee the lavishness and modernity of the Union Army's sustenance, clothing, and equipment. The experience of Great Britain in the Crimean War less than a decade earlier showed that even the most advanced industrial nation of the nineteenth-century world, seconded by the world's largest merchant fleet and navy in using maritime lines of communication, could not support a modern army in the field if the army's own administration was antiquated and incompetent. British economic power notwithstanding, British army strength in the Crimea fell from about 42,000 to about 12,000

effectives in less than a year because British military staffs were too dull-witted and disorganized to maintain the physical health and well-being of the larger force. Thus the Union Army's administrators and logisticians merit considerable credit for translating the economic potential for ample military supplies into reality.

Quartermaster General Meigs deserves the foremost share of this credit. Not a modest man, he described his job of procuring all the Union Army's supplies except ordnance, foodstuffs, and medical items, and transporting everything, including the three latter categories, as the second most important position in the Army, next only to the post of general-in-chief. His assessment was correct. Many of Meigs's lieutenants in the field accomplished similarly impressive work within their spheres, especially Ingalls and the railroad men Colonel Daniel C. McCallum and Brigadier General Herman Haupt. McCallum

*Mechanics at the government repair shops pose for the camera, armed with
the weapons of their war—wrenches, mauls, hammers, and leather aprons.*
(USAMHI)

was director of the United States Military Railroads, Haupt director of railroads in the northeastern theater of war through much of 1862
and 1863.

The Union Secretaries of War contributed
much also, even the frequently abused Simon
Cameron. It is true that Cameron presided over
the initial outfitting of the Union Army with excessive financial laxity and excessive regard for
rewarding political friends. As Quartermaster
General Meigs put it, however, in responding to
criticisms of the quality of the materials purchased when the Army's numbers of men multiplied twenty-seven times during the first four
months—a growth much more rapid than that of
either world war—"the troops were clothed and

rescued from severe suffering, and those who
saw sentinels walking post in the capital of the
United States in freezing weather in their draw-
ers, without trousers or overcoats, will not blame
the department for its efforts to clothe them,
even in materials not quite so durable as army
blue kersey." Cameron accomplished more than
is sometimes acknowledged toward creating the
army of which General McDowell could testify,
while Cameron still headed the War Department: "There never was an army in the world
that began to be supplied as well as ours is."

Cameron's more efficient successor, Secretary
of War Edwin M. Stanton, contributed much to
the continuing workability of the whole administrative and logistical system. The contributions

It was the same at the government trimming shop, where leather and canvas were fitted to make awnings and harnesses and whatever else needed to be "trimmed." (USAMHI)

of such individuals to Union military supply have to be stressed because success was achieved largely through a triumph of human talents over organizational arrangements that were not much better than those that wrecked the British Army in the Crimea. The various supply bureaus of the United States Army and the related administrative bureaus—the Adjutant General's Department, the Inspector General's Department, the Judge Advocate General's Department, and the Pay Department—along with the Corps of Engineers and the newly created Signal Corps, each habitually had gone its own way with little overall coordination, let alone any combined planning for the development of a coherent supply system for the entire army. Called the General Staff, the heads of these departments in no way constituted the slightest approximation of a modern general staff in the sense of a planning body. It was Stanton's contribution to the making of a modern army that by dominating the War Department, not through the medium of organization charts, but by force of an overpowering, even sometimes ruthless personality, he imposed a functional coordination upon the administrative and supply bureaus. Without him, Civil War logistics in the Union Army might well have been as chaotic as those of the later Spanish-American War, for the relationships among the bureaus were otherwise the same as in 1898.

*There were special government shops for repairing and fitting out
ambulances, its glum-looking crew wielding their squares and saws, augurs
and broadaxes.* (USAMHI)

Stanton had to deal also with the problem of establishing a modern command system for the combat operations of an army modern in scale. A lawyer by profession, he could intervene to less direct effect in the technical military issues of combat than in administration because combat was too far removed from his own expertise. The regulations of the Army, furthermore, seemed to confine the jurisdiction of the Secretary of War to administration and finance, leaving combat command to the ranking military professional, the general-in-chief—though thus excluding the President's civilian deputy raised questions involving the constitutional principle of civilian control of the military. When to these various difficulties was added the fact that a capable combat commander for an army of from half a million to a million men is never easy to

find, most of the war had been fought before the command system of the Union Army matched the effectiveness of the Army's administration and logistics.

In the beginning, the general-in-chief was Brevet Lieutenant General Winfield Scott, who had occupied this lofty post for twenty years and had been a general officer since the War of 1812. A hero of the latter war and of his great campaign from Vera Cruz to the City of Mexico in the Mexican War, Scott had grown fat, dropsical, and tired by 1861. His military brain was still good, and he was the principal designer of the "Anaconda Plan" for strangling the Confederacy by naval blockade as well as pressure by land. But as a strategist Scott had always favored the pre-Napoleonic, eighteenth-century mode of limited war, and even if he had been younger

The blacksmiths were probably more numerous than the rest, for they worked in iron, and it was a war fought on iron—iron rails, iron rims, iron horseshoes. (USAMHI)

and more vigorous, he might never have developed enough ruthlessness to seek that utter destruction of Confederate armies and resources which was probably necessary to achieve so sweeping a war aim as the complete extinction of Confederate claims to independence.

President Abraham Lincoln therefore acquiesced when a much younger and seemingly much more vigorous soldier, Major General George B. McClellan, maneuvered Scott aside in November 1861. Already commanding the Army of the Potomac, McClellan moved up to be general-in-chief as well. Unfortunately for the Union, McClellan's youth—he was only thirty-five—proved to assure no more resolution than Scott had shown when it came to risking bold in-

vasions of the South; and if ruthlessness was needed, McClellan possessed less of that commodity than the old man. McClellan at least recognized, however, that an overall strategy would be necessary for the winning of the war, that it was not enough simply to have tactical ideas for the winning of particular battles; and for this reason, "Little Mac" despite his faults was a better choice for the top Union command than most of the available generals would have been.

Yet McClellan proved to lack a narrower but essential ingredient of generalship—the tactical skills to win the particular battles. Consequently he could not give his strategic design—to push the Confederacy militarily just hard enough to

Another small legion of workers fought with brushes, their battlefield the government paint shop. They stand, buckets and brushes in hand, posing with a pile of wheels and boxes awaiting their attention. (USAMHI)

convince the South it could not win, while otherwise conciliating the Southerners with promises of the safety of their property, especially slavery —a real test to demonstrate whether it could work. Lincoln became dissatisfied with McClellan and removed him from the office of general-in-chief as early as March 11, 1862, though for the time being he permitted the general to keep command of the Army of the Potomac. Finding, however, no one else with a strategic grasp comparable to McClellan's, Lincoln now undertook the direct, personal exercise of the role of Commander in Chief, giving orders to the armies himself, with Stanton's help.

In the process, Lincoln oversaw the riposte to Major General Thomas J. "Stonewall" Jackson's

Valley Campaign, and the maneuvers he designed might have trapped Jackson had the President enjoyed better cooperation from the Union generals on the scene. Jackson's escape, however, helped prove that Lincoln had too many other duties to be able to exercise sufficiently precise direct command over field forces, so the President decided he had to find a new professional general-in-chief, notwithstanding the dearth of strategists. He turned to an officer who had at least written and translated books about strategy, Major General Henry Wager Halleck. As commander of much of the Western theater of war from November 1861 to Lincoln's choosing him as general-in-chief in July 1862, Halleck had shown only the most limited promise of trans-

Nearby the wheelwrights work at making and repairing the wheels that the painters paint. Downtown Washington was a sea of enterprise as the government repair shops proliferated. (USAMHI)

forming book learning into strategic accomplishment. Still, he merited some of the credit for his subordinate Grant's Fort Henry, Fort Donelson, and Shiloh campaigns, and all in all he was the most suitable choice on the horizon.

Halleck reinforced the War Department's administrative skills, and his presence assured yet further that the Union Army would be managed and supplied as befitted a modern mass army. But far from exerting a strong strategic grasp, Halleck refused to risk taking responsibility for most of the command decisions on which might turn the outcome of battles or the war. He would give Lincoln and Stanton strategic advice;

he would not take strategic command. After July 1862 Lincoln found himself by default still the architect of Union strategy.

Fortunately for the Union, the President had grown to be a strategist of considerable accomplishment—so much, indeed, that in 1926 a British soldier, Colin Ballard, was to write a book called *The Military Genius of Abraham Lincoln*, and some other historians were to bestow accolades almost as enthusiastic as Ballard's. Strategy, the conduct of campaigns and the fitting of them together in a pattern designed to win a war, does not demand nearly so much technical, specialized knowledge of war as does tactics, the manipula-

Of course, armies had to be fed, and that called for a legion of white-aproned cooks at the government bakery. The armies in the field usually baked their own bread, so this bakery serviced just the troops around the capital.
(USAMHI)

tion of troops in battle. His strategic vision un-clouded by tactical detail, furthermore, Lincoln perceived certain essential principles of the Union war effort more clearly than did almost any professional military man. The professional soldiers had been taught at West Point and from the study of Napoleon's campaigns, for example, that a military force should be concentrated, gathered up to strike a few strong blows or even a single blow against a key objective such as the enemy's political capital or an important road junction. Lincoln recognized, however, that to concentrate Union power against so obvious an objective as Richmond permitted the enemy to concentrate there also in defense, and the effect was to allow the Confederates to make the most of their limited resources. If, on the contrary, the Union used its superior resources not to concentrate but to attack all around the borders of the Confederacy, the enemy did not have the ability to match Union strength everywhere and

somewhere around the Confederacy's periphery the defenses were sure to cave in. Similarly, Lincoln recognized clearly that the principal strength of the Confederacy resided in its armed forces and that the main objectives of the Union should not be geographical points even as prominent as Richmond but rather the destruction of the enemy armies.

For all that, Lincoln's lack of professional military credentials, as well as the need for him to attend to a multitude of tasks besides military strategy, undercut his efforts to lead his generals to apply his strategic perceptions. He continued to seek a professional soldier who would share those perceptions and assume strategic and operational command of the Union armies in the manner that only a professional soldier could. When the triumphs of Vicksburg and Chattanooga in 1863 brought Grant to the forefront among Union commanders, Lincoln shared the wide conviction in Congress and among the

*And to keep the men garbed, the office of the U.S. Depot of Army Clothing
and Equipage occupied the better part of a city block. A more genteel service
bureau, this office could afford a few frills—an ornate eagle painted above its
door and a lamp post with stars and* CLOTHING DEPOT *illuminated in the glass.*
(USAMHI)

public that Grant should receive the full rank
of lieutenant general, vacant since George Washington, and should displace Halleck as general-
in-chief, which he did in March 1864. When
Lincoln came to know Grant, the conviction
deepened. Grant agreed firmly that the destruction of the Confederate armies should be the
main objective of Union strategy and that apply-
ing pressure against all the enemy armies simultaneously should be a principal means of
achieving their destruction.

To what extent the rise of Grant can be said
to have given the Union's modern mass armies
a modern command system remains nevertheless
debatable. Grant decided that as commanding
general he would take the field with the Army
of the Potomac, directly supervising that army
and its commander, Major General George G.
Meade, while overseeing other armies less directly via the telegraph and General Halleck.
For that purpose, Halleck remained in Washington with the new title of Chief of Staff, but he
was not Chief of Staff of the Army in the
twentieth-century sense, since he was subordinate
to Grant. Halleck's administrative skills and military knowledge made him on the whole an

admirable conduit between Grant and the other
Union generals. But there were awkwardnesses
in these arrangements: in the distance of the
chief professional soldier from Washington and
in his focusing on one of several armies; in his
dependence on a Chief of Staff who remained
reluctant to take on responsibilities and who in
a legal sense was not ultimately responsible; in
Grant's continuing dependence on Secretary
Stanton and the chiefs of the supply bureaus to
sustain the armies, while the bureau chiefs were
under Stanton's, not Grant's, command so that
the relationship between the powers of the
general-in-chief and the Secretary of War remained unclear.

The command system of the Union Army
functioned well in the final year of the war because the personalities involved worked well
together. Lincoln, Stanton, Grant, Halleck, and
Meigs all earned high marks for cooperation
with each other. On any organization chart,
however, the ultimate Union Army command
structure would look like a nightmare. Not least
of the problems, there was still the fundamental
question as to how Grant's authority as general-
in-chief was to be reconciled with the constitu-

To erect all these buildings, as well as to supply the Union armies with the raw materials of forts and bridges and stockades and more, the government used veritable forests of timber. This government lumber yard was in Alexandria, Virginia, probably photographed by Captain A. J. Russell. (USAMHI)

tional power of the President as Commander in Chief. This problem was not to be resolved until long after the Civil War, with the creation in 1903 of the twentieth-century version of the Army Chief of Staff as the ranking professional soldier but, unlike a Civil War general-in-chief, claiming no authority to command independent of the President and the Secretary of War.

Whatever the problems of Grant's status, his method of achieving his and Lincoln's objective of the destruction of the Confederate armies added another modern dimension to the Union Army's waging of war. In the campaign of 1864–65, Grant eventually destroyed the principal enemy field force, General Robert E. Lee's Army of Northern Virginia, by the grim expedient of locking it in battle almost every day and inflicting casualties until Lee's army was no more. The campaign became one of deadly attrition, foreshadowing the long-stalemated bloodbath on the Western Front of the First World War, of the Eastern Front of the Second World War, and of the Korean War. At Appomattox, Lee surrendered only some 26,765 men; his army had num-

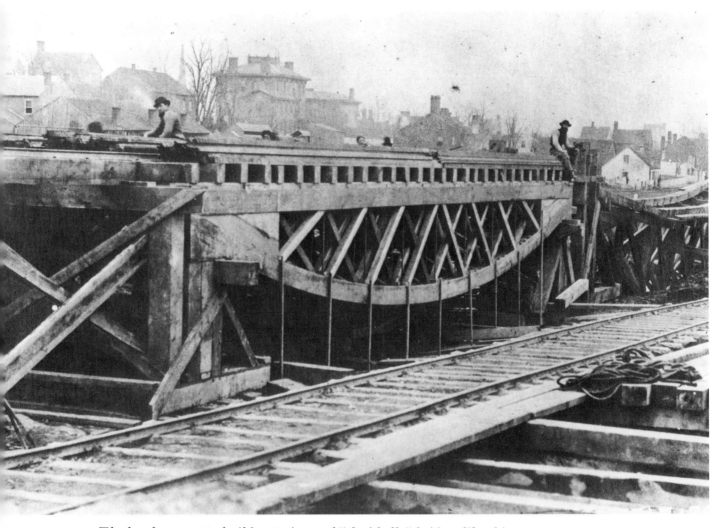

*The lumber went to build experimental "shad-belly" bridges like this one,
photographed by Russell. It had just been subjected to 168,000 pounds of
weight for nine hours and stood the test.* (NATIONAL ARCHIVES)

bered 66,000 just one year before. To be sure,
Grant's strategy of nearly continuous battle imposed tremendous casualties on his own army
as well, but the general-in-chief knew that the
Union could replenish his ranks while the Confederacy could not replenish Lee's.

Nor was Grant merely the strategic butcher
that hostile portrayals have sometimes made him
seem. He had demonstrated a superb capacity
for agile maneuver in his Vicksburg Campaign
before becoming general-in-chief, and he would
have preferred to trap and capture Lee's army by
maneuver in 1864–65 rather than trade casualties with it. But the combination of Lee's tactical
skills and the improved nature of weapons by the

1860s left Grant with no alternative method of
destroying the enemy army than its slow attrition
in protracted combat.

The final modern dimension of the Civil War,
one assuring the resemblance of the Petersburg
trench systems to the elaborate field fortifications of later wars, lay in the firepower of the
rival armies. Fifteen years earlier, the men who
were to be the generals of the Civil War had
fought against Mexico a war whose weapons remained much like those of the American Revolution: smoothbore muskets and cannons. The
Civil War, in contrast, was a war of rifled muskets and to a large extent of rifled artillery. In
the short time between the Mexican and Civil

The wood built platforms like this on which bridge arches were constructed.
Built on the upper flat surface, the arches were then . . . (NA)

wars, the American adoption of mass-production methods of permitting muzzle-loading weapons to fire rifled projectiles despite the difficulties of loading—particularly the American adoption of the French Captain Claude Étienne Minié's "minie ball"—wrought a revolution in warfare out of all proportion to the seeming smallness of the source.

With smoothbore muskets, effective range had been limited to 200 yards or less. As Grant remarked in his memoirs, "At the distance of a few hundred yards a man might fire at you all day without your finding out." With the Model 1855 or 1861 Springfield rifle and other rifled shoulder arms, effective range leaped to 400 or up to 600 yards. Rifled field artillery attained a maximum effective range of some 2,500 yards. Now a defending force could fire so many accurate shots at an attacker during the time he was within range that any frontal assault against reasonably well trained and resolute troops was almost sure to fail. Even attacks against flanks

and rear—in devising which the Union Army's great adversary General Lee was the most skillful tactician since Napoleon—no longer produced quite the devastating effect that they had in Napoleon's day; the firepower of rifled weapons much enhanced the possibility that the victim of such maneuvers might be able to form a new front. Even the best generalship failed to preserve attacking forces from devastating casualties under the defenders' rifles. At Second Bull Run, in August 1862, and Chancellorsville, in May 1863, Lee achieved masterpieces of Napoleonic maneuver against his enemy's flanks, but the Union Army's rifled firepower nevertheless extracted from Lee's forces in those battles casualties of some 19 and 22 percent, respectively. The victor's losses were too high for the victory to yield decisive advantage.

The appalling casualty rates of Civil War battles—at Gettysburg, in July 1863, 23,000 out of some 85,000 for the Union Army, 28,000 out of 75,000 for the Confederate Army—were achieved

. . . tipped over on the hinged platform, to be joined into finished sections of bridge. (NA)

mainly with single-shot, muzzle-loading shoulder arms and artillery. A relatively small number of breech-loading cannon were used, but problems in satisfactorily locking the breech to permit the firing of adequate powder charges were not yet fully solved. Controversy has always swirled around the question whether the Union Army should have made itself still more modern through a speedier adoption of breech-loading and even repeating muskets and carbines. Both Union and Confederate armies used some such weapons, more often cavalry carbines than infantry rifles because cavalry did not have so much need of long range and sustained firing capacity; breechloaders tended to suffer from gas leakage and fouling of the breech mechanism to the detriment of these qualities.

About 100,000 Sharps carbines and rifles are estimated to have been used by both sides, employing a single-shot breech-loading mechanism patented by Christian Sharps in 1848. By the time of Gettysburg in July 1863, some Spencer breech-loading repeating rifles were in Union service; on July 13, 1863, just after Gettysburg, the Federal Ordnance Department placed its first order for Spencer repeating carbines. Eventually the department ordered 64,685 Spencer carbines and 11,471 Spencer rifles. The seven-shot Spencer repeating carbine, using copper rim-fire cartridges, became the standard arm of the Union cavalry by 1864. But like all breechloaders of the era, it still had problems. The cartridge contained only forty-five grains of black powder, so the weapon lacked range and power.

Bridge sections such as this were used to build a new span over the Potomac for the Washington, Alexandria & Georgetown Railroad. They would make a bridge 5,104 feet in length. (KEAN ARCHIVES)

When the carbine grew hot, the cartridges tended to stick in the chamber.

In its rejection of breechloaders as the standard infantry weapon, the Ordnance Department was not obtusely conservative. The famous Prussian needle gun, adopted as early as 1843, had less range than standard Union Army muzzle-loaders. Brigadier General John Buford reported that at Gettysburg some of his Union cavalry troopers armed themselves with muzzle-loading infantry muskets in place of their breech-loading carbines; the soldiers knew which was the better weapon in a hard fight.

The rifled muzzle-loading musket and rifled muzzle-loading artillery could do damage enough. They pushed the Civil War armies finally into entrenchments that foreshadowed the Western Front in World War I. They deprived individual battles of decisiveness and transformed the war into a prolonged tactical deadlock resolved only when harsh attrition had brought one of the contestants to exhaustion. They gave the modernity of the Union Army its fullest but most disturbing dimension. Like other modern armies in subsequent modern wars, the Union Army, despite all its resources, could gain the political objectives for which it fought only through the grim strategies of Grant and Sherman. It had to annihilate the enemy armed forces through day-by-day attrition, or it had to carry destruction beyond the enemy armies to the enemy's economy and civilian population.

It was a model of wartime engineering. Off in the extreme right distance, the Capitol dome looks across to the wonders being done by Lincoln's modern army. (KA)

Furthermore, the builders of the U.S. Military Railroad could erect major depots anywhere they could lay a rail. Here on the James River, at City Point, Virginia, they made the terminus of the road that kept Grant supplied at Petersburg for nearly a year. A Russell image. (USAMHI)

And when boxcars could not go by rail to their final destination, they were put aboard the first "container ships"—steamers and schooners that could hold the cars on their decks. (NA)

Besides rail communications, the Union Army expanded the use of the telegraph to previously undreamed limits for the military. Here in Georgetown, photographer William Morris Smith captures a view of the Signal Corps "camp of instruction," where hundreds of men were trained in Morse code and communication by "wigwag" flags. (LIBRARY OF CONGRESS)

Signal corpsmen erecting telegraph poles and preparing to string wire.
Lincoln's armies, by 1865, could carry instant communication along with
them almost anywhere. (AMERICANA IMAGE GALLERY)

The photos of the several balloons used by the Union Army observation are well known, but less well remembered are the gas generators used to inflate them. T. S. Lowe's generators Nos. 7 and 8 were government property, just part of an ever-expanding arsenal of weapons. (NA)

So that no waterway might present an impassable obstacle for the marching Union armies, special wagons were designed and equipped with canvas pontoons as well as an anchor to hold the pontoons in place. (P-M)

Whole trains of pontoons, equipped with oars for maneuvering, followed the marching Union armies. (NA)

And when a bridge was not available, "blanket boats" were made by stretching rubberized blankets or canvas over wooden frames, lashing them together, and launching away. It could carry a squad of soldiers and a cannon and limber, as in this Russell photo. (LC)

One photographer, perhaps Russell, recorded the building by Union engineers of a pontoon span near Washington. Here the pontoons are ready for "laying." (USAMHI)

Here another view as the working parties assemble. It is to be a timed test. (USAMHI)

Some 450 men are working at wooden boats and canvas pontoons, some of them joined in giant rafts. In the first twenty minutes they have 1,300 feet ready for the passage of heavy vehicles, including artillery. (USAMHI)

The bridge assembled in record time, the proud engineers pose in squads along its length. It is a marvel of hasty yet serviceable construction. Again and again in the war, Yankee engineers will "throw" bridges across every stream in their path. (USAMHI)

They would do it with huge trains of boats like these beside the camp of the 50th New York Engineers at Rappahannock Station, Virginia, in February 1864. A Timothy O'Sullivan image. (KA)

When something more substantial than pontoons were needed, the engineers could make indestructible bridges out of river barges. (COURTESY OF TERENCE P. O'LEARY)

The man in charge of all these ingenious builders was Brigadier General Joseph G. Totten, Chief Engineer of the U.S. Army and one of the oldest men in the service. He was seventy-three when the war began and still a man of active mind. He died in 1864 while still on active duty. (USAMHI)

The camps of the engineers were to be found wherever the Yankee armies went. Here at Chattanooga in 1864 sits the camp of the 1st Michigan Engineers and Mechanics, with Lookout Mountain in the distance. (MICHIGAN STATE ARCHIVES, LANSING)

And here in Chattanooga, near the Tennessee River, is a waterworks under construction by Federal engineers in 1864. (NA)

And here it is finished. They did good work. (NA)

Government sawmills like this one on Lookout Mountain, Tennessee, fed the voracious appetites of the engineers. The army simply took the machinery with it wherever it went. (USAMHI)

A good sharp saw-toothed blade, steam-powered, could make as much of a contribution to the Union war effort as a cannon on the field, and sometimes more. (USAMHI)

Wherever the Yankees went, they adapted to their environment, using their skill and engineering ingenuity to the profit of the march to victory. Here at Beaufort, South Carolina, they erected a massive condenser to distill pure water from seawater, leaving vital salt as a by-product. A Samuel Cooley image from November 1864. (NA)

Here in Beaufort, too, arose the carpenters' shops, this one doing just a little bit of everything. Wagons are repaired, building skylights made, and signs manufactured. Leaning against the wide door at the left is a billboard headed INSTRUCTIONS FOR THE OFFICER OF THE GUARD. *More somber reminders of the war sit to the left of it—grave markers for Privates Charles Williams and Blainwell Sweatt.* (NA)

Of course, the Beaufort paint shop put the lettering on the signs, and the grave markers. Two more of each rest against the wall here. (NA)

On Hilton Head Island, South Carolina, the U.S. Government established a slaughterhouse to provide freshly butchered meat for the soldiers. The piles of hooves and horns outside attest to recent work. Soldiering, it seemed, was not all glory and fighting after all. They also served who only made steaks. (NA)

All across the North and the South, signs of Union might and organization were evident. In Nashville, Tennessee, the vast Taylor Depot went up. (PRIVATE COLLECTION)

In Cincinnati, Ohio, the U.S. Government wagon yard occupied a huge park at Eighth and Freeman streets. (NA)

A few blocks away stood the "tent manufactory," not only where canvas tents were made, but also where mass-produced uniforms were cut from patterns. (NA)

All of this organization required a lot of fuel for the steam engines, the locomotives, and the ships. Here in Alexandria Russell's camera looks at only a part of the government wharves, with their mountains of cordwood for the fuel burners and another mountain of alfalfa for the hay burners. (USAMHI)

Next door the yard of the Cumberland Coal & Iron Company promised plenty of food for the smoke-belching furnaces aboard the John Brooks *and other steamers.* (USAMHI)

Union transport fleets like this one kept all these supplies moving from major centers such as Alexandria to the supply bases established with the advancing armies. Such supply was a marvel of modern logistical design. (NA)

The man who kept all of these supplies coming to the Union armies was Quartermaster General Montgomery C. Meigs, himself an amateur photographer and an organizer of wonderful efficiency. The men in blue rarely went hungry. (RONN PALM COLLECTION)

Each army in the field had its own quartermaster as well, and with the Army of the Potomac it was the capable Brigadier General Rufus Ingalls. He was the only staff officer with that army to serve from beginning to end of the war, enjoying the esteem of every commander he served under. (USAMHI)

Generals like U. S. Grant had sophisticated docks and wharves built to receive their supplies, understanding that armies did move on their stomachs. City Point, Virginia, in 1864. (USAMHI)

The James teemed with every variety of ship, once the City Point docks were ready, all bringing in massive stockpiles of supplies. (NA)

Supplies came straight off the ships and onto the cars of the railroad built by Grant, or into mountainous piles like these barrels of potatoes and salt pork and boxes of hardtack. (P-M)

The commissary depot at Cedar Level, Virginia, in August 1864 actually looked like a mountain. (USAMHI)

*Lesser but still imposing supply depots lay everywhere in the wake of the
Union Army. Here at Stoneman's Station, Virginia, in June 1863, sat a
depot that tempted Confederate cavalry into dashing raids to destroy or
capture much-needed supplies.* (USAMHI)

*And from those depots massive wagon trains like this Army of the Potomac
supply train at Brandy Station, Virginia, in October 1863, brought the
life-sustaining food and matériel to the front. A Timothy O'Sullivan image.*
(CHICAGO HISTORICAL SOCIETY)

Along with the Union armies themselves moved large herds of cattle for fresh meat. This herd is seen at Giesboro, in Southeast Washington, D.C. So prized was beef during the Civil War that in 1864 Confederate Major General Wade Hampton would lead one of the most daring raids of the war—to capture a cattle herd. (NA)

All the Union services that were so comfortably ensconced back in Washington and the other major centers had their counterparts with the armies themselves. Here at Petersburg, Virginia, in August 1864, an engineer battalion is engaged in making gabions—wicker baskets filled with earth for defenses. (P-M)

Here, too, Union repair shops replaced bad wheels or made new signs. (P-M)

*Communities of vendors and mechanics made tiny villages with the armies.
Here a church, a sutler, and a photographer advertising his* AMBROTYPE &
PHOTOGRAPHIC GALLERY *stand side by side.* (NA)

Keeping the men in the field happy meant keeping the mail running between them and their homes. These field desks are for the Union Army's postal service, for sorting letters and packages. A box of "Honey Soap" is in the large pigeonhole of the desk at the left. (USAMHI)

In the more permanent Union installations, the camp cooks in the kitchen became men of particular importance, as the third fellow from the left in the front row seems to appreciate. He stands hand in apron in the same Napoleonic stance so beloved of the officers. After all, he was a soldier too. (USAMHI)

The soldiers had to keep clean somehow, and for many of them that was something new. Huge laundries like this one at Camp Holt in Jeffersonville, Indiana, made it a little easier for them. (INDIANA HISTORICAL SOCIETY LIBRARY, INDIANAPOLIS)

But all of this was ancillary to the Union Army's constant and pressing need to keep those men, clean or dirty, armed with the weapons necessary to do their job. This infantryman in full field equipment, with Sharps rifle and saber bayonet, is ready for the enemy, thanks to the work of thousands who served behind the lines. (MICHAEL J. MC AFEE COLLECTION)

Without that work, these men of the 118th New York, the "Adirondack Regiment," would not be armed with modern Spencer repeating rifles and carbines. (MICHAEL J. MC AFEE COLLECTION)

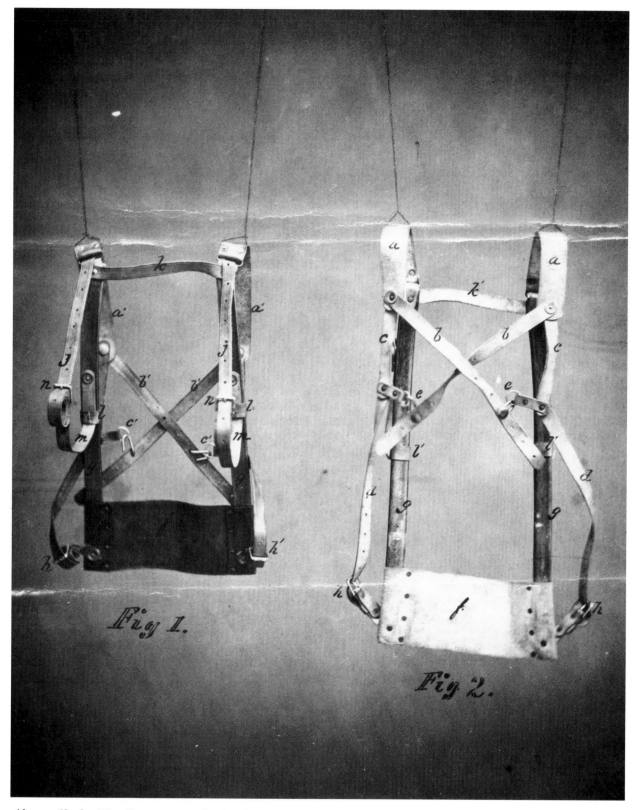

Above all, the War Department had to be willing to try things that were new, something nineteenth-century armies all too often resisted. Inventors bombarded it with contraptions like Baxter's knapsack supporter, designed to give the wearer full mobility and freedom of movement in the field. (NA)

Inventor Baxter even supplied demonstration photographs with his petition, apparently not realizing that the Civil War soldier rarely if ever went into battle wearing his knapsack. (NA)

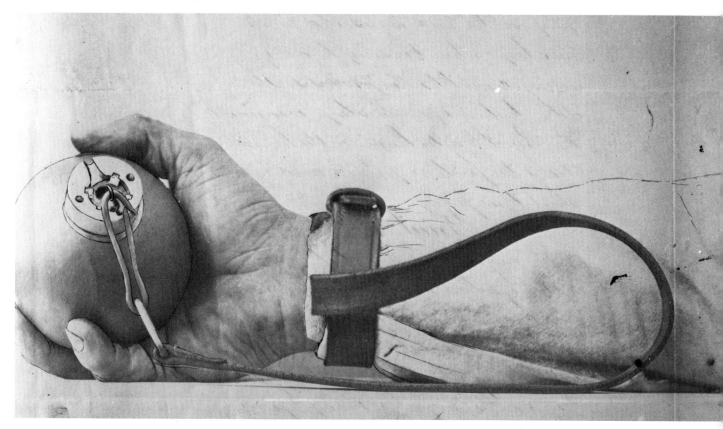

Then there was the Adams hand grenade, here attached to the wrist of its inventor, perhaps. It was little more than a hollow shell filled with powder and balls, with a fuse attached. By throwing it, the user set off the timed fuse when the leather strap attached to his wrist jerked a priming pin. It could have been embarrassing if his throw was a little too weak. (NA)

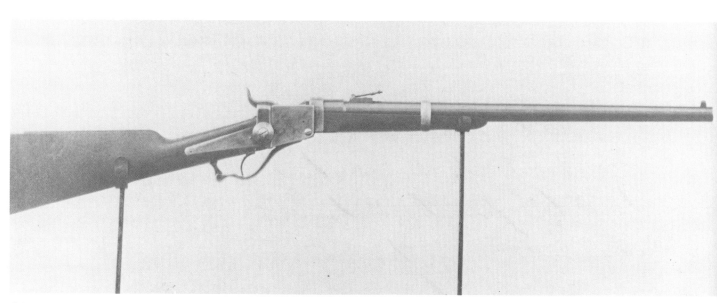

Of more conventional weapons, the War Department considered an untold number, all of them subjected to performance and accuracy tests. The Starr carbine went through tests on October 31, 1864, and was approved for limited use by cavalry. (NA)

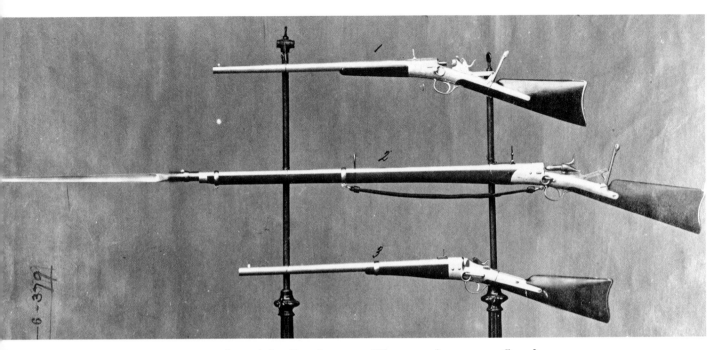

Not so Brand's patent breech-loading firearms. Three versions were offered, the .44 caliber carbine at the top, the .54 caliber rifled musket in the center, and the .54 caliber carbine at the bottom. The weapon at the top was fired some 3,000 times in testing. A self-contained cartridge is shown partially inserted in the breech. For the musket in the center the entire cartridge in the loading and ejecting mechanism are shown. The carbine at the bottom is ready to fire. Inventors would continue designing breechloaders, and all too often a conservative War Department would reject them. (NA)

Lee's breechloader was tested in April 1864. The barrel slipped sideways to allow a cartridge to be slid in. The thing projecting backward from the breech provided one solution to the biggest problem with breechloaders— how to eject the spent casing. This one just pushed backward, forcing the shell out. (NA)

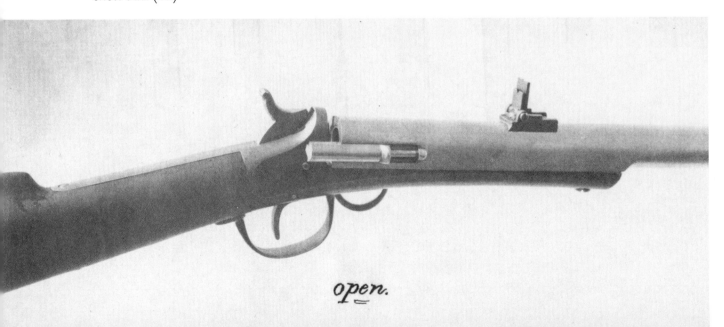

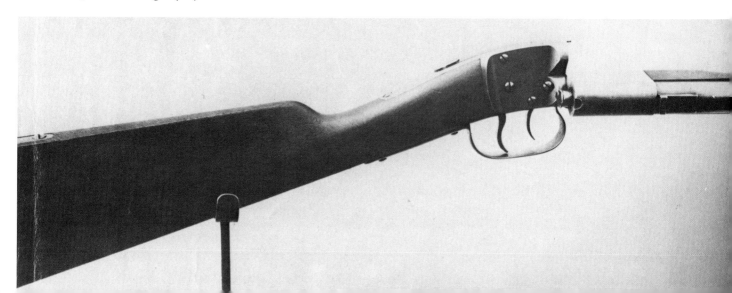

Johnson's breech-loading carbine was even more novel. The whole breech twisted to allow insertion of the cartridge. It is shown here closed. Carbines like this were tested against the standard Sharps carbine. (NA)

Here the barrel and breech of the Johnson carbine are twisted open, to allow insertion of the cartridge. (NA)

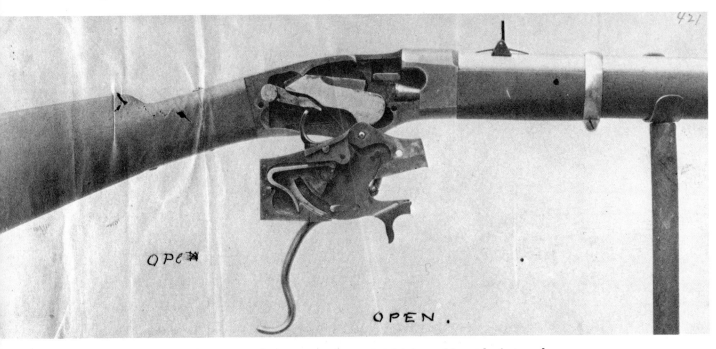

OPEN

OPEN.

Now and then, of course, a design came through which could not be ignored.
That is what happened when Lamson's repeating carbine was examined in
May 1864. The government did not adopt it—it was too similar to the
Spencer already in use—but the increased rate of fire offered by the repeaters
caught the attention of men in Washington. (NA)

What finally caught their attention for good, and that of the next generation
with them, was Henry's repeating carbine. Its serviceability and simplicity
of design made it stand above the others. (NA)

Oliver F. Winchester, president of the New Haven Arms Company, who wanted to produce the Henry, was present for its trials. The carbine performed badly that first time out, but in time it would see limited use in the war and afterward it would be the progenitor of the "gun that won the West." (NA)

Because a rifle, no matter what kind, was only as good as its sighting, experiments were made with telescopic sights for sharpshooters' weapons. This one was attached to an American rifle with the massive barrel used for big game like buffalo or for very long-range shooting. (NA)

Equally important to the U.S. Government were the designs coming in for the bigger guns. The yard here at the Washington Arsenal was packed with all manner of cannon during the war, including the Wiard gun supporting the officers at right. (USAMHI)

Every army in the field had a chief of ordnance, officers like Union Captain Stephen Vincent Benét, grandfather of the distinguished American poet. They had to take what Washington sent them and keep it serviceable. (USAMHI)

Massive seacoast cannon, like this 15-inch Dahlgren smoothbore, were cast and tested in Washington. Next door to the Dahlgren sits a huge Parrott rifle, its projectiles lined neatly about its carriage. (LC)

The big guns were favorites for play and posing. It took a special gun cradle to transport them by rail, one that could support the 42,500 pounds of iron in such a weapon, not to mention the man inside. (MICHAEL J. HAMMERSON)

Many of them were brought here to Fort Monroe, Virginia, for testing, firing at targets out in Hampton Roads. A cannon like this could hurl its 440-pound shot well over four miles. A Rodman smoothbore. (USAMHI)

*It took a special apparatus to move the big guns in the field. William Browne
made this 1865 image of a captured Confederate 8-inch Brooke rifle slung
from a huge Confederate sling cart. (CHS)*

*Without one, a mammoth gun tube
could not be managed. (USAMHI)*

And of course, whatever the size of the guns, the artillery required mountains of projectiles, like those in this scene at the Washington Arsenal made by Captain A. J. Russell, military photographer. Several projectile sizes are evident, including a stack of British Whitworth rifle solid bolts, probably 5-inch, directly in front of the men at left. In the background cannon and mortars and carriages and targets are scattered all about. (AIG)

Schooners like these transported the ammunition to the Union armies in Virginia or to major supply stations like Fort Monroe. (USAMHI)

It was in U.S. Army laboratories like this one, at Sixth and Oxford streets in Philadelphia, that much of the ammunition was designed and even produced. The window at upper right sports a distinctly unmilitary adornment, a window box with plants. (LLOYD OSTENDORF COLLECTION)

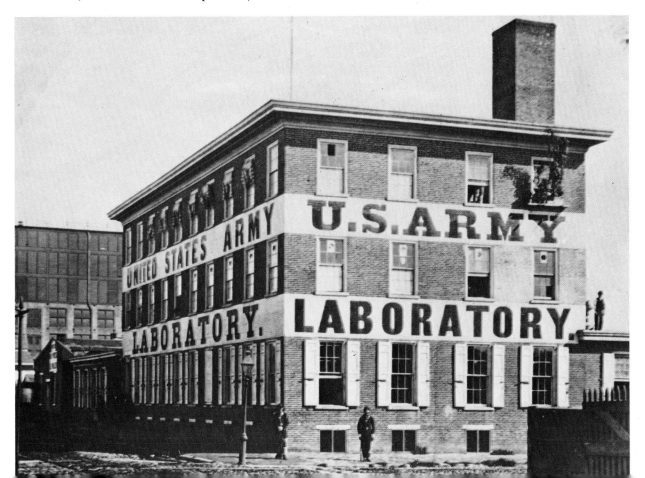

The work of the inventors did not stop at small arms. They looked also to ammunition, with items such as Dodge's cartridge filler. By a series of shiftings and pumpings, powder was automatically placed in the tubes, ready to be topped with bullets and then wrapped in waxed paper. The War Department wisely did not adopt it. (NA)

The so-called wire gun had a barrel made up largely of steel wire wrapped tightly around the bore. It was not an impressive success. (NA)

Major testing for experimental new big guns for the Union armies was done either at Fort Monroe or in Washington. Here in the former, a cast-iron 15-inch Rodman sits ready for a series of stress tests. (NA)

And here it is after one charge too many, a still-intact counterpart quietly awaiting its turn in the distance. (NA)

A steel and iron gun fared no better. (NA)

Piece of Steel Gun

The rifling inside the bore shows handsomely in this "exploded" view of the pieces of the steel and iron gun. The ordnance testers were fascinated with the camera for recording the results of their experiments. (NA)

This cast-iron cannon managed to stand up after 1,600 firings. That was more like it. (NA)

The inventors never gave up. H. B. Mann stands here behind his new breech-loading cannon. This early version is being admired by an onlooker and his dog. Mann would refine it considerably before . . . (NA)

. . . *submitting it for testing by the U.S. Government in June 1865. By that time the war was done, of course, and Mann was out of luck. Just what he did with his 2,000-pound toy is unknown.* (NA)

Lee's breechloader fared no better. It went through U.S. Government trials in August 1865, with little hope of a contract now that the fighting was over. In the testing, the supervising officer revealed the prejudice against this type of weapon when he referred to "the arguments against breech-loading guns as a class." Washington learned slowly sometimes. (NA)

Broadwell's breechloader was wonderfully simple. The slide sitting on the ammunition box was inserted in the slot in the side of the gun's breech. With the slide pulled out, the shell at left could be inserted into the barrel. Then the slide was pushed in behind it, sealing off the chamber ready for firing. In the distance above the barrel is a target used for testing. (NA)

Broadwell's gun with the slide in place. (NA)

It took constant attention to the projectiles those guns fired to keep the armies in the field well supplied. Shot and shell were experimented with just as much as cannon. The shells at bottom are fitted with experimental fuses, made up of the rings at the center, with the fuse plug at the upper left and right inserted using the tool in the top center. It all had to work. (NA)

The Pevey shell was another such experiment, and one not adopted by the government. The soft tin or lead casing at its base was intended to expand into a gun's rifling grooves, to give the shell a spin as it emerged. (NA)

And here another Pevey shell designed for antipersonnel work—a hollow sphere with powder in the center cavity and iron balls in the outer chamber. American inventors could create decidedly lethal concepts in their pursuit of profits. (NA)

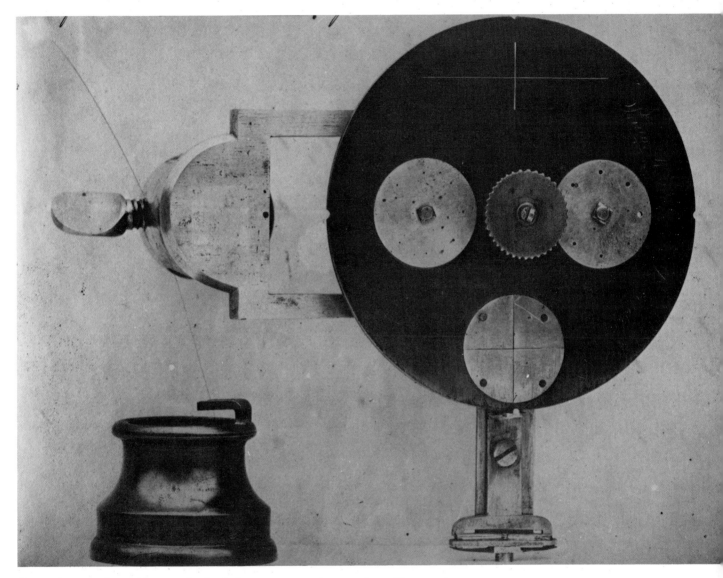

Even the men in uniform, who had the most experience, after all, sometimes turned tinkerer. Philo Maltby of the 14th Ohio Artillery designed this Rotary Sight for siege or seacoast guns. It could adapt to changes in light and was on the whole very refined. Indeed, the examining officer complimented the inventor: "It was constructed by Artificer Maltby in the field with such tools as a soldier in his vocation would there have at his command, and whatever may be said of its adaptability to general service, certainly reflects great credit on his skill and perseverance." Having said that, the officer then concluded that Maltby's was "misdirected ingenuity," condemning all such attempts as "the efforts of a class of persons, ingenius [sic] and well meaning it may be, but who have mistaken the desideratum in the field of invention on which they have entered." The closed mind was already well entrenched in the U.S. military in August 1864. (NA)

*Items like the iron siege carriage for heavy guns got a little more attention,
but proved to be simply too heavy for horses to pull.* (NA)

*Real ingenuity came when the imagination tried to fire more than one shot
at once. It produced specimens like the volley gun, a simple clustering of
121 barrels inside a cylinder and a breechblock containing 121 charges and
bullets.* (NA)

The volley gun required a fair amount of special apparatus and, after all, only sent its hail of bullets out into a very limited area. (NA)

Somewhat more to the point was the Requia battery, which actually saw limited service with the Union forces at Charleston, South Carolina. It was just twenty-five barrels side by side, with a strip of brass holding the charges and bullets inserted in the breech. The lanyard-controlled firing hammer is just visible at the rear center. (NA)

If all these weapons of war worked even a fraction as well as their inventors expected, then there were going to be a lot of wounded. And so the designers tried also to perfect the ambulance. E. Hayes & Company of Wheeling, West Virginia, submitted this prototype army ambulance to the U.S. Government in February 1862. Besides being very attractively appointed, it also boasted two water or spirit casks built right into the back panel. (NA)

And for those who did not survive the ingenious means of death being devised for them, the Union laid out cemeteries. It was all part of the job of a modern, organized army that left little to chance. Here in 1864 surveyors are at work laying out a major military cemetery . . . (NA)

. . . on Arlington Heights, Virginia, across the Potomac from Washington.
(NA)

*Here, on ground which had been the home of Confederate General Robert E.
Lee, they began the work of what would become Arlington National
Cemetery. From enlistment to arming to death, the organized war was
complete.* (NA)

"Damn the Torpedoes!"

CHARLES R. HABERLEIN, JR.

Ships of iron, and men to match, battle on an August morning for Mobile

REAR ADMIRAL David Glasgow Farragut returned to the Gulf in January 1864. Refreshed by five months in the North, with his flagship *Hartford* refitted, he was eager to begin the next step in reducing the Confederacy's south coast.

Farragut had begun this work nearly two years previously by boldly running past the fortifications defending New Orleans. With the South's greatest seaport in Federal hands, he had continued with vigorous thrusts up the Mississippi River. Now but one important Rebel port remained on the long Gulf of Mexico shore.

Mobile, Alabama, with its fine rail and water links to the Confederate heartland, was a valuable asset to the South. Located at the head of large, shallow Mobile Bay, the port was well defended. On the mainland an earthwork, Fort Powell, guarded the bay's southwestern "back door." Between Dauphin Island on the west and Mobile Point on the east, on the bay's lower edge, the main entrance was flanked by twin antebellum masonry fortifications, Fort Gaines and Fort Morgan. Since 1861 additional batteries had been added to each. The waterway between them had been largely obstructed by driven pilings and moored mines, or "torpedoes," in the contemporary terminology. A few hundred feet

of deep channel remained open, directly under Fort Morgan's heavy guns.

Through this channel passed fast little Confederate steamers with exports of cotton and imports of war-sustaining munitions. The blockade-running trade was harassed, but not prevented, by Federal warships lurking offshore and cruising in the sea-lanes. Only direct occupation of the entryway would effectively blockade Mobile. To effect this was Farragut's intention.

Naval assaults on well-defended fortifications would not succeed without cooperating troops, and these were unavailable during the winter and spring of 1864. As the latter season progressed through May, another factor appeared on Mobile Bay: the new Confederate ironclad ram *Tennessee*. Her long-anticipated arrival provoked a brief outbreak of "ram fever" even in the intrepid Farragut. Fretting over the prospect of the Rebel ironclad steaming out into the Gulf, laying waste to the blockaders and perhaps even spearheading efforts to wrest Pensacola, Florida, and New Orleans, Louisiana, from their Northern occupiers, he badly wanted ironclads of his own.

Enemy plans worried the other side, too. Confederate Admiral Franklin Buchanan was ulti-

people I can get at." The routine blockading and patrolling continued from the Rio Grande to Florida, occasionally punctuated by minor raids and counter raids.

Unknown to the West Gulf Blockading Squadron, Washington had in fact decided on Mobile. The end of the ill-conceived Red River expedition in May and lack of progress in capturing Charleston freed monitors for other employment. Major General William Tecumseh Sherman's army, marching on Atlanta, needed diversionary support. In June orders went out to four Union monitors to proceed gulfward. Major General E. R. S. Canby, the area's army commander, received instructions from Washington to cooperate with the navy in a Union attack on Mobile.

There was a gleam in the eyes of Rear Admiral David Glasgow Farragut. When C. D. Fredericks photographed him in New York, the loyal old Tennessean was laden with glory from his capture of New Orleans and the opening of the Mississippi. In 1864 he wanted another assignment and looked to Mobile, Alabama. (WILLIAM GLADSTONE COLLECTION)

So did Union Major General E. R. S. Canby. After the fiasco of the Red River Campaign in May, his troops needed active and successful employment. A joint move against Mobile with the navy would serve the purpose. (USAMHI)

mately too cautious for a dash into the Gulf. *Tennessee* and her three wooden consorts, the gunboats *Selma*, *Gaines*, and *Morgan*, remained inside the bay, assigned to help defend the forts.

Since his return, Farragut had bombarded the Navy Department with requests for ironclad monitors and army support. He did not delude himself about the response, writing a colleague: "The Government appears to plan the campaigns, and Mobile does not appear to be included just yet. . . . I shall have to content myself going along the coast and pestering all the

The Union had been interested in Mobile and its bay, center for Confederate West Gulf blockade-running operations, for some time. Converted "tinclad" steamers like the USS Elk *patrolled regularly off Mobile's waters.* (USAMHI)

Hints of these developments reached Farragut within a few weeks. Solid confirmation, in the form of the monitor USS *Manhattan*, steamed into Pensacola harbor early in July. With three more monitors on the way, Farragut and Canby perfected their plans.

Farragut's fleet was to steam past Fort Morgan into Mobile Bay and eliminate the Confederate squadron. Simultaneously, Union Army forces would land on Dauphin Island to assault Fort Gaines. If Fort Powell was taken, so much the better. Once communication was secured between the fleet inside, the logistics system outside, and the troops in between, Fort Morgan

would be doomed. Canby put together a 2,000-man contingent with enough transports for the job and appointed Major General Gordon Granger to command them.

In the fleet, ships were coaled, stored, and stripped for action. Superfluous spars and rigging were taken down and stowed. Anchor chain, sandbags, and spare sails were worked in around vital spaces for additional protection. Guns were shifted to the right, or starboard, sides to increase the firepower bearing on Fort Morgan.

Farragut ordered his ships to double up. Each of the more powerful sloops of war would have a gunboat or smaller sloop lashed to its unengaged port side. The lighter ships could then pass into the bay protected by the thicker bulwarks and heavier armament of their partners. In return, the big ships received backup propulsion in case they were disabled.

The four monitors were instructed to stand inshore of—and parallel to—the sloops and gunboats and to bombard Fort Morgan vigorously, to suppress its fire and prevent the *Tennessee* from interfering. All ships were warned to stay east of the black buoys anchored a few hundred yards out from the Fort Morgan shore. These, it was correctly assumed, marked the location of the minefield. The fort's gunfire was less dangerous than a catastrophic explosion of a big torpedo.

Granger's troops went ashore on Dauphin Island as planned, on the third of August, covered by several minor warships. Fort Gaines was immediately invested. However, the Union monitor *Tecumseh* arrived late, forcing postponement of the navy's mission. Farragut was mortified because he could not uphold his end of the plan, but admitted later that the delay was beneficial. During the intervening hours, the Confederates pushed reinforcements into Fort Gaines, where they were easily captured a few days later.

In the wee hours of August 5 the fleet formed up. An unfortunate change of plan, reluctantly adopted by Farragut, assigned the lead to the big sloop *Brooklyn*. Her forward-firing battery was heavier than his flagship *Hartford*'s, and she had a torpedo rake on her bow, presumably capable of fending off any mines encountered. The flagship took second position, followed by the other big sloop, *Richmond*. These three were paired with the fast, light-draft paddle-wheelers *Octorara, Metacomet,* and *Port Royal.* Once past the fort, these "double-ender" gunboats would be cast off to drive away the *Selma, Gaines,* and *Morgan,* which were of similar force.

Following the lead trio were four more pairs: sloops *Lackawanna* and *Seminole,* sloop *Monongahela* and gunboat *Kennebec,* smaller sloop *Ossipee* and gunboat *Itaska,* and, at the rear, small sloops *Oneida* and *Galena.* The ironclad squadron, parallel and inshore, was led by the single-turret *Tecumseh,* followed by the identical *Manhattan.* Each had two 15-inch guns, the most effective weapons available for countering the *Tennessee.* Light-draft monitors *Winnebago* and *Chickasaw,* each with twin turrets and four 11-inch Dahlgren guns, completed the inshore force.

At 6 A.M. the lines of ships stood in over the bar and headed slowly toward Fort Morgan. Under cloudy skies, the westerly wind fluttered battle ensigns out from every masthead and peak. The flood tide would help carry the ships past the fort, and the breeze was just right for blowing dense black-powder smoke directly into Confederate gunners' eyes. Conditions were virtually ideal for Farragut's scheme.

In Fort Morgan, Brigadier General Richard L. Page sent his men to their guns. Nearly twenty heavy smoothbores and rifled cannon and a similar number of medium guns prepared to rake the ships as they approached, bludgeon their sides as they passed, and rake them again as they stood up into Mobile Bay. Admiral Buchanan, on board the *Tennessee,* hovered near the fort's north side, ready to attack any Union ships that got past the batteries. Farther north his three gunboats were positioned to fire freely at oncoming Federals with little risk of effective reply. A short distance out in the channel the torpedoes waited silently.

Fort Morgan boomed out its initial challenge at six minutes past seven. *Brooklyn*'s 100-pounder Parrott bow rifles answered, followed by *Hartford*'s. Other ships opened up as they came into range. Farragut had climbed into the mainmast rigging of his ship, the better to see over the gunsmoke. From there he had good communication with his pilot in the maintop, with *Hartford*'s captain on the quarterdeck, and with *Meta-*

Men like Lieutenant Commander George U. Morris, whose first ship, the USS Cumberland, *had been sunk by the Rebel ironclad* Virginia (Merrimack), *commanded the* Port Royal *in constant blockade duty off Mobile during 1864.* (USAMHI)

comet's commander alongside. Below the admiral the twelve broadside gun crews stood by, ready to throw 9-inch shells as soon as Fort Morgan loomed into their field of fire. On the forecastle, Parrott-rifle gunners were already loading another round.

The monitor *Manhattan,* second in her line, began slow fire from her one serviceable 15-inch gun. The whole ship shuddered as the piece discharged. Thick smoke wafted down into the hull below the turret. From there, smoke penetrated the hot, poorly ventilated machinery spaces, where conditions were so hellish that sweating coal heavers and engineers required frequent relief. Smoke was so intense topside that the captain, in his tiny conning tower over the turret, could see his consorts and target only with difficulty.

Union blockaders in the Gulf were hard pressed for adequate bases and sometimes had to use far-flung spots like Florida's Fort Taylor on Key West. (USAMHI)

The commanders of the faster-firing double-turret monitors elected to conn from out in the open, where vision was better. *Chickasaw's* young captain, George H. Perkins, was so excited that he stood atop one of his turrets "waving his hat and dancing about with delight and excitement." Despite the heavy surrounding cannonade, neither he nor *Winnebago's* captain were touched.

In the leader, *Tecumseh*, Commander T. A. M. Craven sent off a pair of heavy shells at the very start of the engagement, then reloaded with solid shot and the heaviest powder charges. He was saving his power for the *Tennessee.*

Buchanan watched the Union lines nearing the midpoint of their passage, exchanging a spirited fire with Fort Morgan. He ordered his ponderous ship into motion out into the channel, only a few hundred yards from the *Tecumseh.* Craven turned to port to intercept. Through his conning tower slits he saw a black buoy ahead, seemingly closer inshore than it should have been. Obsessed with stopping the *Tennessee,* he set his course just to the west of the buoy and in the path of the second column of slower-moving ships.

Brooklyn's captain James Alden was surprised and confused by Craven's move. He signaled the flagship: "The monitors are right ahead. We can not go on without passing them. What shall we do?" Farragut was also perplexed. His orders were very clear. Nothing was to prevent the column's advance. Slowing or stopping under the intense fire of the fort risked disaster. The ironclads had been strictly enjoined to keep out of the wooden ships' way. Now, five hundred yards ahead, the *Tecumseh* had turned into his path, and the *Brooklyn* was turning, too.

Suddenly, in what seemed only a matter of seconds, *Tecumseh* shuddered, lurched from side to side, pitched bow down, capsized, and disappeared. Then the *Brooklyn* stopped and began backing hard. Her lookouts had spotted torpedoes in the channel just ahead.

All the careful plans were collapsing, as the battle line began to pile up behind the wayward *Brooklyn.* The ironclads blocked the right-hand route. Above the surface, only the course through the minefield lay clear.

Farragut offered up a hasty prayer for guidance and received the only answer consistent with his character: "Go on!" He called out to those below: "Damn the torpedoes! Four bells!"

Responding to this order, *Hartford's* engines

Farragut, if he could, would make a Yankee base out of Mobile. In July 1864
he staged his mighty fleet in the Gulf, ready to move on Mobile Bay when
the moment was right. Flagship of the fleet was his legendary Hartford, *here*
photographed by McPherson & Oliver, wearing the coat of gray paint used to
make her less visible at sea. The first-class sloop appears shortly after her
fight in Mobile Bay. (MARINERS MUSEUM)

went ahead full. *Metacomet* backed hard. The two ships pivoted to port, the double-ender put her engines back ahead, and the two sped past the *Brooklyn* into the lines of torpedoes. At that instant, two shells struck *Hartford*'s battery directly below the admiral's perch, sweeping away most of two gun crews. While the survivors silently removed the bodies of their comrades and brought their guns back into action, other men felt the torpedoes thudding against the hull. Some thought they heard primers snapping.

Nothing happened. Apparently the mine cases were leaky, and their powder had been rendered inert.

Leaving a boat to rescue the *Tecumseh*'s few survivors, *Hartford* and *Metacomet* pressed northward. *Tennessee* tried to ram them, but was evaded amid an exchange of broadsides. Fire from the Confederate gunboats was more serious. All three peppered the *Hartford* freely, since her bow guns could engage but one enemy ship at a time. One of these rifles was soon knocked out. Another shell exploded between the two foremost broadside guns, causing severe casualties. Again *Hartford*'s dead and wounded were quickly removed and the two guns returned to action.

Bearing this murderous fire for several painful minutes, the *Hartford* finally reached a point where her broadside would bear on the enemy. Successive discharges put *Morgan, Gaines,* and *Selma* to flight. The *Metacomet* shot off in pur-

Farragut leans against a howitzer on the poop deck of the Hartford, *with the ship's commander, Captain Percival Drayton, leaning against the opposite wheel. The two complemented each other perfectly, Drayton highly organized and efficient and Farragut brilliant, intuitive, and impatient for action.* (NAVAL HISTORICAL CENTER)

suit, running down and capturing the *Selma* within an hour. The mortally injured *Gaines* beached herself to avoid sinking. Only the *Morgan* survived; sheltering under the fort's protection until nightfall, she escaped up the bay in the darkness.

West of Fort Morgan, it was about 8 A.M. when *Brooklyn* got the situation sorted out and started forward again. Her captain's indecision had left her the center of attention for the Rebel gunners, who made many damaging hits on her battery, hull, and rigging. Astern, the *Richmond* was hardly struck at all. Both rapidly steamed up the channel, engaging the *Tennessee* in turn. Once clear of that enemy, they also sent their consorts off to chase the fleeing Confederate gunboats.

The intense fire of the monitors and leading three sloops apparently drove many of Fort Morgan's gunners under cover, for the next three pairs of wooden ships passed through with modest damage. Rearguard *Oneida*, smallest of the sloops, received a redoubled fire. In a rain of shot and shell, her starboard boiler was hit and exploded, scalding many of her engineers. The other boiler supplied some steam to the engine, and with the *Galena* gamely pulling at full power, the *Oneida* was able to continue on, pursued by enemy fire until out of range.

Tennessee continued to contest the passage of the follow-up ships. Too slow for successful employment of her ram, she fired as rapidly as a four-gun maximum broadside and unreliable gun primers permitted, making some hits. One

Here McPherson & Oliver capture the Yankee fleet as it rests at anchor outside Mobile Bay, above the parapets of Fort Morgan. Though taken sometime after the battle, the photograph gives a fair idea of what the Confederates might have seen the day before the fight. (NA)

hit badly injured long-suffering *Oneida*'s captain. The ironclad received in return a forceful but ineffective ramming from the *Monongahela* and a number of inconsequential shot hits from the wooden fleet. By 8:40 *Tennessee* had been left behind and returned to the fort to assess the situation.

Farragut had achieved his initial objective. His fleet had entered Mobile Bay, still fit for action. The bay was now closed to enemy use. The forts were isolated. Only the *Tennessee* remained as an unpredictable factor, and he could deal with her in due time. His ships anchored in the pocket of deep water northwest of Fort Morgan and prepared to stand down from the tension and horror of the early morning.

Within minutes, however, lookouts saw the *Tennessee* steaming toward them. Admiral Buchanan had decided to expend her modest coal supply in a desperate last attempt to prevent the loss of Mobile Bay. Even if this failed to destroy the Union fleet, he reasoned, his iron-sided ship could still return to Fort Morgan and do what she could to buy time for strengthening the upbay defenses.

It was a forlorn hope. Farragut quickly sent *Lackawanna* and *Monongahela* off to intercept and ram the enemy ironclad while the rest of the fleet got ready. Receiving his orders to engage, *Chickasaw*'s Perkins almost somersaulted overboard with joy. Exuberant as he appeared, Perkins' cool conduct in the following hour largely determined the outcome.

The *Monongahela* went full speed at the *Ten-*

Mobile's defenses had been well designed. Confederate Brigadier General Danville Leadbetter was a native of Maine and as an engineer in the U.S. Army and after 1857 as a civilian had spent years here building harbor works. In 1863 he returned to Mobile to supervise the defenses being erected by Southerners. (USAMHI)

nessee, hit her sharply on the starboard side, shuddered to a halt, and backed away. She received a crushed bow and two shots into the berth deck for her trouble. *Tennessee* seemed unscathed. *Lackawanna* followed with a similar blow to the ironclad's other beam, with like result. The opponents exchanged shots, musketry, insults, and thrown debris as they separated.

Close behind, the *Hartford* also tried to ram, but struck obliquely. Her unshipped anchor took the blow and was bent beyond use. Ironclad and sloop passed port side to port side, a few feet apart. Admiral Farragut watched from an impromptu battle station in the port mizzen shrouds as *Hartford*'s massed 9-inch smoothbores blasted away with solid shot and heavy charges,

making a negligible impression on *Tennessee*'s iron casemate. The latter's low-set broadside discharged directly into the *Hartford*'s berth deck, causing heavy casualties among her ammunition party. Farragut's flagship steamed away to try again, but collided with the *Lackawanna*. The battle was over for both of them, though their injuries were not crippling.

The Federal monitors arrived. A Confederate officer watched as "a hideous-looking monster came creeping up on our Port side, whose slowly revolving turret revealed the cavernous depths of a mammoth gun." It was the *Manhattan*. Only one of her 15-inchers worked that day, but it made damaging hits, smashing away armor plate, crushing backing timbers and shocking the enemy with the force of her blows. The *Chickasaw* doggedly clung to the *Tennessee*'s flanks, hammering away at the aft part of her casemate with 11-inch shot. Other ships fired from a distance. In less than half an hour, *Tennessee*'s steering was destroyed, her smokestack knocked away, most of her gunport shutters jammed and her casemate smashed nearly to collapse.

Inside, Admiral Buchanan and a working party were trying to clear one of the after port shutters, so some reply could be made. A shot hit directly opposite them. Despite armor, the concussion and splinters devastated those nearby. Two men were killed and Buchanan's leg so badly broken that he had to be carried below.

Although no Federal projectiles had entered the protected casemate, the *Tennessee* was by this time "sore beset." Unable to steer, unable to fire, power plant crippled by the loss of the smokestack, hull leaking from the effects of rammings, and the casemate aft wall on the verge of falling in, she had little choice. Reluctantly, inevitably, a white flag was pushed up from the battery grating. Firing ceased. The onrushing *Ossipee*, bent on another ramming attempt and unable to stop in time, struck one final blow. Sending a boat, *Ossipee* took possession of the prize. With that, just at ten o'clock in the morning of August 5, 1864, the Battle of Mobile Bay was over.

Months earlier, Farragut had commented: "How unequal the contest is between ironclads and wooden vessels in loss of life." How correct he was. His fleet had suffered more than fifty

The Alabama shorefront bristled with water batteries like this captured Confederate one outside Fort Morgan, photographed by New Orleans artists Moses & Piffet in September 1864. (NA)

men killed, nearly half of them on his own flagship, plus over ninety souls carried down with the torpedoed *Tecumseh*. Confederate casualties were almost trivial by comparison: a dozen killed in the ships, one man dead in the fort.

But battles are not decided on ''points.'' The Southern squadron had been swept away. Within

a few days, Fort Powell had been evacuated and Fort Gaines surrendered. On August 23, after General Granger's siege lines reached Fort Morgan's walls and heavy shellfire threatened to destroy its garrison inside inadequate ''bombproof'' bunkers, General Page capitulated. Mobile city remained in Confederate hands nearly until

*McPherson & Oliver made a better image of the batteries that September and
followed it with others . . .* (USAMHI)

war's end, but its value to the Confederacy was
gone.

Strategically, the Battle of Mobile Bay was a
sideshow to the vast campaigns then underway
in Georgia and Virginia. Even within the blockading effort, it was not more than a junior part-
ner to the greater undertakings at Charleston,
South Carolina, and Wilmington, North Carolina. The numbers of men and ships involved
were slight—a few thousand troops and a modest
fraction of the navy on the Northern side, even

fewer on the Confederate. Mobile's neutraliza-
tion was simply another ratchet notch in the
great Union windlass that was by then inexo-
rably reeling in the South.

However, this August morning with Farragut
provides a peerless object lesson in the benefits
of close, friendly cooperation between army and
navy. Most importantly, it is an unexcelled in-
stance of inspired leadership and heroic determination. More than a century later, it still
commands attention and respect.

. . . like this picture of three more captured Confederate guns facing the sea. (NA)

The Confederate commander of Mobile was a distinguished officer with a hopeless task, Major General Dabney H. Maury of Virginia. He had too few men with too little weaponry against too much. It was the old Confederate story. (P-M)

Maury's subordinate commanding the post of Mobile was Brigadier General Thomas H. Taylor of Kentucky, a veteran of Vicksburg where he was captured, who came back into the service after his parole and exchange only to be assigned to another doomed city. (VALENTINE MUSEUM)

There were several forts protecting Mobile, but the only one of real consequence was powerful Fort Morgan, a giant masonry and earth fortification built several years before the war. McPherson & Oliver made a series of views of the place after the fight, including this one of the front facade. The wreckage left by the bombardment it suffered is plain to see. (CHS)

Another front view of the fort shows a row of mortars awaiting emplacement,
several Union soldiers with their arms stacked, and on the horizon the badly
battered lighthouse. (CHS)

The southwest face looks much the same, battered and damaged, belying the
tranquil form of the lounger in the foreground. (CHS)

The front and west side of Fort Morgan shows a little less damage, but the poor lighthouse seems barely able to stand. (USAMHI)

On August 5, 1864, Farragut, seated right, ordered his fleet to steam past Fort Morgan's batteries and into the bay. Drayton, left, was flag captain for the day, commanding the Hartford. (NHC)

The USS Hartford's helm, manned just as it was that morning of the attack, with, left to right, Seaman Joseph Cassier, Captain of the Forecastle John McFarland, Landsman James Reddington, and Quartermaster James Wood. McFarland in particular distinguished himself, receiving the Medal of Honor for outstanding performance of his duty in the battle. (NHC)

Here men of the Hartford's *after guard pose near one of her 9-inch guns. Directly behind them, rising out of the picture, are the mizzen shrouds where Farragut placed himself during the battle with the ironclad* Tennessee. (NHC)

The Hartford's *gun deck, by McPherson & Oliver. The starboard battery of 9-inch Dahlgrens is at the right, these being the guns that engaged Fort Morgan during the passage of the fleet. Here was done terrible carnage among Farragut's gun crews. The two officers standing at the left are Lieutenants George Mundy and La Rue P. Adams, who commanded most of those guns. Adams himself was wounded.* (NHC)

Captain James Alden was supposed to take the lead with his sloop Brooklyn, *but he ran into a problem and caused considerable confusion before* Hartford *surged on past him. He and the admiral were never very friendly again.* (NHC)

The USS Ossipee, *photographed at Honolulu in 1867, was a light sloop that Farragut stationed toward the rear of his line as it braved Fort Morgan's guns. She suffered almost no damage at all.* (NHC)

This Winnebago-*class monitor is probably the* Kickapoo, *sister ship of the monitors* Chickasaw *and* Winnebago *that brought up the rear of Farragut's line. Neither the admiral nor the monitors' commanders had too much faith in them, and* Winnebago *was nearly put out of action in the battle. The* Kickapoo *joined the fleet at Mobile some weeks after the battle.*
(U.S. MILITARY ACADEMY, WEST POINT)

Only one ship was actually crippled by Confederate fire, the sloop Oneida *commanded by Commander J. R. Madison Mullany. He had begged to get into the action that day, and Farragut temporarily assigned him to the* Oneida. *Fire from the CSS* Tennessee *damaged his left arm so badly that it had to be amputated.* (NHC)

One of the greatest heroes of the fight, however, was Ensign Henry C. Nields of Metacomet. *When the USS* Tecumseh *hit a mine and sank, he took a boat out into the channel under heavy fire to rescue her survivors. He saved ten of them.* (NHC)

The most feared enemy for Farragut were not the mines—called "torpedoes"—but the dreaded Rebel ironclad Tennessee, *shown here after her surrender in a photo probably made in New Orleans. Built like almost all Confederate ironclads, she had the strengths and weaknesses of her type. Her four 6.4-inch and two 7-inch Brooke rifles were no match for some of Farragut's heavy cannon.* (LC)

Still, she was a formidable vessel and well handled under the command of a real veteran of ironclad warfare . . . (NHC)

. . . Admiral Franklin Buchanan. He it was who commanded the CSS Virginia *in her fight with the* Cumberland *two years before, taking a wound in the battle. In the fight with Farragut, Buchanan's leg was badly shattered.* (NHC)

Buchanan's chief adversary was Commander James Strong, who brought his sloop Monongahela *in close and repeatedly rammed the Rebel ironclad with his specially prepared prow. This portrait is by Gurney & Son of New York.* (CIVIL WAR TIMES ILLUSTRATED COLLECTION)

And all the while, Fort Morgan's guns were bombarding the Union fleet as it passed. The fort's batteries were so arranged that Farragut had either to risk coming in close to them and taking a heavy shelling or passing through a more distant channel filled with torpedoes. By accident he chose the latter. Fort Morgan itself came in for its share of bombardment later on. (NA)

An elevated view of the fort shows the extensive damage it suffered from the land bombardment on August 22 that followed Farragut's passage. Like all masonry forts in the war, Fort Morgan did not stand up well under siege artillery. (CHS)

The bombardment made a mess of its parapets. (NA)

*The so-called citadel of Fort Morgan, viewed from the south by McPherson &
Oliver, shows the collapsed roofs and toppled chimneys of a beleaguered
fortress. The Confederate gunners did not dare serve their guns on the top
tier.* (KA)

Instead, they had to hide below in equally unstable "bombproofs" while the Yankees sent shell after shell at them. (KA)

It proved very frustrating indeed for the fort's commander, Brigadier General Richard L. Page of Virginia. He had been a captain in the Confederate Navy, then switched to the Army. Fort Morgan was to be his only command. He stands here with his family. (WILLIAM ALBAUGH COLLECTION)

The main gate, or sally port, of Fort Morgan. Even though the damage from the bombardment is not yet cleaned up, already the conquering Yankees have built ornamental shot pyramids beside the portals. A giant gun sling stands at far right. (NA)

Part of the interior of the fort shows a reinforced bombproof and sandbagged parapet, hasty measures to futilely resist the enemy's heavy siege guns. (NA)

The parade of the fort looks like a wasteland after its surrender. (NA)

The Civil War almost ended the era of the masonry seacoast fortification, and the damage done to Fort Morgan shows why. Page and his garrison were fortunate to hold long enough to surrender without being buried alive. (NA)

Their guns, like this 8-inch British Blakely, were no match for what the Yankees could throw at them. (NA)

Fort Morgan's southeast bastion in September 1864, the guns now silent, looked out upon nothing but the quarters of some of the victorious Federals. (KA)

The fort's once thundering parapet is now a place for loungers and sightseers.
(NA)

*There they could see the damage done to this dismounted Columbiad by
accurate Yankee fire.* (NA)

They could also view the whole scene of destruction and read in it some metaphor for the doom of the Confederacy. (KA)

Fort Morgan was a great scene of devastation, so overwhelming that McPherson & Oliver could not stop photographing it, though some of their shots were becoming redundant. (KA)

Though not itself a target, the lighthouse on Mobile Point, near the fort, was particularly damaged by shots that went high and passed over the fort. In the distance stands a makeshift signal tower, while at the foot of the lighthouse sits the hot-shot furnace. Out on the parapet, men have placed comfortable chairs to enjoy the midday air and sea breezes. (KA)

Somehow the battered lighthouse seems symbolic of the fallen fortress and of the Southern cause for independence that by this time was teetering in precarious balance. (NA)

While Farragut handled the naval end of the victory at Mobile Bay, it was Major General Gordon Granger, a hero of Chickamauga, who besieged Fort Morgan into submission. (USAMHI)

The fort surrendered on August 23, 1864, almost three weeks after the naval battle was over. After the surrender Farragut and Granger met for a camera sitting, having offered in their operations a model of Army-Navy cooperation not often emulated. Granger's commanding officer, Major General E. R. S. Canby, would remark later that "the relations that have existed between the two services . . . have been of the most intimate and cordial character and have resulted in successes of which friends of both the Army and the Navy have reason to be proud." (USAMHI)

Later the old USS Potomac, *a sailing frigate more than thirty years old, played host to the captured officers of the Rebel ironclad* Tennessee. *Too old for active fighting, the proud old wooden ship played its support role to the end.* (USAMHI)

It was a welcome rest when the operations for Mobile Bay were complete, and officers of the USS Hartford *could relax on deck. All of these men were aboard during the battle. They are ensigns, lieutenants, and surgeons and a captain of marines. It is a well-earned rest.* (NHC)

As for the CSS Tennessee, *there will be no rest for her. Here she is in New Orleans, being refitted to go into service as the USS* Tennessee. *Having done their best to destroy her, her captors are now ready to add the ship to the ever-growing arsenal of Union naval might.* (USAMHI)

Houghton at the Front

A PORTFOLIO

The little-known Vermont photographer G. H. Houghton
went to the war in 1862 for an unforgettable series

AS WITH SO MANY of the war's camera artists, little is known of the Green Mountain photographer G. H. Houghton, of Brattleboro, Vermont. This is all the more unfortunate given the unusually high quality of his work. In at least two trips to the Virginia front in early 1862 and early 1863, Houghton made nearly a hundred images that survive, and probably more that do not. He photographed Vermont soldiers on the Peninsula in what was a considerable change of pace for an artist whose usual work was outdoor scenes of his native state. But Houghton was an unusual artist. Though few hometown photographers went any farther than the army camps when they came to the war zone, Houghton went beyond the camps and took his camera very close indeed to the front. And unlike those of many of his contemporaries, his war views eschewed the modest carte de visite format and appeared instead in large, beautifully detailed prints which he marketed back home in Brattleboro.

A brave, able, and innovative artist, G. H. Houghton of Vermont exemplified the hundreds of unknown photographers who recognized that in this war lay the greatest event of their generation, something worth the effort and the danger to record.

*"Photographer's Home," Houghton called this scene. It was one seen
throughout the war-torn country—the itinerant artist's tent studio or hastily
erected "Picture Gallery," ready to capture for the boys in blue or gray their
likenesses. Houghton's establishment here at Camp Griffin, Virginia, was a
bit different, however, for he came to record the look of his fellow Vermonters
in the field as they battled on the Peninsula in the spring of 1862.* (VERMONT
HISTORICAL SOCIETY)

Few photographers of the war could surpass Houghton's ability with the lens. There was a tranquillity about his work that belied the deadly business that populated these tents with fighting men around Brigadier General William F. Smith's headquarters at Camp Griffin. (VHS)

*Houghton, in fact, began chronicling the career of Green Mountain soldiers
even before they left home. Here he records the camp of the 1st Vermont
near Brattleboro. (VHS)*

*And now, down in Virginia, he captures the scene of the 4th Vermont in
Camp Griffin, the regiment drawn up, company after company, off to the
left, while their band prepares to enspirit them with martial song. (VHS)*

The 2d Vermont was here in Camp Griffin, too, less formal for the camera.
The man in the center of the standing group appears to hold a newspaper.
(VHS)

Houghton caught the 16th Vermont in their "winterized" tents at Union
Mills. (VHS)

And the men of the 12th Vermont at Wolf Run Shoals. The men of Company B are ready for a hard winter. The leaves have left the trees, and already the stumps left by ravenous firewood parties testify to the cold. (VHS)

*The 3d Vermont camp in Virginia revealed an unusual, if rude, bit of
construction, probably a stable for the wagon teams or a commissary
storehouse. It would not provide much obstruction to the wind.* (VHS)

*Company A of the 13th Vermont went into camp directly next to a battery it
was supporting. Between clearing the woods for a field of fire for the cannon,
and foraging for firewood, the forest is representative of the devastation done
to Virginia's woodlands by the war.* (VHS)

The 6th Vermont made its headquarters here at Camp Griffin, its bandsmen standing proudly—if somewhat chilly in their greatcoats—with their instruments. (VHS)

Houghton turned his camera to the places where power stayed, like General Smith's headquarters at a place called Becky Lee's Opening. (VHS)

Smith's favorite campaign horse made a more than fitting subject for the lens, seemingly as casual about the camera as the young "contraband" holding his head. (VHS)

The generals themselves, as always, were happy to pose for Houghton. Brigadier General William F. Smith, standing in the center, a Vermonter, was soon to command a division in the VI Corps. His hat conceals the thin hair that led to his nickname "Baldy." Standing at the right is Brigadier General John Newton, a Virginian who remained loyal to the Union. And at the left is Brigadier General Winfield Scott Hancock. Eighteen years from now he will narrowly lose a bid for the presidency to another former Civil War general, James A. Garfield. (VHS)

Hancock himself made his headquarters under this mulberry tree at Cold Harbor, Virginia. He sits at the left of the shadowy group under its branches. (VHS)

And he sits at the left here, too, legs crossed and looking casual as he is joined by one of his fellow brigade commanders in Smith's division, Brigadier General William T. H. Brooks, seated next to him. Ironically, in 1864, even before the war was over, Brooks resigned his commission and began farming —in Alabama! (VHS)

*Houghton turned his camera to a group of officers in Fort Lincoln that
winter as well. Colonel Hiram Berdan, leader of the famed Berdan's
Sharpshooters, leans backward (left center) against the cannon tube. Leaning
on it with him, his foot on the carriage trail, is Brigadier General John W.
Davidson, a native Virginian now commanding a brigade in Smith's division.*
(VHS)

For all the attention he gave the officers, Houghton was really more interested in the common soldiers. He came to the camp of Company F, 4th Vermont, where the Green Mountain boys agreeably struck the variety of camp poses that the people back home liked to see. (VHS)

Even some of the company officers struck a homey pose. For reasons of their own, they dubbed the agreeable young lieutenant seated right "Infant John." (VHS)

Sergeant Rogers' men of Company A, 4th Vermont, look suitably rustic. It is to be hoped that the tiny tent was not supposed to hold all four of them. (VHS)

Houghton caught the teamsters and mechanics attached to Smith's headquarters at their work. All manner of tools—shovels, wagon jacks, axes, and mauls—litter the ground at the left; a portable forge and smithy stands at the far right. (VHS)

Regimental bands like that of the 4th Vermont were always happy to dress up for the camera. (VHS)

Less formally attired, the bandsmen relax in camp amid their instruments and boxes of "pilot bread" (hardtack) like the one making a seat for the soldier at the left. (VHS)

One might have expected a lot of sour notes from all those dour Vermont faces. (VHS)

But dour or no, these Vermonters could look splendid when they wanted to. The 12th Vermont presents an immaculate line for Houghton at Wolf Run Shoals. (VHS)

Company A of the 4th Vermont looks formidable indeed as they pose at charge of bayonet. Yet there is still a lot of innocence in some of those young faces. War has not yet hardened them. (VHS)

One of Smith's batteries runs through its drill. (VHS)

And here Houghton views a so-called masked battery of 10-pounder Parrott rifles near the Golding farm on the Peninsula. (VHS)

Here an entire battery stands in position, banner flying and officers leaning on their swords. This is dress rehearsal for the sake of the camera, not the way they would look in battle. (VHS)

Houghton, like other photographers, did not focus his lens on actual battle scenes, but he did follow the army's movements a little in Virginia. Here he shows part of one regiment breaking camp near Newport News, the wagons loading tents and equipment for the march. (VHS)

*And here at Lee's Mill, Houghton watches as a battery of Major General
Romeyn Ayres's Union artillery crosses an earth dam built by the
Confederates. Defenses once occupied by the enemy show in the background.*
(VHS)

The previous image must have been taken sometime after this one was made, showing the same scene from a different angle. Houghton later claimed that the Rebels were still in their works when he exposed this negative. If so, the graycoats were acting very camera shy. (VHS)

Houghton also looked at some of the country through which his Vermont compatriots tramped and fought, finding some marvelous scenes like this one of Ford's old mill at Wolf Run Shoals. Soldiers are popping out of the windows. (VHS)

He found this slave family at the Gaines house, facing untold changes in their lives in the years to come. (VHS)

And Houghton found some Vermont boys for whom life's last change had just taken place. Soldiers stand quietly, out of respect for their dead comrades at Camp Griffin. (VHS)

Alas, it was the most oft-repeated scene of the war. Men of the 6th Vermont, alive just before the fight at Lee's Mill, are now reduced to names on rude headboards in the Virginia soil. (VHS)

There they would wait until their government or their families could have them brought home. (VHS)

Happily for those who lived, there was a return to home as well, and to a jubilant reception. Here the 4th Vermont comes home to Brattleboro, their uniforms and posture showing that they are hardened veterans now. It is no wonder that the admiring schoolboys cluster and caper around them. They are all local heroes. And so, too, is G. H. Houghton, who went to war with them and brought home the record of their time of trial. (VHS)

The Great March

JOHN G. BARRETT

"From Atlanta to the sea" and on through the Carolinas,
the indomitable Sherman could not be stopped

IN THE LATE AUTUMN of 1864 Major General William T. Sherman with 62,000 men; 35,000 horses, mules, and cattle; 2,500 wagons; 600 ambulances; and a horde of followers marched across the heart of Georgia, leveling much of the countryside and demoralizing the civilian population. This campaign, from Atlanta to Savannah, known as the "March to the Sea," was but one part of a larger operation which had begun the previous May at Chattanooga, Tennessee, and was to end near Durham, North Carolina, in April 1865.

Only in the mountains of northwest Georgia and around Atlanta did the Federal army meet sustained resistance. Thus the moves from Atlanta to the coast and up through the Carolinas were important for reasons other than victories on the battlefield. Their primary significance rests upon the fact that these campaigns provided a glimpse of what later was called "total war."

Two years earlier, while on duty in western Tennessee, Sherman had evolved his philosophy of total war. Concluding that it was impossible to change the hearts of the people of the South, he decided that he could "make war so terrible" that Southerners would exhaust all peaceful remedies before starting another conflict. He stated that while the Southern people "cannot be made to love us, [they] can be made to fear us and dread the passage of troops through their country." Considering all of the people of the South as enemies of the Union, Sherman planned to use his military forces against the civilian population as well as against the armies of the enemy. He believed this plan of action would demoralize not only the noncombatants but also the men under arms. His program of warfare also called for the destruction of the enemy's economic resources. In bringing the war to the home front he hoped to destroy the South's will to fight. With Sherman war was not "popularity seeking." War was "hell." Still, it was not a sense of cruelty and barbarism that prompted him to formulate his new theory of war. It was more a search for the quickest and surest means to end a bloody conflict.

The first application of this new philosophy of war was to be in Mississippi. In Georgia and the Carolinas, however, Sherman repeated the performance but on a much larger scale.

On November 15, 1864, Sherman's army moved out of Atlanta, which had been in its possession since early September, to begin the

*On the march again. Major General William T. Sherman would not stop
with the capture of Atlanta in early September 1864. There was the rest of
Georgia to conquer and a war to win.* (NEW-YORK HISTORICAL SOCIETY)

And now his goal would be one of the loveliest cities in all the South, a
perfect jewel untouched by the ravages of the war, Savannah. George N.
Barnard captured this image of the peaceful river town shortly after the war.
(LC)

March to the Sea. This move was a bold, im-
aginative stroke, but not one designed to draw
off enemy troops. Confederate General John
Bell Hood, after losing Atlanta, had hoped, by
assuming the offensive in late September and
marching for Tennessee, to checkmate his foe.
But Sherman, after a futile pursuit, decided to
abandon the chase and to move, instead, into
the interior of Georgia "to smash things up." So
in mid-November one of the curiosities of the
war occurred. This date found the two main
armies in the Western theater, bitter antagonists
for three years, purposely moving in opposite
directions, never to meet again.

The Federal army on its March to the Sea
was divided into two parts. Major General
Oliver O. Howard commanded the right wing
which was composed of the XV and XVII Corps

commanded respectively by Major Generals
Peter J. Osterhaus and Francis P. Blair, Jr. The
left wing, under Major General Henry W. Slocum, consisted of Brigadier General Jefferson C.
Davis' XIV Corps and Brigadier General Alpheus S. Williams' XX Corps. The cavalry was
led by Brigadier General Hugh Judson Kilpatrick.

This army marched from Atlanta in three
parallel columns, five to fifteen miles apart, and
forming a thirty- to sixty-mile front. Averaging
ten to fifteen miles a day, it pushed relentlessly
toward the coast. The right wing moved
through Jonesboro and then to Monticello,
Gordon, and Irwinton. The left wing headed
toward Covington, Madison, Eatonton, and
Milledgeville, the state capital. In the meantime,
Kilpatrick's cavalry struck toward Macon and

*It was a rested and ready army that Sherman led on its March to the Sea. A
close friend from Missouri, Major General Francis Preston Blair, Jr.,
commanded the XVII Corps. Seated here in the center with his staff, Blair
finished the war a bankrupt, having spent himself dry in behalf of the Union
cause.* (USAMHI)

then withdrew to Gordon and rejoined Sherman
at Milledgeville. The general was traveling with
the left wing. By November 23 Slocum's entire
command was united in and around the capital
city. The right wing was close by at Gordon,
twelve miles to the south.

In Milledgeville the governor's mansion,
which served as Sherman's headquarters, and the
capitol were spared the torch by the Federal
soldiers. The penitentiary, arsenal, and depot,
however, were destroyed by the men in blue,
who also took great delight in holding a mock
session of the Georgia legislature. They declared
the ordinance of secession repealed and voted the
state back into the Union.

The next day the march resumed. Sherman
accompanied the XX Corps which took the direct road to Sandersville. This small community
was reached simultaneously with the XIV Corps
two days later. Earlier, Howard's right wing had
started its movement along the Georgia Central

Railroad toward the coast, tearing up the track
as it went. By December 10 all four of the
Federal corps had reached the vicinity of
Savannah.

When Sherman learned that the city's defenses
had recently been strengthened by the arrival of
15,000 troops under Lieutenant General William J. Hardee, he decided that before launching
an attack he should first establish contact with
the Federal fleet in Ossabaw Sound, south of the
city. The quickest route to the water was along
the banks of the Ogeechee River which flowed
into the sound. But on the south side of the
Ogeechee, near its mouth and fifteen miles from
Savannah, stood small yet formidable Fort Mc-
Allister.

Sherman ordered Brigadier General William
B. Hazen's division to cross the river and take
the fort. The successful assault, lasting barely
fifteen minutes, took place late on the afternoon
of December 13 under the approving eyes of

Leading the XIV Corps was Brevet Major General Jefferson C. Davis, a veteran of the ill-fated defense of Fort Sumter in April 1861, a man who had shot and killed—some said murdered—a fellow Union general in an argument, and a fighter of unquestioned ability. He sits, gloves and sword in hand, among his staff in a photograph made in Washington in July 1865. (USAMHI)

General Sherman who remained on the north bank of the Ogeechee. Hazen's casualties were three times those of the enemy. Still, he managed to capture the entire Confederate garrison along with fifteen guns.

That night, aboard the gunboat *Dandelion* in Ossabaw Sound, Sherman wrote Secretary of War Edwin Stanton that he regarded "Savannah as already gained," and so it was. Hardee abandoned the city on the night of December 20, retreating across the Savannah River on pontoon bridges covered with rice straw to muffle the sound of horses and wagons. By the next morning the port city was in Federal hands, and on December 22 Sherman wired President Lincoln: "I beg to present you as a Christmas-gift the city of Savannah, with one hundred and fifty guns and plenty of ammunition, also about twenty-five thousand bales of cotton."

For the Federal soldiers the march through Georgia had been "one big picnic." Having destroyed the railroad to his rear, Sherman was dependent upon the countryside for supplies. The army, in order to subsist, was permitted to forage freely as it moved through the fertile lands of the state. Meeting only token resistance from Major General Joseph Wheeler's cavalry and the Georgia militia, the men, as one of them put it, "rioted and feasted on the country," and the order to "forage freely" was interpreted by some to loot and burn. On a sixty-mile front the army had devastated the land as it moved toward the coast.

By all of the accepted rules of strategy, Sherman's veterans should have been transferred immediately to a theater where they "could pull their own weight." The Federal Navy had the ships to transport them to Virginia where Lieu-

One of the foremost non-West Point-trained officers of the war led the XV Corps after January 8, 1865, as the Union Army made its way north from Savannah. Major General John A. Logan was a politician with a natural bent for war. In this portrait made at war's end, he wears mourning crape for President Lincoln on his sleeve, and a XV Corps badge on his blouse. (CWTI)

Brigadier General Alpheus S. Williams temporarily commanded the XX Corps on the March to the Sea. He wears on his blouse the star badge of his corps. (USAMHI)

tenant General Ulysses S. Grant had General Robert E. Lee bottled up behind fortifications at Petersburg. Grant was desirous of this move but Sherman was not. He wanted, instead, to apply total war to the Carolinas. Every step northward from Savannah, he felt, was as much a direct attack on Lee at Petersburg as would be operations within sound of the artillery of the Army of Northern Virginia. Furthermore, Sherman was not adverse in the least to the idea of punishing South Carolina for her role in bringing on the war.

When the news of Major General George Thomas' resounding Union victory over Hood at Nashville, Tennessee, reached Grant on December 18, he penned Sherman a confidential note giving him permission to move through the Carolinas. This communication reached Savannah on Christmas eve. An elated Sherman immediately informed his chief that he expected "to be ready to sally forth again" in about ten days.

In Savannah the Federal troops were generally well behaved. Brigadier General John W. Geary's division of Easterners garrisoned the city and, with the exception of a few minor incidents, all depredations ceased. Sherman even went so far as to permit Episcopal churches to omit prayers for the President of the United

The men that these and other generals led would really decide the outcome of the campaign, and they were the raw, toughened Western fighters who had already been blooded at places like Shiloh and Chickamauga. "In my judgment," said Sherman, they were "the most magnificent army in existence." (USAMHI)

States, saying at the same time to ministers who asked if they might pray for the Confederate President, "Yes, Jeff Davis and the devil both need it." Also, the general wisely allowed the city officials to retain their posts, and he strengthened the hand of the mayor, Dr. Richard D. Arnold, whom he had known before the war. In fact, the situation was so peaceful in "handsome" Savannah that every day seemed like a Sunday to Sherman.

During this period of relative tranquillity, preparations for the march north were not neglected. It was a busy time. Nevertheless, very few changes were made in the organization of the army. As during the March to the Sea, it comprised two wings of two corps each. The cavalry remained under Judson Kilpatrick. In the upper command posts there was only one major change. Major General John A. Logan replaced Osterhaus as commander of the XV Corps.

Sherman's plan of campaign called for feints on both Augusta, Georgia, and Charleston, South Carolina, and a march directly on Columbia, the South Carolina capital, and then to Goldsboro, North Carolina, by way of Fayetteville, on the Cape Fear River. Goldsboro was chosen as the destination because that city was connected to the North Carolina coast by two rail lines running, respectively, from Morehead City (via New Bern) and Wilmington, to the south. By this circuit the Federal army could destroy the two chief railroads of the Carolinas, disrupt enemy supply transportation, and devastate the heart of the two states.

The officers, like these of the 82d Illinois posing in Atlanta, could look civilized enough, indeed resplendent at times. (CHS)

Sherman planned to cut himself off completely from his base in Savannah, hence he could expect no government supplies until he reached the Cape Fear River. His wagons could carry only limited provisions. Thus the army once again would have to "forage liberally on the country during the march." To regulate the foraging parties, very strict orders were issued. But, as was the case in Georgia, there was a wide discrepancy between the orders and the actions of some of the men. Foraging parties many times degenerated into marauding bands of mounted robbers which operated not under the supervision of an officer but on their own. Most of the pillage and wanton destruction of property in both Georgia and the Carolinas was the work of the "bummers," as this peripheral minority of self-constituted parties of foragers was called.

When Sherman crossed the Savannah River and commenced his march through the Carolinas

the latter part of January 1865, the meager Confederate forces that could possibly be brought to oppose him were scattered from Virginia to Mississippi. So by February 7 the major part of the Federal army had penetrated without difficulty well into South Carolina and was encamped along the South Carolina Railroad. Five days later Orangeburg, to the north, was in Sherman's hands.

From Orangeburg the army moved out in the direction of the capital city of Columbia, destroying the railroad as it went. By late afternoon of February 15, only two weeks and a day after the invasion of the Palmetto State had begun in earnest, Sherman's troopers were within four miles of Columbia, called by them the "hellhole of secession." That evening the so-called Battle of Columbia began when a division of the XV Corps quite carelessly camped within range of the Confederate artillery east of the

But the boys in the ranks, unlike their counterparts in the Army of the Potomac, never took the spit and polish of soldiering to heart. They were as content with informality as these men of the 17th Ohio, posing with friends back home. (LO)

Congaree River and got a mild shelling. The next morning, February 16, Federal skirmishers carried the Confederate defenses around the Congaree River bridge but found only the charred timbers of the structures remaining. On this same date Sherman issued his instructions for the occupation of the city. General Howard was to "destroy public buildings, railroad property, manufacturing, and machine shops" but was to "spare libraries, and asylums, and private dwellings."

By this time Columbia had become a city without law and order. Chaos prevailed. The establishment of martial law on February 17 had not prevented acts of robbery and pillage. Negroes, soldiers, and local citizens either vied with one another for government provisions or turned their attention to the looting of shops and stores.

Early on the morning of the same day Columbia was awakened by a tremendous explosion at the South Carolina Railroad depot, caused in all probability by a looter accidentally igniting the powder stored there. And with the coming of daylight the looting got worse. The state commissary was plundered and in some parts of Main Street, it was reported, "corn and flour and sugar cover[ed] the ground." All the while Lieutenant General Wade Hampton's Confederate cavalry was slowly withdrawing from the city along the Camden and Winnsboro roads.

Columbia, undefended and deranged, was now at the complete mercy of the enemy. Sometime before noon Sherman, with a few members of his staff, rode into the city. Fewer than twelve hours later a large part of South Carolina's capital, including the state house and other public buildings, scores of private homes, several churches, and even a convent lay in smoldering ruins, the result of a great fire that had raged uncontrolled throughout the night. The origin of this conflagration has been the subject of considerable controversy from the day it occurred.

The most likely explanation is that it began from burning cotton. Columbia at this time was a virtual firetrap because of the hundreds of cotton bales in her streets. Some of these had been ignited before Sherman arrived, and a high wind spread tufts of the burning fiber over the city. Also, poorly disciplined troops, many of whom were intoxicated, became incendiaries. In a laconic statement made after the war General Sherman summed up his sentiments on the burning of Columbia: "Though I never ordered it and never wished it, I have never shed any tears over the event, because I believe that it hastened what we all fought for, the end of the war."

The Federal army remained in the city for two days, destroying under orders railroad and public property. The Evans & Cogswell Company, which held the contract for printing Confederate money, was burned, as was the state armory on Arsenal Hill. "They destroyed everything which the most infernal Yankee ingenuity could devise means to destroy," said one native of

But such an army could march and fight. Indeed, Sherman's wagon trains, like this one photographed near Savannah, were often hard put to keep pace. (USAMHI)

Columbia. Then, on February 20, to the accompaniment of hisses and boos from the people along the streets, the troops moved out in the direction of Winnsboro.

This historic old town, as well as Camden to the southeast, and Cheraw to the northeast, suffered much at the hands of the Federal troops. At Cheraw, the army's last stop in South Carolina, Sherman learned that his former antagonist in Georgia, General Joseph E. Johnston, had replaced General P. G. T. Beauregard as commander of the Confederate Army of Tennessee in North and South Carolina. He now concluded that Johnston would unite his widely scattered forces and, at a place of his own choosing, strike one of the Federal corps on the move. Fully aware that the battle he wished to avoid was, in all probability, unavoidable, Sherman put his army in motion for Fayetteville, North Carolina, some seventy miles northeast of Cheraw.

South Carolina was now free of this army which had applied total war in its severest terms within her borders. Lieutenant Charles S. Brown of the 21st Michigan never spoke truer words

They also had to be wary of lightning raids by Confederate cavalrymen like Major General Joseph Wheeler, who accounted for much of the Southern attempt to keep Sherman at bay during the March to the Sea. It was a hopeless task. And it came at a price, for the dashing Wheeler could not control his men. One superior wanted him relieved "for the good of the cause, and for his own reputation." Yet he would go on fighting, and thirty-four years later he would fight again, this time for the United States. In the Spanish-American War, old Joe Wheeler became a Major General of U.S. Volunteers. (LC)

than when he said: "South Carolina may have been the cause of the whole thing, but she has had an awful punishment."

General Sherman entered North Carolina at the beginning of March with the confident expectation of receiving a friendly welcome from its supposedly large number of pro-Union citizens. Thus he had his officers issue orders for the gentler treatment of the inhabitants, and when the state line was crossed, he circulated new instructions regulating foraging activities. But no orders were drafted prohibiting the burning of the great pine forests within the state.

North Carolina's turpentine woods blazed in fantastic splendor as "bummers touched matches to congealed sap in notches on tree trunks." Seldom did the soldiers pass up an opportunity to fire these pine forests, for the burning rosin and tar created a spectacle of flame and smoke that surpassed in grandeur anything they had ever seen before.

On March 8 North Carolina for the first time felt the full weight of the Federal army, the right wing having crossed the state line on this date. General Sherman, traveling with the XV Corps, made his headquarters near the Laurel Hill Presbyterian Church, a region his soldiers thought looked "real Northernlike," but tor-

Major General Ambrose R. Wright commanded one of several Confederate defense lines across portions of Georgia, designed in the futile hope of stopping Sherman. Wright was also president of the Georgia state senate, next in line for the governorship, and when Yankee invasion split part of the state away from the capital in Milledgeville, Wright proclaimed himself governor of the remnant. No one paid any attention. (VM)

Another erstwhile politico trying to stop the Yankee invasion was Brigadier General William M. Browne. An Irishman by birth, he had been on Confederate President Jefferson Davis' personal staff, and for a little over a month in 1862 served as temporary Secretary of State of the Confederacy. (LC)

rential rains soon turned the roads into a sea of mud and water, making them almost impassable for either man or beast. The most formidable obstacle in the path of the army lay in the dark, swirling waters of the Lumber River and its adjacent swamps. It took a tremendous effort on the part of the Pioneer or Engineer units to get the army through this region. Sherman called it "the damnest marching I ever saw."

To the southeast, in South Carolina, the Federal cavalry under General Kilpatrick crossed the Pee Dee River on March 8. Here Kilpatrick learned that the Confederate cavalry under Wade Hampton was only a few miles behind

him and moving rapidly on Fayetteville. Hoping to intercept the enemy, the Federal general set a trap for the Confederates only to have his own camp at Monroe's Crossroads surprised and his troops put to flight on March 9 by the enemy horsemen. To make his own escape, Kilpatrick, clad only in his underclothes, had to spring from the bed of a lady companion, mount the nearest saddleless horse, and disappear into a neighboring swamp.

Since the Federal cavalrymen eventually drove the Confederates out of their camp, there was considerable disagreement over who got the better of the fighting, contemptuously tagged by the Federal infantry as "Kilpatrick's Shirttail Skedaddle." Yet the fact stands that by engaging

*None of the Confederates, amateur or professional, could keep Sherman from
the sea. On December 13, 1864, the Federals launched their attack on Fort
McAllister, principal coastal guardian of Savannah, and that same day it was
all over.* (LC)

Kilpatrick in battle, Hampton was able to open
the road to Fayetteville which the Federal camp
blocked. The Confederate cavalry joined General Hardee's army near Fayetteville the evening
of March 10.

The Confederate forces withdrew across the
Cape Fear River on March 11, burning the
bridge behind them. At the same time the Federal advance entered Fayetteville from the
south. The city suffered a great deal as a result
of the Federal occupation. Besides the destruction of numerous public buildings, including
the United States arsenal which had served the
Confederacy for four years, there was considerable pillaging by the bummers before Major
General Absalom Baird garrisoned the city with
three brigades.

While at Fayetteville Sherman took the opportunity to replace all the rejected animals of
his trains with those taken from the local citizens
and to clear his columns of the vast crowd of
white and black refugees that followed the army.
He called these followers "20,000 to 30,000 useless mouths." To Major General Alfred H. Terry
at Wilmington, North Carolina, he wrote: "They
are dead weight to me and consume our supplies."

By the middle of March Sherman had his
entire force across the Cape Fear, and the move
on Goldsboro had begun. The general was in a
happy frame of mind as he watched his troops
march by. The campaign was running smoothly.
Goldsboro, he felt sure, would be his in a few
days.

Though the fort's parapets like this one were well constructed, there were too few defenders inside. Samuel Cooley photographed the fort a few months after its fall. (LC)

From Savannah to Fayetteville Sherman had moved his army in flawless fashion, but from this latter place to Goldsboro his operations were definitely characterized by carelessness in the management of a large command. He placed little importance on Hardee's delaying action at Averasborough on March 16. Also, he allowed his columns to become strung out to such an extent that the Confederates came close to crushing his XIV Corps at Bentonville. At this small village west of Goldsboro General Johnston had skillfully managed on March 19 to concentrate his sparse and widely scattered Confederate forces. They totaled only 21,000 effectives, and

this included both junior and senior reserves as well as the battered remnants of the Army of Tennessee. Fortunately for Johnston there were many able lieutenants in his small command. In no engagement of the Civil War were so few men led in battle by so many veteran officers of high rank. Two full generals of the Confederacy and four lieutenant generals were among the galaxy of officers present at Bentonville. For a while it looked as though the day would be carried, but Federal reinforcements late on the afternoon of March 19 blunted the Confederate offensive.

More Federal troops reached the field on March 20, and by the next day Sherman had his

The Savannah River, in the distance, flows by Fort McAllister, where Yankee sentinels now stand post. (LC)

entire command in the vicinity of Bentonville. That night Johnston withdrew his small force to Smithfield fifteen miles to the north. Rather than pursue his badly outnumbered opponent, Sherman decided to march his victorious troops into Goldsboro. There they were joined by the command of Brigadier General John M. Schofield which had marched up from Wilmington and New Bern.

This completed the task Sherman had set out to do upon leaving Savannah. His army was now united with that of Schofield's. Large supply bases on the North Carolina coast were available by rail and the countryside from Savannah to Goldsboro, in a swath an average of forty miles across, had been laid waste.

Sherman now decided it was time to discuss with Grant the plans for a possible junction of their armies around Richmond. He was a na-

tional hero as a result of his Georgia and Carolinas campaigns, and as yet the climactic battle of the war had not been fought. So, with Grant's permission, he could still share with the Army of the Potomac the glory of capturing the Confederate capital.

Late in the day of March 25 Sherman boarded a train for City Point, Virginia, Grant's headquarters. In a festive mood before departure, the general told friends that he planned to see Grant in order "to stir him up" because he had been behind fortifications so long "that he had got fossilized."

Back in North Carolina, at Smithfield, Johnston, uncertain of Sherman's next move, used the time to reorganize his hodgepodge forces. He even held a review for Governor "Zeb" Vance of North Carolina and several ladies from Raleigh. It was thought that the troops "once

Mortars like this were absolutely useless against Sherman's attack on the fort. It fell with almost the entire garrison within hours. (USAMHI)

Fighting was hand to hand for a time, as the defenders were pushed back into their bombproofs like the openings behind this cannon. The hole behind the cannon is a powder magazine. (LC)

Then commenced the inevitable cleanup, and the conversion of Fort McAllister into a Union strongpoint. A work party is removing a Confederate Columbiad from its carriage. (LC)

more" looked "like soldiers." The general was well pleased with the way his men had fought at Bentonville, but in early April, when rumors began to circulate around the camps that Richmond had fallen, morale among the troops started to wane badly. Desertions increased dramatically. Patrols were busy night and day arresting men absent from camp without leave. "Heavens the gloom and how terrible our feelings," wrote a staff officer.

Johnston had no illusions about the future. Shortly after Bentonville he had informed General Lee that "Sherman's force cannot be hindered by the small force I have. I can do no more than annoy him." More and more he became convinced that the only hope lay in bringing the Confederate armies in Virginia and North Carolina together. Even so, Johnston must have thought that hostilities were about to end for at this time he ordered Lieutenant General A. P. Stewart to suspend all executions of deserters. The time for all killing to stop was almost at hand. If the South could go on at all now, the decision rested in the hands of Lee at Petersburg.

And here an endless procession of workmen is hauling projectiles for big guns like that Columbiad, as McAllister is rearmed and fortified for the Union. (UNIVERSITY OF GEORGIA LIBRARY, ATHENS)

Now the Columbiad must guard a Yankee-controlled Savannah River and provide a strong base in his rear. For "Uncle Billy" Sherman is going to turn north toward the Carolinas. (LC)

From signal towers like this one, Federal messages will pass to the ships in the river or to outposts on the other side. Savannah will be ringed with Yankees. (NA)

It is all Union territory now. When George Barnard turned his lens toward the river soon after the war's close, almost all sign of the conflict had been erased. (LC)

The fighting done, Savannah and its people returned quickly enough to peaceful pursuits. Here at Buena Ventura plantation Barnard might well have wondered if there had ever been a war at all. (LC)

*Few occupied cities in Sherman's path suffered so little from their
conquerors as Savannah. Sherman put Brigadier General John W. Geary in
charge as military governor. Geary, shown here at the table with his staff, his
finger pointing, ruled fairly and firmly. He would later become governor of
Pennsylvania.* (LC)

*A Savannah photographer named Beckett captured several views of the city
during its occupation, and they attest to its tranquillity. Here is the Pulaski
Hotel on Broughton Street . . .* (LO)

. . . and here the customs house and post office. (LO)

Colonel Henry A. Barnum became Geary's provost in the city, carefully keeping order and a tight rein on unruly soldiers. Repeatedly wounded during the war, he had actually been proclaimed dead and buried two years before, until someone discovered that they had misidentified the man in the ground. He appears here at war's end in his new rank as brigadier. (P-M)

*Savannah city hall at the foot of Bull Street attracted Beckett's camera one
day at 12:23 by the tower clock.* (LO)

*Only a few outward signs show that there was still a war going on. This
beautiful Greek Revival building became an ordnance depot for a time . . .*
(LO)

. . . and Oglethorpe Barracks, once home to Confederate units, now bristles with bluecoats, who would hold Savannah while Sherman marched on, at the end of January 1865, toward the Carolinas. (USAMHI)

Oddly, the Confederates had done little to anticipate defending South Carolina from Sherman. Worse, they had a surplus of generals and a dearth of soldiers. Major General D. H. Hill and others tried to plan a defense of the state, but their counsels were divided and their troops too few and too scattered. (CWTI)

Once again it fell largely to the cavalry to try to retard Sherman's progress. Brigadier General Pierce M. B. Young led his tiny mounted division in repeated attempts to slow the enemy advance, all to no avail. (LC)

The Southerners tried their best to block passage of the rivers in Sherman's path. Brigadier General Zachariah Deas attempted to guard the crossings of the Edisto River, but when the enemy approached, he had to retire to avoid being overwhelmed. (CWTI)

And so, inevitably, on February 17, 1865, Sherman captured Columbia, capital of South Carolina. When he arrived, he found the new state house, still uncompleted. (USAMHI)

And in the wake of occupation came the burning and near destruction of the city. Barnard put his camera on the state house grounds to view the ruins of the city in 1865, a devastation that would unjustly mar Sherman's reputation for a long time to come. (LC)

The state house itself did not survive the conflagration. (LC)

The burned-out offices of the South Carolina Railroad. (SOUTH CAROLINIANA LIBRARY)

The remains of Hunts Hotel, now only chimneys and rubble. (SCL)

All that remains of the South Carolina Railroad's freight depot . . . (SCL)

. . . of the bridge over the Congaree River . . . (SCL)

. . . of the state armory on Arsenal Hill, with the photographer's wagon in the foreground. (SCL)

Even the Presbyterian lecture room fell to the flames. (SCL)

Here is what is left of the printing establishment of Evans & Cogswell on West Gervais Street. Confederate treasury notes had been printed here for years. Now even though some of the presses were gotten away safely before Sherman came, the building is as worthless as the scrip it had been printing. (SCL)

When Sherman's march brought him into North Carolina at the beginning of March, he came face to face once more with his old adversary from the Atlanta Campaign, General Joseph E. Johnston. It would be their final confrontation, and Uncle Billy would have it all his own way. (VM)

The first real fight in North Carolina came at Averasborough on March 16, with the division of Brigadier General William T. Ward of the XX Corps in place for an attack. Ward is seated here with his brigade commanders. Brevet Brigadier General William Cogswell stands at right, next to Brevet Brigadier General Daniel Dustin. And standing at far left is another brevet brigadier, Benjamin Harrison of Ohio. Twenty-three years from now he will be elected President. This very image was widely distributed in the 1888 campaign. (USAMHI)

Major General Henry W. Slocum was one of Sherman's favorites and exercised overall command of two corps that pushed back the Confederates at Averasborough. He advanced immediately toward Bentonville, North Carolina. (USAMHI)

The erratic cavalryman Brigadier General Hugh Judson Kilpatrick helped bring the enemy to bay at Bentonville. Sherman called him "a hell of a damned fool." (USAMHI)

And in the battle that followed at Bentonville, on March 19, Slocum made his headquarters in this home, the Harper house. (WESTERN RESERVE HISTORICAL SOCIETY)

The first Confederate force on the scene to meet Slocum was the corps of Lieutenant General A. P. Stewart of Tennessee. Johnston hoped for a surprise attack against Slocum at Bentonville. (VM)

The first fighting came in the Confederate center, where the North Carolina division of Major General Robert F. Hoke repulsed an attack by the Federals. (SOUTHERN HISTORICAL COLLECTION, UNIVERSITY OF NORTH CAROLINA)

One of Hoke's regiments was the 31st North Carolina, led by dapper Colonel J. V. Jordan. The enemy had long known what he looked like, for this portrait of him was captured in New Bern, North Carolina, when the town and its photographer's studio fell to the Federals in 1862. (USAMHI)

Among the Confederates in the ranks was Private William Washington Cavender of the 1st Georgia Cavalry. Reputed to be an excellent marksman with the pistol, he apparently took his skill seriously enough to point it directly at the camera. (DALE SNAIR COLLECTION)

Sherman had such a surfeit of troops by this time that whole army corps were left out of the fighting. Major General Alfred H. Terry and the X Corps spent most of the campaign marching rather than in battle, much to the derision of the combat veterans from other commands. Against such numbers, the Confederates were almost powerless. (NA)

And so, by the end of March 1865, the Carolinas, like Georgia before them, were conquered. Shortly after the war George N. Barnard came back to Savannah to make a series of images, among them this one of a fountain. Standing in the distance, to the right of the fountain, are two officers, apparently Confederates still wearing their uniforms. If so, it is fitting that one of the photographs with which Barnard concluded his Civil War coverage should include men that he and Sherman had spent so many months pursuing. (IMPERIAL WAR MUSEUM, LONDON)

Petersburg Besieged

RICHARD J. SOMMERS

After three years the Union finally has Lee at bay,
but the quarry goes to ground and Grant can only wait

CONFIDENT CAPITAL of a nascent nation, Richmond for two years owed her redemption and salvation to General R. E. Lee's Army of Northern Virginia. Lee defended her best by keeping the enemy far afield. By late spring 1864, however, Lieutenant General U. S. Grant's Federals forced Lee back to Richmond's immediate vicinity. Then in the final decisive struggle the two great chieftains grappled for Petersburg, guardian of Richmond's lifeline to the Southern heartland. Through the Cockade City, as Petersburg called herself, ran the railroads linking the capital to the upper Shenandoah Valley and to the blockade runners' Atlantic ports. Whoever controlled Petersburg would control Richmond.

As early as May 1864, while Grant and Lee battled at Spotsylvania, Major General Benjamin F. Butler's Army of the James seized a central position on Bermuda Hundred and briefly threatened both cities. Confederate General Pierre G. T. Beauregard's victory at Drewry's Bluff on May 16 contained that danger, and Petersburg's tiny garrison under Brigadier Generals Henry A. Wise and James Dearing and Lieutenant Colonel Fletcher Archer checked another threat on June 9—a date the city thereafter celebrated as her time of deliverance. Sal-

vation looked short-lived, though, as Grant's main force assaulted the rail center a week later. Major General William F. Smith's XVIII Corps stormed Petersburg's outer defenses on June 15. Behind him came Major General George G. Meade's Army of the Potomac, which had moved through Charles City Court House and crossed the broad James River at Wilcox's Landing by boat and pontoon bridge. Still, Union hesitancy and Confederate valor, especially that of Major General Bushrod Johnson's division, stopped the onslaught short of Petersburg itself between June 16 and 18.

As he had since May 7, Grant responded to a frontal check by extending his left around the graycoats' right. His severe defeat in the resulting Battle of the Weldon Railroad on June 22—and his recognition that his troops needed rest after seven weeks of incessant fighting—caused him to settle down before the Confederate works east of Petersburg. Grant's war of maneuver was over. The Siege of Petersburg had begun. Here would be decided the fate of the rail center, the capital—perhaps even of Lee's army and the Confederacy itself.

This decision would not come in one great Napoleonic battle. No Civil War battle—except

Petersburg, Virginia, major railroad city of the state and key to the capture of Richmond. In June 1864, after months of fighting in the Wilderness and at Spotsylvania, Lieutenant General U. S. Grant and his Union Army were finally close enough to Petersburg to strike. (USAMHI)

Nashville—achieved those results, and the Petersburg operation did not even aspire to them. Yet Petersburg was not really a siege in the classical European sense, either. Rather it was a grim, relentless effort through which Grant fixed the Southerners in place strategically and tactically to wear them down in a war of attrition. Rather it was, too, a valiant and increasingly desperate effort by Lee to retain tactical mobility, regain strategic mobility, and avert impending disaster. "We must destroy this army of Grant's before he gets to James River," Lee had warned in May. "If he gets there, it will become a siege, and then it will be a mere question of time." Yet as ever, the Virginian did not resign himself to apparent ill fate but strove against the odds to make his own fate. Petersburg would be his greatest such effort—and virtually his last.

For nine and one-half months he and Grant vied for Petersburg and Richmond. Their clash involved battles, of course: flare-ups of heavy but brief fighting punctuating weeks and even months of relative quiescence. But still more it involved supply lines and supplies, permanent fortifications and light fieldworks, and ever expanding fields of operations eventually spanning two rivers and stretching for almost fifty miles.

Supply lines, after all, were what made Petersburg militarily important. A short north–south railroad just west of Bermuda Hundred linked Richmond to Petersburg. Four other railroads fanned out from the city—one northeast toward City Point; one southeast toward Norfolk; one south toward Weldon and Wilmington, in North Carolina; and one—the Southside Railroad—west toward Burkeville and Lynchburg. The two easterly lines fell to Grant when he arrived before Petersburg in mid-June. Not until two months and four tries later, though, did he finally get a permanent choke hold on the Weldon Railroad at Globe Tavern. Even then the

For the first time in the campaign, Grant managed to steal a march on his adversary . . . (ROBERT J. YOUNGER)

creasing numbers of sick and wounded, and Provost Marshal General Marsena Patrick's "bull pen" for captured graycoats awaiting transfer to Federal prisons in the North.

Also near City Point Grant established his permanent headquarters and eventually his 1864–65 winter living quarters. From that central location he initiated his onslaughts against Southern positions; some battles he waged on distant sectors without even leaving City Point, though he usually preferred riding to the front to observe events.

From City Point, too, flowed the supplies for his command. Some went to nearby garrisons. Other supplies crossed the lower Appomattox at Broadway Landing and Point of Rocks to Bermuda Hundred. From Bermuda Hundred the supply lines eventually bridged the James— from Jones's Neck to Deep Bottom in June, from Jones's Landing to Aiken's (Varina) Landing in September—to support the growing Northern presence on the Peninsula that threatened Richmond directly. Most supplies meantime headed southwest toward the main body aiming for Petersburg. To haul these supplies, the Federals operated the captured City Point and Weldon railroads, connected them via the U.S. Military Railroad that provided lateral service along the Union battle line to Globe Tavern, and ran spur lines westward to Poplar Spring Church and Cummings' farm.

These railroads were the final link that brought the North's vast agricultural and industrial resources to City Point, and thence to Grant's soldiers in the field. Superior numbers, backed by superior matériel, could better endure the hot, dry summer when the siege began and the cold winter through which it continued —could better endure the grueling ordeal of close trench warfare and the bitterness of repeated checks—than could the starving, tattered, thinning ranks in gray. In the long run, such superiority could not help but tell. To Grant's credit, he understood how to convert these potential advantages—which, after all, his predecessors in the East had enjoyed, too—into positive achievements.

Over against Federal advantages, the Confederates increasingly suffered from their deteriorating logistical situation. Temporary or

graycoats could use the latter tracks northward to Stony Creek Depot, from where they transshipped supplies to Petersburg by wagon. Five Federal drives westward against those wagon roads and against the Southside Railroad set the course for the rest of the campaign. The Yankees finally severed the Southside tracks on April 2, 1865; that night Lee abandoned Petersburg.

Long before Grant reached that final Confederate supply line, he made sure his own forces remained in good supply. The James River, controlled by the U.S. Navy and guarded by six Union garrisons, afforded an unbreakable supply link from Hampton Roads westward to City Point, seven miles northeast of Petersburg, at the mouth of the Appomattox River. The City Point hamlet soon swelled into the well-fortified nerve center of a mighty army. To its rapidly expanded wharves came ships bearing reinforcements, munitions, and supplies. In its environs grew up warehouses for those supplies, hospitals for in-

. . . the seemingly unbeatable General Robert E. Lee. Seen here in a portrait by Richmond photographer Julian Vannerson, the Gray Fox seems invincible. (VM)

*Grant already held an outpost on the James River about fourteen miles
northeast of Petersburg, at Bermuda Hundred, shown here months later as
supplies of hay for the Union Army's animals grow into virtual mountains.*
(USAMHI)

permanent loss of supply lines into Petersburg
produced immediate problems. Widespread
destruction of supplies and communications
elsewhere in the Confederacy by Major Generals William T. Sherman, Philip H. Sheridan,
and Alfred H. Terry created even graver difficulties. These hostile actions hastened the
collapse of the always primitive Southern supply system, and its revitalization in the war's
waning weeks came too late to accomplish much.
Hungry, ill-clad, outnumbered troops could still
win battles but were not likely to win a long
campaign—especially against such well-supplied
opponents as the Federals.

This increasing disparity lowered some
Secessionists' morale. Awareness that their
families were also suffering added to their dis-
may. And the overwhelming reelection of
President Lincoln on November 8—with its
unmistakable mandate of four more years of
unrelenting war—drastically intensified some

soldiers' disaffection. Over the winter of 1864–
65 their desertion—to the Union forces, to the
hills, or to home—increased dramatically. Their
departure made the disparity between Southern
and Northern armies even worse.

Yet Lee had always striven against long odds,
and to the very end at Petersburg he continued
doing so—through daring feints, bold counterattacks, and great reliance on earthworks—to
offset his numerical weakness. More than any
other Civil War campaign, Petersburg was
marked by extensive use of fortifications.

Both that city and Richmond were ringed
with permanent defenses when the campaign
began. The capital, indeed, had three such rings,
plus two forward water batteries on the James
at Chaffin's and Drewry's bluffs. When Union
Major General Benjamin Butler occupied Deep
Bottom, the Rebels dug a trench eastward from
Chaffin's to New Market Heights to contain him.
His big breakthrough at Fort Harrison on

Then, on June 15, Grant completely fooled Lee with a surprise crossing by portions of his army over the James River. Over this speedily erected pontoon bridge at Weyanoke Point, some 2,200 feet long, the IX Corps sped toward unprotected Petersburg. A James Gardner photo. (P-M)

September 29 rendered that trench and much of the Exterior Line of Richmond's permanent defenses untenable—indeed, breached the main camp on Chaffin's Bluff itself. Lee, however, soon stopped that threat and retained the main Richmond works—and the city they guarded—until the final collapse. Yet he could not hurl back the bluecoats, secure in their own field-works from Fort Brady through Fort Burnham and thence curving back east toward Deep Bottom.

Comparable stalemate settled over the James itself and Chesterfield County between the two cities. Because the Union Army and Navy had obstructed shallow Trent's Reach to prevent the Confederate Navy disrupting Grant's crossing of the James in mid-June, for the assault on Petersburg, the Yankee vessels were subse-

quently unable to move upriver above the reach. To bypass those obstructions, Butler dug a canal through narrow Dutch Gap neck between August 1864 and January 1865. Beset with engineering difficulties and annoying but not particularly damaging mortar fire, the canal proved a fiasco, unusable by the Union squadron (though after the war it became the river's main channel), because the graycoats established three major batteries along the right bank between the existing defenses at Drewry's and Howlett's bluffs to blast the ships if they came. Even more needed by the Rebels were the fieldworks running south from Howlett's to protect the railroad and "cork Butler in his bottle" at Bermuda Hundred. Yet corresponding Federal trenches across the mouth of the "bottle" twice stopped Beauregard's efforts to overrun the area. And Northern

Awaiting them to the east of the city was an old and familiar face, that of General P. G. T. Beauregard. Yankees had fought him at Fort Sumter and First Bull Run and Shiloh, and now, with a handful of defenders, he would meet them again. (USAMHI)

It fell to Major General William F. "Baldy" Smith to make the first Union attack on Petersburg before Confederate reinforcements could arrive. Alas, everything went wrong. (USAMHI)

batteries, along with river obstructions and the characteristic breakdown of Confederate iron-clads, checked the one Southern naval sortie down the James on January 24, 1865.

Meanwhile, the military situation south of the Appomattox in mid-1864 was more fluid, and the ever extending fieldworks there reflected that fact. The initial Northern onslaught on Petersburg on June 15 overran the permanent defenses to the east, but first one, then another line of trenches that Beauregard hastily threw

up halted the drive short of the city. Those temporary works connected with the original permanent defenses at Rives's Salient on the Jerusalem Plank Road, the great southeastern angle where the Confederate ramparts bent back westward before turning northward to reach the Appomattox above Petersburg.

The bluecoats promptly dug their own field-works close up against Beauregard's position east of town, from the lower Appomattox to the Jerusalem Plank Road. West of that highway, the fortifications drew apart, out of rifle range. As the Army of the Potomac drove west—to Globe Tavern, to Poplar Spring Church, to Hatcher's Run—it dug trenches to secure each new conquest and link it to previous gains. Moreover, a rear line from the church back northeastward to Blackwater Creek guarded against cavalry raids.

The Confederates, though, made little effort against the Union rear except for sabotaging an

Beauregard held out, assisted by able subordinates such as Brigadier General Alfred H. Colquitt of Georgia. So sparse were Confederate troops by now that within weeks Colquitt would be ordered off to North Carolina to counter threats there. (VM)

ordnance barge to explode at City Point on August 9, rustling a large cattle herd downriver from there on September 15–17, and constantly committing guerrilla depredations. Their main concern, however, lay in protecting their own front, so they dug two lines of fieldworks running southwestward from the city's main fortifications. The forward line guarding the vital supply routes along the Boydton Plank Road and the Southside Railroad remained in Lee's possession until the end. Its eventual capture on April 2, 1865, was what doomed Petersburg.

For fifty-one miles—from west of Richmond on around Petersburg—these Confederate lines eventually stretched. The corresponding North-

ern front line, thirty miles long, whether fieldworks or permanent defenses, constituted a series of redoubts connected by trenches or infantry parapets. Most such Northern forts were named for officers killed from the Wilderness in May 1864 through Petersburg. The Confederates preferred naming strongholds after living commanders on those sectors—such as Lee himself. The respective practices eventually proved less dissimilar, though. Several of those Confederate generals, too, would lose their lives in or near their redoubts or would ultimately die of wounds received there.

Generals could give their names to forts, but trained engineer officers had to design and refine the works. Moreover, special engineer units—the 1st, 15th, and 50th New York Engineers, the U.S. Engineer Battalion, and the 1st and part of the 2d Confederate Engineers—performed much of the sophisticated technical construction, such as assuring proper slopes and angles and sinking mines and countermines. Most of the actual labor with pick and shovel, however, was provided by fatigue parties of infantry, cavalry, and artillery on both sides and also, on the Southern side, by slaves. Combat troops could establish light works of logs, rails, and earth right on the battlefield. Subsequently, engineer officers and labor parties would strengthen the profile with revetments and gabions, improve angles and fields of fire, and perhaps obstruct approaches with abatis, chevaux-de-frise, or a moat. Such refinements converted the primitive initial sheltering parapets into nearly impregnable fortifications.

Behind those fortifications most soldiers could camp in relative safety and even ease, first in tents, then in winter quarters. But men of both armies holding the sector east of Petersburg where shelling and sniping flared daily knew no such respite. Yet even they could seek shelter—against the parapet or in supposedly "bombproof" dugouts, where they waited out the fire and yearned for transfer to a quieter stretch of line—or, better still, a transfer to reserve or to the unravaged country outside the works.

To view that open country, those reserve positions, and the defenses themselves and to send semaphore messages, signal towers rose over each army's trenches on both sides of the James.

The 25th South Carolina, including whatever remained of this 1861 group from the Washington Light Infantry of Charleston, were among Petersburg's valiant defenders. (WASHINGTON LIGHT INFANTRY, CHARLESTON, SOUTH CAROLINA)

Surer communications clicked along telegraph lines uniting the far-flung sectors to City Point and to Lee's various headquarters: Dunn's Hill, Mrs. Chaffin's, and Edge Hill. Indeed, the relatively static siege was ideal for using telegraph, and within days of units reaching each new position, telegraph wire linked it to the communications net as surely as new earthworks connected it to existing fortifications.

Those fortifications thus provided shelter to the communications and camps behind them and to the garrisons within them. They also afforded platforms for each army's fieldpieces, siege guns, and light and heavy mortars (like the Federal 13-inch seacoast mortar "Dictator") that shelled each other north from the Jerusalem Plank Road to the lower Appomattox. Such artillery fire, however, was generally intended to annoy enemy troops and civilians and to silence enemy fire. Blasting down ramparts, and digging mines—hallmarks of classical European sieges—played little role in the Siege of Petersburg.

Even as Smith's attack was failing and Lee raced to reinforce the city, Major General George G. Meade sped with the bulk of his Army of the Potomac to join in the attacks. This image by Brady & Company was made just days before, on June 12, at Cold Harbor, northeast of Richmond. Meade is seated at center with his legs crossed, surrounded by his staff. Major General Andrew A. Humphreys is on his right, and seated to the right of Humphreys is the army's provost marshal, Brigadier General Marsena Patrick. Standing immediately on Meade's left is his quartermaster, Brigadier General Rufus Ingalls, and the man second to Ingalls' left is Meade's artilleryman Brigadier General Henry J. Hunt. (USAMHI)

Nor were the works—especially the permanent fortifications around the two cities—scenes of heavy fighting. The severe losses and small results from May 5 to June 18, 1864, had made Grant wary of assaulting well-prepared and well-guarded defenses. Thereafter he generally avoided such frontal charges. To him, his own works were not a forward line for delivering direct charges on nearby enemy ramparts. Rather, they were a great entrenched camp, or staging area, from which he could safely launch heavy forays into the relatively unfortified areas beyond either flank. Such forays would either cut the supply lines and capture Richmond or else would at least force the graycoats to leave their works and fight in the open.

Lee was not averse to fighting in the open. His permanent defenses were safe bases from which Beauregard's and Lieutenant General A. P. Hill's infantry and Lieutenant Colonel William Pegram's artillery could sally against the threats, and his fieldworks were ready means for slowing, stopping, or bluffing Union forays until he could counterattack. Also available to him in the open and screening his communications was his usually superior cavalry—an arm that provided extra mobility for meeting threats on several sectors. Such mobility, along with trench defense and surprise attacks, often made three or four Southern brigades the equal or the better of three or four Yankee divisions. Thus, most of the so-called Siege of Petersburg was not a siege at all but a series of forays and counterblows in largely open country.

The defeat of the first Union drive for the Weldon Railroad on June 22 and the rout of Northern cavalry raiders at Reams' Station on June 29 not only converted the mobile maneu-

James Gardner was present at Charles City Court House on June 14 to capture this image, just as Meade's army was moving through the place on its way to the planned attack. (USAMHI)

ver of spring into the static semisiege of summer but also set the tone for the rest of the campaign. For nearly a month the exhausted armies rested. Then, on July 27, three Federal corps under Sheridan and Major General Winfield Scott Hancock crossed the James above Petersburg and burst forth from the Deep Bottom bridgehead toward Richmond itself. Lieutenant General Richard H. Anderson's Rebels, heavily reinforced from Petersburg, stopped that push far short of its goals. Hancock, however, at least succeeded in drawing most of the Confederate army to the Peninsula. He then hastily returned south of Petersburg to support the impending attack against the weakened Southside Railroad.

In a rare frontal blow, Major General Ambrose E. Burnside spearheaded that attack by exploding a mine under Elliott's Salient east of Petersburg in the early morning of July 30. The resulting Battle of the Crater threatened the city with capture, but Yankee blunders, Union Brigadier General James Ledlie's cowardice, the rout of Brigadier General Edward Ferrero's Negro division, a stout defense by Johnson, and repeated counterattacks by Brigadier William Mahone converted the operation into disaster for the Union forces and restored Lee's front.

Upset but undaunted, Grant struck again on August 14. For a second time, Hancock sallied from Deep Bottom, above Petersburg; for a second time, local Rebels under Major Gen-

*When the army reached Wilcox's Landing on the James, it started crossing on
steamers. A Brady cameraman made this image probably on June 15, while
the crossing was under way. The wharf is crowded with steamers and wagons,
as a mighty army is on the move.* (WRHS)

eral Charles Field, reinforced by troops from
the Southside, checked him right away; and
for a second time, the Army of the Potomac
sought to take advantage of the diversion of
enemy units to north of the James. This time,
though, Major General Gouverneur K. Warren's V Corps entered the unfortified country
west of the Jerusalem Plank Road and cut the
key Weldon Railroad at Globe Tavern on August 18. For four days, his Northerners reeled
under Beauregard's and Lee's savage counterattacks, but—reinforced in the nick of time by
Brigadier General Orlando Willcox's IX Corps
divisions—they retained their hold on the railroad. Subsequent efforts by the returned Hancock to tear up track southward from there,
however, met disaster at Reams' Station on
August 25. Lee, reluctantly reconciled to losing
Globe Tavern, thereafter sought to contain the
Federals there and to cover the wagon roads
leading into Petersburg.

After another interlude of five weeks, Grant
drove for those wagon roads and also for Richmond. On September 29 most of Butler's army
crossed the James at Deep Bottom and at a new
bridge at Aiken's Landing. His right wing under Major General David B. Birney was again
checked temporarily at New Market Heights,
but this time his upriver column under Major
General Edward Ord stormed the outer Confederate defenses at Fort Harrison (later renamed Fort Burnham). This breakthrough on
Chaffin's Bluff bade fair to capture the capital, but Unionist errors and the heroic defense
by Brigadier General John Gregg and Lieutenant General Richard Ewell checked the
disjointed attempts to press on. However, Anderson failed bloodily to retake Fort Harrison the
following day. Lee's own effort to roll up the
Northern right on the Darbytown Road on
October 7 met initial success but eventual defeat. Federals in force were on the Peninsula

To maintain instant communications with Grant and the rest of the Union Army, a hasty telegraph office was established at the landing. (USAMHI)

to stay, and all Lee could now do was to erect new works to contain them. At least, he had little difficulty parrying Brigadier General Adelbert Ames's feeble probe against those works on the Darbytown Road on October 13.

The Union story on the Southside line was similar. On September 30, Brigadier General Charles Griffin punched through the outer defenses at Poplar Spring Church. Major General John G. Parke's halting efforts to continue toward the Boydton Plank Road and the Southside Railroad, though, were routed by Major General Cadmus Wilcox's and Lieutenant General Wade Hampton's skillful counterblows. Yet neither Wilcox, Hampton, nor Major General Henry Heth could recapture the ground initially lost. Meade thus retained another sector, linked it to his previous conquests, and established his headquarters in Aiken's house, nearer to the new front and the scene of future action. From this latest gain, he would launch Major General Romeyn Ayres's limited probe up the Squirrel Level Road on October 8 and three massive onslaughts and a major raid later in the siege.

The first big blow fell on October 27, as Meade and Butler struck simultaneously against both Confederate flanks. Lieutenant General James Longstreet easily blunted Butler's hesitant Army of the James at Fair Oaks. The situation below Petersburg was more touch-and-go. Three Union divisions finally reached the Boydton Plank Road below Hatcher's Run, only to be heavily counterattacked from four sides. In this his final battle, that splendid Union tactician Hancock repulsed every charge, then skillfully extricated his imperiled corps. With him recoiled the whole Army of the Potomac. On both flanks Grant had struck simultaneously; on neither had he accomplished anything.

This conspicuous failure of his two-pronged assault led Grant to revise his strategy. Thereafter he would mass his forces on the left for a heavy first strike below Petersburg. The initial effort there was simply Warren's destruction of the Weldon Railroad from Jarratt's Station to Belfield in December. Better indication of the new strategy came on February 5, 1865, as Meade again struck for Hatcher's Run. When fighting ended two days later, Warren's V Corps had been

But despite all Grant's efforts, Confederates in Petersburg held out long enough for Lee to bring the bulk of his army to the city. Major General Bushrod R. Johnson, a native of Ohio, fought valiantly to halt the first assaults.
(DEPARTMENT OF ARCHIVES AND MANUSCRIPTS, LOUISIANA STATE UNIVERSITY, BATON ROUGE)

roughly handled, but Confederate Brigadier General John Pegram was dead, and Hancock's successor, Major General Andrew A. Humphreys, had permanently extended the Union line to that stream.

Thereafter, Lee and Grant became increasingly aware of the impact of military developments in other theaters on their own operations. Throughout the Petersburg siege, for that matter, both generals had sent troops elsewhere to block threats, win victories, suppress treachery, and enhance prospects around Petersburg. Seven Southern and eleven Northern brigades permanently moved to the Carolinas the winter of 1864–65. Even more did the Shenandoah Valley divert forces from the Tidewater

in 1864 (eight of Grant's divisions, five of Lee's). Subsequently, four Gray and five Blue infantry divisions bolstered Lee and Grant from the Shenandoah, and then in early March 1865 Sheridan's two powerful Union cavalry divisions crushed the Confederate Army of the Valley and raided overland from the Blue Ridge to the Peninsula. The two feeble Rebel mounted divisions that rode east from the Shenandoah to resist him hardly offset this mighty build-up of Federal horse at Petersburg.

As this threat to Lee descended from the northwest, even more ominous danger loomed from the south, as Sherman moved irresistibly through the Carolinas, ever closer to Petersburg. Meantime, from north and west, respectively, Hancock's and Major General George Thomas' Union armies threatened Lynchburg. And all the while, Grant tenaciously grappled with the Army of Northern Virginia, determined to pin it down while his subordinates devoured the rest of the Confederacy and then joined him for the final kill.

Lee, as ever, fought back against impending doom. On March 25, 1865, in a daring strike through no-man's land east of Petersburg, Major General John Gordon's Rebels stormed Fort Stedman. But as with so many breakthroughs in the siege, they could not exploit it, and Parke's and Brigadier General John Hartranft's counterattack soon drove them out. Meantime, Humphreys' and Major General Horatio Wright's corps profited from Gordon's diversion to the center and captured the entrenched picket line on the Confederate right.

Holding that picket line proved advantageous when Grant launched his final offensive on March 29. Sheridan, reinforced by Warren, spearheaded the onslaught south of Hatcher's Run. Humphreys engaged just below that stream, and Wright and Parke stood ready farther north. This time most of the Army of the James, now under Ord, left the Peninsula to join the attack below Petersburg. Brave to the last, the Confederates repeatedly counterattacked this new drive, and time and again they trounced Union divisions. On this occasion, however, the Northerners kept coming. Sheridan routed the last mobile flank guard, Major General George Pickett's command, at Five Forks, April 1. In an

*One of many redoubts placed along the outer Confederate line and captured
in the first assaults in June 1864.* (P-M)

even more decisive stroke the following day, Sunday, Wright stormed the works covering the Boydton Plank Road and killed A. P. Hill, long the chief guardian of Petersburg. Later that day, Major General Nelson Miles defeated the last defenders of the Southside Railroad at Sutherland's Station. Only in the fortifications of Petersburg itself did Gordon, Wilcox, and Brigadier General Nathaniel Harris blunt Parke's and Ord's repeated charges until Longstreet's reinforcements could finally arrive from Richmond.

Except for permitting an orderly retreat, though, those reinforcements were too late. This time disaster for the Southern cause was real—and irretrievable. The last wagon road was gone; the last railroad linking Richmond and Petersburg to the outside was gone; and with them was gone the last military justification for holding

Petersburg. To stand siege within the city would simply lose the army, too. Yet there was no place else on the James to stand, either. Richmond was now as untenable as the Cockade City.

Overnight, April 2–3, Lee abandoned them both. In his wake, civilian looters burned much of the capital. With daylight came Major General Godfrey Weitzel's and Parke's bluecoats, who at last entered ruined Richmond and battered Petersburg unresisted. Meantime their triumphant comrades in Grant's main body south of the city were in excellent position to intercept Lee's desperate flight toward North Carolina. The Army of Northern Virginia, once mighty, had been too weakened at Petersburg to continue long in the open field. For Lee and his men, within just one week, the road from Petersburg would lead to Appomattox.

Yankees, too, were heroic in their efforts to break through the enemy lines. Colonel Joshua L. Chamberlain of the 20th Maine won a battlefield promotion to brigadier general on June 18 in one of the last assaults. (WRHS)

Stopped in front of the city, Grant tried to work around it on the south to cut off Confederate communications via the Weldon Railroad. Here, near Globe Tavern, he was turned back. Captain A. J. Russell made this image late in 1864. (KA)

And so Grant had to settle in for a long siege and that meant building a major supply base. He chose City Point, on the James, about seven miles northeast of Petersburg, and here established the greatest such base of the war. Egbert G. Fowx caught this image of City Point, including his own log-built Fowx's Photographic Gallery at the left. (USAMHI)

At City Point Grant built an ordnance wharf that could accommodate the ceaseless comings and goings of the supply steamers. Probably a Russell image. (LC)

Transports like the Neptune *disgorged their supplies directly onto the rail cars that would speed them around Grant's lines wherever needed. Probably a Russell image.* (USAMHI)

Everywhere there were masts and lines of guns and caissons, a ceaseless activity that continued around the clock. (KA)

The trains await whatever they must carry. (NA)

So did the supply wagons that would go where the railroad did not. (LC)

A row of 12-pounders and their carriages, awaiting transportation to the front. (LC)

Maintaining the mammoth City Point supply base required hundreds of
special laborers, and that in turn required a special encampment for them.
Here their winter quarters outside the base kept them close to their unending
work. (USAMHI)

Soon a more sophisticated telegraphic operation was under way as well,
employing a dozen and more key operators, shown here in their rustic
summer quarters. (LC)

Grant set up outdoor summer headquarters at City Point, shown here in a Brady & Company image taken in late June or early July 1864. Grant and his staff are seated under the shade of the tree. (USAMHI)

Another Brady image taken at the same time shows Grant seated third from the left. Already there is at least one war trophy: partially furled on a staff leaning against the tree at left is a Confederate battle flag. (USAMHI)

The bluecoats would be at City Point for a long time, though Grant did not know that this summer. Nearly a year later, in spring 1865, his headquarters looked like this in an E. & H. T. Anthony Company image. (RJY)

Though he was the aggressor here in Virginia, Grant knew that he had to look to his own defense, with the wily Lee as an adversary. Fortifications were built to protect City Point. (P-M)

*And regiments like the resplendent Zouave 114th Pennsylvania were detailed
as provost guard and garrison troops. They pose here in August 1864.* (LC)

*Even then, City Point felt at least one blast of destruction. On August 9,
1864, an explosion went off, set by Confederate saboteurs. It rocked the
ordnance wharves. Russell caught the scene.* (USAMHI)

And it left an enormous mess in its wake. The culprits were never caught.
(USAMHI)

Grant himself was listening to an officer who claimed that enemy spies were infiltrating City Point when they heard the explosion. (KA)

From City Point the supply network spread out wherever the army went. One major route carried succor to Bermuda Hundred by way of Broadway Landing on the Appomattox River. (WRHS)

Much of the ground was like this—too swampy in the winter for passage. An early 1865 image, published by E. & H. T. Anthony Company. (LC)

All this done, there was nothing left for the Federals to do but to start pounding away at Lee. Indeed, even before City Point was well established, Grant's artillery began the work. A Brady photographer made this view of Captain James H. Cooper's Battery B, 1st Pennsylvania Light Artillery, on June 21, 1864. Though long identified as being taken "under fire," Brady's images were made at a time and place when the Confederate lines were about a mile away, and this image was almost certainly posed for the camera. (LC)

Brady himself stepped into the picture in this image of the same battery that day. He stands, hands in pockets, just behind the cannon at center. (LC)

Real fighting was done by men like these Zouaves of the 164th New York, the Corcoran Legion. At Deep Bottom, about fifteen miles north of Petersburg, on July 27–28, they met the enemy, only to be repulsed. (USAMHI)

As a result of the stalemate, the Confederates, too, had to settle down to what would be a long siege. Shown here are some of the Southern winter quarters captured in June 1864, now home to grinning Yankees. (P-M)

To contain the enemy's relentless attempt to encircle and strangle them, the Confederates maintained formidable fortresses like this one at Drewry's Bluff on the James, north of Petersburg, but no naval attack was forthcoming. (USAMHI)

Able defenders like Brigadier General Johnson Hagood turned back Major General Benjamin Butler's May 1864 land attack. (LC)

Following the fighting at Fort Darling, as the earthwork at Drewry's Bluff was called, obstructions placed in the river were intended to interdict ships. (USAMHI)

Old steamers were brought out into the channel and scuttled. (VM)

They made a virtual barricade across the James. (USAMHI)

In Fort Darling itself, the Confederate officers had dug themselves several substantial gun emplacements, with sunken magazines, bombproofs, and a well. (USAMHI)

The officers' quarters were barely a stone's throw from the earthworks. (USAMHI)

Once the fort fell to the Yankees, however, it became a useful bastion for them as well. Federal transports filled with artillery tie up at the tiny dock. (USAMHI)

Elsewhere along the James the Federals secured their hold with water batteries like this one below Fort Brady. (P-M)

Here a large Parrott rifle stares out over the James, not far from Dutch Gap,
above Petersburg. (NA)

Confederate water batteries were also
located near Dutch Gap, mounting
formidable guns like this banded Brooke
rifle. The Union could not make full use
of the James until they could get past
obstructions and batteries like these.
(USAMHI)

The problem led to one of the war's great, unsuccessful schemes, the Dutch Gap Canal. Butler's Army of the James spent months digging a canal across the narrow neck of land left by a great loop in the river. When completed, it would have allowed ships to bypass enemy water batteries. Captain Russell brought his camera to record the work and probably made this image in August or September 1864. (CHS)

Again it was probably Russell who made this fall 1864 image showing the work on the canal well under way, the work parties, surveying instruments, and barges and tracks for removing earth all perfectly visible. (NA)

*The greatcoats on the working parties attest to the coming of the cold season
late in 1864. The workers are almost entirely Negro troops, their white
officers standing on the upper level supervising.* (NA)

*In November Russell made this image showing the last stages of the canal
before the remaining earth was blasted away to complete the ditch.
Everything is ready, and giant crevices have been sliced through the earth. On
January 1, 1865, it needs only the touch of a spark to the powder charges laid
and . . .* (P-M)

. . . the Dutch Gap Canal is open. (P-M)

In succeeding days and weeks the canal mouth will be widened and deepened to allow traffic to pass through, but in fact the canal will prove to be militarily pointless. It was not completed until April 1865 and by then it was too late to be of use. In later years, ironically enough, the James will shift its course slightly and the canal will become part of the main channel. (USAMHI)

Much of the work was done under nagging but largely fruitless artillery fire from Confederate batteries. One shot did manage to sink this dredge. (LC)

Meanwhile, Butler fretted and fumed here in his headquarters, thoroughly disgusted with his bad fortune, and thoroughly out of favor with Grant. (NA)

His engineers, like the 15th New York, went into winter quarters such as these and suffered through the cold and damp and mud. The log breastworks with their sandbag firing posts were never used to repel enemy attack. (KA)

*Butler further fortified Dutch Gap with heavy mortars like these and built
the landmark Crow's Nest signal tower in the background to keep an eye on
the enemy.* (LC)

*To protect themselves from the Confederate shelling, some of Butler's people
dug bombproofs into the side of the hill. This image was made on
Thanksgiving Day in 1864 while Rebel artillery was firing from afar. It is
possibly the work of Captain Russell's assistant Egbert G. Fowx, with whom
Russell would later fondly reminisce about the dangers of making
photographs while under fire.* (USAMHI)

*Meanwhile, back on the main Union lines stretching around Petersburg, the
work of reducing the enemy continued. On June 20, 1864, a Brady
cameraman recorded this image of the 12th New York Battery, now
operating in a captured Confederate earthwork, Battery 8. Brady himself
appears once again, standing in straw hat in the center. Just two days later
this entire battery would be captured in a Confederate attack in another
sector.* (WRHS)

Slowly the ring of Union fortifications grew. Fort Rice shows the winter huts built to keep the men during the siege. (USAMHI)

Fort Sedgwick went up on the Jerusalem Plank Road, south of Petersburg. It was a massive earthwork incorporating gabions, abatis, and chevaux-de-frise. (USAMHI)

The maze of trenches and gabions—earth-filled baskets—soon was dubbed "Fort Hell" by the Confederates. (USAMHI)

There was a lot of engineering going on in both armies and that done by the Federals was chiefly under the direction of Brigadier General John G. Barnard, Grant's chief field engineer. (P-M)

Formidable movable obstructions like these chevaux-de-frise were built to break up enemy assaults. (USAMHI)

Tons of twigs and branches were carefully woven into the gabions that
formed the basis of much of the earthworks. (KA)

The sticks were even woven into mats like these, for a variety of purposes, in
a rat's maze of tunnels and ditches. (LC)

The Confederates meanwhile were doing some engineering of their own.
From Fort Mahone, they began digging a tunnel underground toward Fort
Sedgwick, their intention being to detonate a powder magazine and breach
the fort. It did not work, perhaps because the Yankees had already tried that
trick themselves and were wary. (LC)

Besides, these bombproof quarters at Fort Sedgwick were already such a maze of tunnels and holes in the ground that a mine underneath them could hardly go undetected. (LC)

Everywhere men were living in homes carved out of the dirt. Here is a kitchen among the Union bombproofs. (P-M)

And here just one simple soldiers' shelter from flying enemy shells. (P-M)

Even the horses enjoyed bombproof stables. (P-M)

For the Confederates it was much the same. Here at Gracie's Salient all manner of digging and moving has taken place. To show the proximity of the opposing lines by the end of the siege, the Federal earthworks can be seen in the left distance. (USAMHI)

Atop the works at Gracie's, the camera can see nothing but the results of endless burrowing in the dirt. (USAMHI)

What Union shelling did not ruin, the rain and weather often did, breaking down works and filling the trenches with water and mud. (P-M)

Everywhere the Confederate ditches seemed to stretch to the horizon. (P-M)

Captain Russell's early April 1865 image of one Rebel cannon mounted in the inner line of defenses. In the distance all around it appear more and more lines of works. (LC)

Conditions in the trenches were no different for the Federals. The rain and mud attacked them as well. (USAMHI)

Their work seemed just as endless as, like a colony of ants, they went on with the work of tearing up the soil of Virginia. (USAMHI)

Happy by contrast were those Yankees who could spend their part of the siege in the sky. Grant's engineers built a series of signal towers like this one on Peeble's farm. From it they could watch enemy movements . . . (P-M)

. . . 150 feet below. Winter quarters and log breastworks are evident in the Union lines in the foreground, and beyond them two feathery lines of sharpened stakes or branches stand ready to delay any enemy attack. The redoubt in the center is probably Fort Conahey. (P-M)

Another less tall but more famous signal tower was the Crow's Nest, 136 feet high, near the Dutch Gap Canal. It was a landmark for Yankees all about. (USAMHI)

And particularly for the Federal warships that plied the James River nearby.
The Union monitor Sangamon *rests at her mooring below the Crow's Nest.*
(WILLIAM GLADSTONE COLLECTION)

Farther off, near Bermuda Hundred, yet another tower kept at least a few
Yankees high, if not dry. (USAMHI)

When not building, the Yankees were shooting, often mammoth seacoast mortars like this 13-inch behemoth called the Dictator. Its service at Petersburg was neither distinguished nor unusual except for its railroad mounting, but it captured the interest of more than one photographer, and they subsequently made it one of the most famous cannon of the war. O'Sullivan or his assistant David Knox photographed it here on September 1, 1864, mounted on the railroad flatcar that transported it. The officer standing at right center, holding the field glasses, is Brigadier General H. J. Hunt, Meade's chief of artillery. (LC)

And here that same day O'Sullivan or an assistant recorded the scene as the Dictator pointed toward the enemy works beyond the ridge. (USAMHI)

Certainly the most notorious endeavor of the Yankee engineers, however, was the Great Mine. Dug by coal miners in the 48th Pennsylvania, it ran across the no-man's land between the lines and under the Confederate works. It fell to Major General Ambrose Burnside, standing in the center, his hand in his blouse, here with his staff, to make the attack that would follow the explosion of four tons of powder at the end of the 511-foot shaft. He was a poor choice. (NA)

When the charge went off—on July 30, 1864—this "crater" was formed, 30 feet deep, 170 feet long, and from 60 to 80 feet wide. It literally blew a whole section of Confederate works—with their defenders—out of existence. Portions of the shaft are still visible in this 1865 image. (USAMHI)

*Burnside's troops rushed in, one brigade commanded by Brigadier General
W. F. Bartlett, seated here fourth from the right with his staff at war's end.
He already wore an artificial cork leg, and now it was shattered in the attack
and he taken prisoner.* (USAMHI)

*Occupying the salient that was blown up was
Brigadier General Stephen Elliott. He was
himself seriously wounded in repulsing
Burnside's poorly organized assaults and would
not see service again until Bentonville, North
Carolina, at the end of the war.* (USAMHI)

By the time the Federals were falling into confusion after the explosion, some of them trapped in the crater itself, Brigadier General William Mahone had rushed his Confederate division to the threatened spot. In time he drove the bluecoats out and won for himself a battlefield promotion. (CHS)

After Petersburg's fall a cameraman made this view from the hole, looking off toward the Union lines in the near distance. It shows just how close the opposing parties came in their mole's work. (USAMHI)

The whole Union effort had been a shambles, thanks chiefly to dreadful leadership. Brigadier General James Ledlie, commander of the Federal attack, hid, drinking, in a bombproof while his division went into the slaughter. (NA)

Brigadier General Edward Ferrero, shown seated at the center a few days after the attack, commanded the Negro division that supported Ledlie. Ferrero, too, hid with Ledlie while his command was torn apart. He managed to survive the resulting court of inquiry, though not without censure, but Ledlie would soon leave the service in disgrace. (USAMHI)

The crater itself would survive down to the present, but 5,500 good men of both sides perished or were wounded in the fight for it. Even among regiments like the 40th Massachusetts, assigned as a reserve and never thrown into the actual battle, men fell. This image shows them at drill in the winter of 1862–63 at Miner's Hill, Virginia. It is an important image for another reason. It is one of the two photographs that were the start of the massive 40,000-image collection of the Massachusetts Commandery of the Military Order of the Loyal Legion of the United States (MOLLUS), the largest collection of Civil War images in existence, now at Carlisle Barracks, Pennsylvania. (USAMHI)

In August 1864, still smarting from the setback at the crater, Grant sent part of his army farther out around the Confederate fortifications south of Petersburg and had them strike at Globe Tavern on the Weldon Railroad. (USAMHI)

The subsequent fighting was savage. Confederate Brigadier General Thomas Clingman was so seriously wounded that he never again saw real field service. Regarded as incompetent, he was not sorely missed. (NA)

*It was the reinforcing Union division of Brigadier General Orlando B.
Willcox, seated second from the right, that finally secured the Weldon line.
This image was made in August 1864, a few days before the fighting.*
(USAMHI)

*Grant's September offensive involved swift river crossings. The slender finger
of land on the other side in this view of a Union pontoon bridge across the
James is Jones' Neck. Captain Russell probably made this image that same
month.* (USAMHI)

There was another crossing at Aiken's Landing, this one a bridge with a removable section to allow Union steamers to pass through. It is just being opened in this image. (USAMHI)

And here the bridge is ready to allow river traffic passage. The engineers could accommodate anything they set their minds to. (MINNESOTA HISTORICAL SOCIETY)

Over these boards tramped the Union army corps of men like . . . (KA)

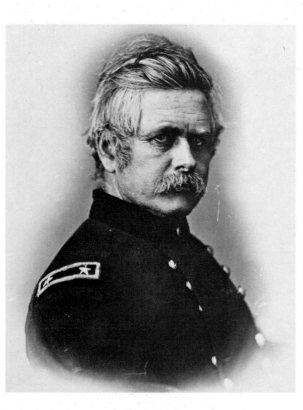

. . . Major General Edward O. C. Ord. He was on his way toward Chaffin's Bluff, there to assault . . . (USAMHI)

. . . Confederate Fort Harrison. It was one of the strongest of all Southern forts north of Petersburg. Should it fall, the Federals would have taken a major step on the road to Richmond. A bombproof in the fort after the Federals took it and renamed it Fort Burnham. (KA)

Here, in the rear of Fort Gilmer, near Fort Harrison, sits a 27-foot ditch dug to prevent another underground tunnel like that which led to the Great Mine outside Petersburg. (LC)

Even Confederate ships like the ironclad Richmond *supported the defense of the capital by firing from the river on Ord's attacking Federals. Robert Wright was an engineer aboard the vessel.* (PAUL DE HAAN)

Brigadier General John Gregg was one of the defenders of Fort Harrison. Only a week later he was killed in fighting a few miles away. (VM)

Brigadier General Adelbert Ames, seated center, poses here with his staff in the winter of 1864–65, not long after his attempt to penetrate Lee's new defenses south of Richmond failed. (SOPHIA SMITH COLLECTION, SMITH COLLEGE, NORTHAMPTON, MASS.)

There were Yankee probes and attacks everywhere, it seemed, and most of them were turned back by skillful and desperate commanders like the Confederate Cadmus M. Wilcox, the major general who later at the siege's end managed to hold off the Federals long enough for his army to escape. (WRHS)

Late in October 1864 Major General Benjamin Butler became actively engaged north of the James again, but failed. Butler sits on the chair at left center, with Brigadier General Godfrey Weitzel seated on the floor next to him. A Brady operator made the image at Bermuda Hundred in the late summer of 1864. (USAMHI)

While Butler was being repulsed, Meade was fighting a desperate battle near Hatcher's Run, southwest of Petersburg, one of his divisions in the fray being led by Major General Gershom Mott. They narrowly averted disaster before a skillful withdrawal. (USAMHI)

*There were hard losses, too, for the Confederates. On December 2 the capable and well-liked Brigadier General Archibald Gracie was killed by a sharpshooter. A New Yorker by birth, he had a large family who remained loyal to the Union. An unpublished ambrotype. (*MUSEUM OF THE CONFEDERACY*)*

*Upon Gracie's death, his command was turned over to Colonel Young M. Moody, a Virginian who would make brigadier in March 1865, one of the last generals appointed in the Confederacy. He stands here at right. (*VM*)*

Finally, in late March 1865, the last Union push for Petersburg began.
Trying to preempt such an offensive, Lee launched his last great attack of the
war, the March 25 assault on Fort Stedman, a Union strongpoint west of the
city. (P-M)

Leading the attack was one of the last of Lee's
premier fighting officers, Major General John B.
Gordon. With no formal military training, he
yet became one of the ablest battlefield
commanders of the war. Fort Stedman was just
the last of many courageous assaults for the
combative Georgian. (NA)

Within these defenses at Fort Stedman the Federals were taken by surprise by the advancing enemy and nearly put to flight. (P-M)

As he led his brigade against the fort, Brigadier General Philip Cook suffered a dangerous wound that ended his war service. (VM)

It was in this sector that the Rebels broke through—the line between Fort McGilvery and Fort Stedman. (USAMHI)

But in the end, the Federals behind these Fort Stedman defenses retook what was lost. (USAMHI)

Then on March 29 Yankee divisions led by commanders like Major General Gouverneur K. Warren began to strike at the last available avenue of retreat for the Confederates. (USAMHI)

There were too few Confederates left to stop them. The attrition in Lee's high command had been dreadful. Just the month before, the brilliant and handsome young Brigadier General John Pegram was killed on Hatcher's Run, three weeks after his marriage. (VM)

Major General Andrew Humphreys, standing hat in hand at the center, led his Union corps in the attack on Hatcher's Run late in March, having become one of Meade's most capable corps commanders. (USAMHI)

Major General Horatio Wright sent his VI Corps into the fight against the Rebels at the same time. (MHS)

There was fighting all along the line as Grant pressed Lee everywhere. Brevet Brigadier General Robert Nugent, seated holding his sword, led his "Irish Brigade" in the fighting on the Southside Railroad on April 2, helping cut off the Confederates' final avenues of escape. (USAMHI)

That same day the IX Corps launched its assaults from Fort Sedgwick, the oft-dubbed "Fort Hell." Captain Russell probably made this view two or three days later, with the battle barely done. (MJH)

*Fort Sedgwick fascinated the photographers, who covered every inch of it
with their cameras.* (USAMHI)

*Another Russell image looking along the
Union lines from which the attackers
sprang on April 2.* (USAMHI)

*The rains that preceded the final assaults left Fort Sedgwick a muddy mess
by the time a cameraman arrived to capture the scene.* (LC)

The fall of Five Forks, some thirteen miles southwest of Petersburg, sealed the fate of the city. There, on April 1, the Yankees had pushed aside the valiant resistance of Brigadier General Eppa Hunton and others, cutting Lee's dwindling lines of retreat. (VM)

Units like the 17th Virginia, commanded by Colonel Arthur Herbert, could not withstand the overwhelming numbers of the enemy. With Five Forks lost, Lee had to abandon Petersburg. (LEE WALLACE)

In the collapse of the Petersburg line, the Confederates lost good men everywhere, but no loss was more disastrous than the death of Lieutenant General A. P. Hill. He had been a pillar of support for Lee. His death was emblematic of the loss of thousands who could not be replaced. (USAMHI)

Among the last Confederate commands to hold out was the brigade of Brigadier General Nathaniel H. Harris. His men bought time for the rest of the army to make its escape. (USAMHI)

The loss of Petersburg was a heavy blow to Lee. According to tradition, sometime during the siege of Petersburg the tired old warrior mounted his warhorse Traveller and posed outdoors for an unknown photographer. The war was slowly killing him, but still there is the firmness and stature of the leader about him. This is how his soldiers would ever after remember "Marse Robert." (DEMENTI STUDIO, RICHMOND)

And here, at last, lay Grant's prize. All he had to do was march in. The spires that had for nearly a year been distant landmarks, were now in his grasp. (NA)

James Reekie probably made this image of a street scene in Petersburg. Taken around April 10, it depicts a commonplace sight of train after train of Union supply wagons rolling through the city on their way to the army that followed Lee to Appomattox. (LC)

Captain Russell's image of the principal rail junction in the city, the reason for its military importance and the reason that Lee had to defend the city to the last. Burned cars rest on the tracks at right. The crooked and broken ribbons of rails attest to the inability of the Confederacy to maintain its railroad lines against wear and tear. (LC)

Signs of damage were visible everywhere. The Dunlop house shows where a Federal shell managed to find a nonmilitary target. (USAMHI)

Inside the house all was rubble and ruin.
(MHS)

Russell's camera found one bridge that was torched with an engine still upon it, leaving the whole a twisted mess of masonry and iron. (KA)

With Petersburg fallen, the Federal soldiers rushed to the parapets of the Confederate forts to play the tourist and to pose for the cameras. Here Russell found them at Fort Mahone, perhaps as early as April 3. (USAMHI)

Their curiosity seems boundless, that and the relief in at last being able to stand up straight on top of the ground without fear. (USAMHI)

A few had fun posing behind now captured Confederate picket posts like these gabions. T. C. Roche photographed them on April 3. (USAMHI)

The cannonballs and impedimenta strewn about the ground lent an added touch of realism to scenes that were entirely posed. (USAMHI)

*So did the dead, and the photographer found them everywhere, Confederates
who died in the attempts to stave off Grant's final onslaught. Roche found
this body in the trenches at Fort Mahone on April 3.* (MHS)

Lying almost as if asleep, this man died in "Fort Damnation," the nickname for Fort Mahone. The bare feet attest to the dreadful scarcity of shoes in the Southern army. Either he simply did not have shoes when he died or else a fleeing comrade took time out from the evacuation to remove what the dead soldier no longer needed. (CHS)

Only a few yards away from this fallen soldier stands the picket post that Federals posed in for Roche's camera. (RJY)

Roche seemingly could not stop recording scenes of death as he took his camera into Fort Mahone on April 3. They were all over the place. (MHS)

A Confederate artilleryman who has done his best and rests forever. For him, as for all of his comrades, living and dead, the Siege of Petersburg is over. (CHS)

To the victor belongs the glory, but U. S. Grant will spend precious little time riding about his prize on his old warhorse Cincinnati. For Grant's quarry was never a city—it was a man. And though Petersburg has fallen, Lee is still in the field, and with him the Confederacy still lives. (USAMHI)

Richmond, City and Capital at War

EMORY M. THOMAS

Symbol of the Confederacy, the Virginia metropolis
fights to the last

RICHMOND IN 1860 was an amalgam of mills and magnolias. The place was at once an old Southern town and a young "modern" city.

Located at the falls of the James River, Richmond had been for some time essentially the trading-post community her founder William Byrd II had projected in 1733 and established in 1737. The Virginia legislature during the Revolution had voted in 1779 to move the state capital from Williamsburg to Richmond, and soon after, in 1781, Benedict Arnold honored this distinction by leading a British force into the new capital to raid and burn the town. During the nineteenth century Richmond attracted national attention as the scene of Gabriel Prosser's abortive slave insurrection in 1800, the site of Aaron Burr's treason trial in 1807, and the home of John Marshall and Edgar Allan Poe. The city continued to attract political interest as a state capital and developed a fairly active mercantile economy as a commercial link between the regional countryside and the wider world.

On the eve of the Civil War, though, Richmond was more than a sophisticated trading post. Her principal distinction among Southern cities lay in a somewhat "un-Southern" emphasis upon manufacturing. Much of this activity involved the elemental refinement of local agricultural products, especially tobacco and grain. Twelve mills produced annually three million dollars' worth of flour and meal, and fifty-two tobacco manufacturers processed a gross product worth five million dollars. However important were grains and tobacco to Richmond's economy, the city's iron industry was even more significant. No other city south of the Potomac possessed more than a fraction of Richmond's iron production, which was worth nearly two million dollars in 1860. Joseph R. Anderson's Tredegar Iron Works was the city's largest and most versatile plant and the only establishment in the South capable of producing cannon and railroad rails. Tredegar also led the way in two other atypical Southern activities, the attraction of immigrants (mostly German and Irish) and the adaptation of slave labor to industry. In total value of manufactures, Richmond ranked thirteenth among American cities in 1860 and first among cities that soon after composed the Confederacy.

Richmond boasted a relatively sophisticated financial community in 1860—strong banks and insurance companies. The city's slave traders, too, did a brisk business; Richmond ranked

*Richmond, capital of the Confederacy, for almost four years symbol of
Southern independence and determination. It had been a lovely, rather quiet
city in 1861 and looks little different in this 1865 view by the Philadelphia
partners Levy & Cohen. The state house stands at right, while to the left is
the spire of Broad Street Methodist Church and, beside it, an equestrian
statue of George Washington. Confederates looked to the example of the
"Father of His Country." He was father to theirs as well.* (KA)

second only to New Orleans among the nation's
slave markets during the 1850s. At the same
time that some Richmonders were manipulating
capital with the facility of "Yankees," others
were trading with equal facility upon the South's
"peculiar institution." And no one seemed to
notice the irony.

Despite the urban influence of trade, finance,
and manufacturing in Richmond, the place was
in many ways still an overgrown town in 1860.
The city's population—37,910 total, 23,635
white, 2,576 free Negro, and 11,699 slave—
ranked third in 1860 among "Confederate"
cities, but twenty-fifth among all American cities.
Roughly 38,000 people were not very many,
compared to urban centers like New York

(1,080,330), Philadelphia (565,529), and Baltimore (212,418). Perhaps even more significant
was the dominance of planters and professionals
in the upper strata of Richmond social life. As
one astute observer noted, "Trade, progressive
spirit, and self-made personality were excluded
from the plain of the elect, as though germini-
ferous. The 'sacred soil' and the sacred social
circle were paralleled in the mind of their
possessors."

Mayor Joseph Mayo served as the city's executive and also as a sort of urban "overseer."
The city attempted to act as surrogate master,
not only to the slave population, but to the free
Negroes, as well. Mayo held court daily to deal
with breaches of the city's peace and of Rich-

Here Virginia's wartime governors lived and tried their mightiest to manage the state's government separate from that of the Confederacy. In time, Richmond, Virginia, and the C.S.A. seemed indistinguishable. (USAMHI)

mond's "Negro Ordinance" which proscribed a rigid code of conduct for both free and bonded Negroes.

Prosperous burgers who occupied a majority of the twelve City Council seats had proven themselves quite capable of running the city. Mayor Mayo was a vigorous man despite his seventy-six years. Whether the men and governmental machinery which ran the small, stable city could rise to the challenges of a swollen, wartime capital was an unanswered question in 1860.

Indeed the question was unasked. Richmond was a conservative city in 1860, and she gave few political indications that she even desired membership in a Southern Confederacy, much less the leadership role implied in becoming its capital. Traditionally the vast major-

ity of Richmond voters were Whigs; Democrats referred to themselves as "the Spartan band." In the presidential election of 1860 Richmonders went Constitutional Union, giving neo-Whig moderate John Bell a two-to-one majority. Then in the selection of delegates to the Virginia convention that considered secession, the city's voters chose two Unionists and one Secessionist. Throughout the winter months of 1861 Virginia's convention sat in the capitol in Richmond and voted moderation while the states of the Deep South seceded and formed the Confederacy at Montgomery.

As the crisis at Fort Sumter between the United States and the Confederate States intensified during the early spring of 1861, the mood in Richmond shifted. By April editorials in all four of the city's newspapers were

In April 1865 a Northern cameraman, probably Alexander Gardner, made a broad multi-image panorama of the city. Two of his images are joined here, and it presents a scene that would be little different from the look of the capital two or three years before. The state house, as always, dominates the skyline in the left-hand image. (USAMHI, NA)

One governor, William Smith, spent two years in the Confederate Army as a brigadier general before going to the state house to lead Virginia in the last years of the war. He was called "Extra Billy" because of his penchant for expanding his one-time mail route in return for extra fees from the United States Government back before the war. In battle he wore a beaver hat and carried an umbrella if rain threatened. (VM)

threatening secession if the Washington government attempted to coerce the seceded states back into the Union. On April 4 the radicals in the state convention failed by only three votes to have a secession referendum put to Virginia voters. Former Virginia Governor Henry A. Wise then called a kind of counterconvention, the "Spontaneous Southern Rights Convention," to meet in Richmond in an effort to stampede the state into radical action.

Then on April 12 came news of the firing on Fort Sumter. Overnight, it seemed, Richmond was transformed. Amid demonstrations of Southern fervor, the state convention passed an ordinance of secession on April 17, and two days

later the city exploded in celebration. Ten thousand people, nearly half the white population, poured into the streets, and bonfires, bands, torches, bells, and fireworks hailed the revolution.

A few days later Confederate Vice President Alexander H. Stephens journeyed to Richmond to hasten Virginia's alliance with the Confederacy. In the process he stated, "It is quite within the range of probability that . . . the seat of our government will, within a few weeks be moved to this place." Stephens' remark became prophecy on May 20, when the Confederate Congress voted to move the capital from Montgomery, Alabama, to Richmond.

The presence and influence of Virginia's delegation to the Congress played some role in the decision. Other considerations, however, were also significant. Montgomery in 1861 was small (10,000 people) and ill-prepared to be the seat of a sizable government. Some congressmen were reportedly ready to move anywhere to escape Montgomery's crowded hotels and voracious mosquitoes, and Richmond promised the new government more adequate accommodations and facilities. Perhaps most important, Richmond seemed to offer a war government in proximity to its war. The Confederates assumed that Virginia would become the major battleground in their conflict, and thus moving the government to Richmond seemed a natural way to facilitate the conduct of the war.

Hindsight has offered a set of serious reservations about the wisdom of establishing the Confederate capital at Richmond. Located on the geographical fringe of the nation, the new capital tended to isolate its government from the vast Southern interior. Too, proximity to Washington rendered Richmond a tempting target for Union armies and thus, as one scholar has suggested, a "beleaguered city." And because the South's war eventually included many battlefronts, Richmond's location and defense may have overpreoccupied the Confederate government and precluded attention to other theaters which had equal or greater strategic significance. Such latter-day judgments are not unjust, and certainly the Confederacy's prime reason for moving to Richmond (to be close to the war) proved tragically naïve.

St. Paul's Episcopal Church stood on Capitol Square, while the square itself was always a popular gathering place for loungers and idle gossipers. (LC)

Yet Richmond was not a bad choice for the capital. To be sure, the location imposed some military strain upon Southern armies; but during the first two years of the war the Tredegar Iron Works were perhaps as crucial to the Confederacy as the government. Southern arms had to hold Richmond whether or not the capital was there. More important, Richmond's role as magnet in attracting Federal armies probably cost the Union more than it did the Confederacy.

The North's "on-to-Richmond" enthusiasm drained men, matériel, and energy that might have been used more effectively elsewhere, and for four years Richmond's defenders defied the invaders and their hope of quick victory. Far from leading to a quick victory, the hundred miles between capitals became a killing ground on which the North suffered its greatest frustration. Near the end, Richmond's role changed from magnet to "millstone"—hung about the

The view looking west on Main Street. Taken in April 1865, it shows Yankee wagons rolling off in the distance. (LC)

neck of Lee's Army of Northern Virginia. But by then the war had brought about Southern exhaustion everywhere, and though the trenches prolonged the life of Lee's Richmond army, they also trapped them.

In May of 1861, however, the Confederacy lived in blissful ignorance of these gloomy second thoughts, as Jefferson Davis led his government's exodus from Montgomery. Richmond became very quickly the center of intense political and military activity. War was at first parades

and picnics in Richmond. "We ought to be miserable and anxious," wrote Mary Chesnut in her famous diary, "and yet these are pleasant days. Perhaps we are unnaturally exhilarated and excited."

The new capital's euphoria certainly lasted through midsummer of 1861, and Richmonders rejoiced over the Southern victory at First Bull Run. But then came the ambulances and trains bearing wounded soldiers and with them an initiation into sobering reality. Richmond be-

The view from the Confederate "White House" of the Shockoe Valley and the section of Richmond called Butcher Town. It had been, literally, the place where cattle were slaughtered. (NA)

came a hospital center in 1861 and continued as one throughout the war. Richmond also became a prison center for captured Federals, and despite efforts to move the captives to prison camps established farther South, Richmond often held 10,000 enemy soldiers on Belle Isle (enlisted men) and in Libby Prison (officers). Wounded friends and captured foes represented only the most obvious challenges faced by Richmond as wartime capital.

Richmond became quickly overcrowded; her population grew eventually to an estimated 100,000, an increase of 150 percent since 1860. The city's crime rate increased as well. Drunken soldiers thought it great sport to seize watermelons, throw them into the air, and try to catch them on their bayonets. Gambling houses,

"hells," as they were called, flourished despite repeated raids by the city police force, and Richmond became, according to the leading historian of soldier life in the Confederacy, "the true mecca of prostitutes." One madam was so bold as to open for business across the street from a YMCA hospital. There "ladies of the evening" advertised themselves from the windows and enticed convalescent soldiers from one bed to another. Although the City Council increased the size of the police force and Mayor Mayo reactivated the "chain gang" for lesser offenders, Richmond remained in the newspaper *Examiner*'s phrase a "bloated metropolis of Vice." Perhaps the most effective method of combating lawbreakers was the policy of the surgeon-in-charge of one of the city's military hospitals.

There were several nationally famous hostelries in the city, none more so than the Spotswood Hotel, shown here in an April 1865 image by Gardner's assistant James Reekie. Here President Jefferson Davis lived in 1861 until the executive mansion could be readied for him. Here General Robert E. Lee stayed when he "went South" in 1861, and throughout the war the greatest luminaries in the Confederate constellation passed through its doors. (USAMHI)

Less well known but still popular was the Ballard House, at left, in this April 14, 1865, Reekie image. Its unusual walkway over Franklin Street connected it with the unseen Exchange Hotel. (USAMHI)

Of course, as a major city in war, Richmond offered a few guest
accommodations that were less desirable, such as those afforded to enemy
prisoners. Belle Isle in the James River rises in the center distance, a place
where thousands of Yankees languished and not a few died. (USAMHI)

Lacking a guardhouse, the officer detained un-ruly patients and staff in the hospital "dead house" (morgue). Thereafter, he reported, he "never heard anything more from them."

Crowding and crime were both symptom and source of chaotic economic conditions. Rich-mond did become a center of war industry; the shops and laboratories of Major Josiah Gorgas' Ordnance Bureau multiplied in number and grew in size, as did other government enterprises that produced everything from cannon to cur-rency. Among private enterprises the Tredegar Iron Works, for example, nearly tripled its work force and increased its production to the limit of its ability to secure pig iron. In competition with the wartime prosperity that affected every-one from "iron puddlers" to prostitutes, though, was the inflationary spiral of Confederate cur-rency and the scarcity of life's necessities in the city. Wages never kept pace with prices, and crowding compounded the difficulty of supply-ing the capital with food and fuel. To make mat-ters worse, many of the fields that normally pro-duced food for the city became fields of battle.

Prices rose to the point at which the Rich-mond *Dispatch* estimated that a family's weekly groceries that cost $6.65 in 1860, cost $68.25 in 1863. Rumors circulated of vast profits made by "extortioners" who hoarded large quantities of provisions and became rich from the sufferings of others. Early spring was the leanest time; new crops were not ready to harvest and stored sup-plies ran low. In mid-March of 1863, to make a bad situation worse, the Confederate Congress authorized the Army to impress foodstuffs. The new law had the effect of unleashing army com-

The man in Richmond given charge of these prisons, and all Confederate prisons, was Brigadier General John H. Winder, shown in this unpublished portrait in his prewar uniform as an officer in the United States Army. His task so exhausted him that, like many prisoners in his charge, he died before the war was done. (VM)

missary agents upon the city's marketplaces. Civilian food supplies became quite scarce, and prices of what was available rose alarmingly.

The *Whig* spoke of being "gouged by heartless extortioners and robbed by official rogues," and a War Department official recorded in his diary, "There is a manifest uneasiness in the public mind different from anything I have noticed heretofore."

Then on March 19 and 20, 1863, nine inches of snow blanketed the city and rendered travel in and out of Richmond all but impossible. The weather soon warmed, but as a result roads became quagmires. Those farmers and gardeners who still had food to sell and who were willing to risk impressment at prices now below the

market level were all but unable to transport their produce into the city.

On the morning of April 2 a group of working-class housewives gathered at Belvidere Hill Baptist Church. Their neighborhood of Oregon Hill was near the outskirts of the city, and many of their husbands worked in the nearby ironworks. The women talked about their plight and their empty cupboards and then decided to petition the governor for immediate relief. The walk from Oregon Hill to Capitol Square was long, but the day was mild, and as the women walked others joined the march. By the time they reached the governor's mansion the group was sizable, and men and boys had joined the housewives. Governor John Letcher listened to

More somber to Richmonders was the Virginia State Penitentiary, shown here in an April 1865 image. When the city fell, its 287 inmates escaped, fired the place, and rampaged through the city. (USAMHI)

their problems and offered his sympathy, but nothing else. When he had made his offering, Letcher went back inside the mansion, leaving the several hundred people in his front yard to mill about in frustration.

The gathering attracted attention and greater numbers. Soon the gathering became a mob and a leader emerged. Mary Jackson, "a tall, daring Amazonian-looking woman," with a "white feather standing erect, from her hat," urged the people to action. And they followed her white feather away from the governor's mansion toward Richmond's commercial district.

Waving knives, hatchets, and even a few pistols, the mob swept down Main Street shouting for bread. The mob then became a riot. Throughout an area of ten square blocks the rioters broke into shops and warehouses and took food. Some seized the opportunity to take jewelry and clothing as well.

Governor Letcher appeared on the scene and

attempted to stop some of the looting, but no one seemed to notice him. Mayor Mayo tried to read the riot act, but no one heard him. Then a company of soldiers, reserve troops from the Tredegar Iron Works, came marching up Main Street. The column drove the advanced rioters back upon the rest and was rapidly clearing the street until someone pulled a horseless wagon across the soldiers' path. The wagon formed a hasty barricade between the troops and the mob, and into the impasse strode the President of the Confederacy.

Jefferson Davis stepped onto the wagon and shouted to the mob. Women hissed while Davis tried to make himself heard. He emptied his pockets, threw his money into the crowd, and then he took out his pocketwatch and gestured at the company of troops. "I will give you five minutes to disperse," he stated, "otherwise you will be fired on."

As if to punctuate the President's demand, the

Yet there were quieter, more peaceful places. Richmond was a city of churches, and not just the great steepled edifices on Capitol Hill. St. John's Church stood at Broad and 24th streets in the eastern part of the city. A Brady cameraman made this image, and his employer, Mathew Brady himself, stands behind and just right of the tombstone. Here in this church ninety years before, in 1775, Patrick Henry made—or is said to have made— his "Give me liberty" speech. (USAMHI)

captain of the company commanded, "Load!" The men complied, although no one knew for sure whether they would enforce the President's ultimatum by firing on the crowd of their fellow citizens, some of whom may have been neighbors and relatives. Davis kept his eyes on his watch, and for what seemed a long time no one moved. Then the mob began to drift away, and soon the President and the soldiers were alone in the street. The riot was over.

The City Council met in emergency session the same afternoon and concluded that the riot had been instigated by "outsiders." And instead of hunger the councilmen attributed the riot to "devilish and selfish motives." After resolving that Richmond's "honor, dignity, and safety will be preserved," the city fathers adjourned. During the night artillery batteries unlimbered their pieces on Main Street. The Secretary of War ordered the telegraph office to transmit "nothing of the unfortunate disturbance of today over the wires for any purpose" and made a "special appeal" to Richmond's newspapers "to avoid all reference directly or indirectly to the affair." Thus, on April 3, 1863, the *Dispatch* carried a lead editorial headed "Sufferings in the North."

Although several days later Mayor Mayo was still requesting more troops to prevent further

Monument Church, or the Monumental Church of Richmond, stood on Broad Street, not far from the Capitol. It was built by private subscription in memory of seventy-two people who died in the 1811 Richmond Theater fire on this site. (USAMHI)

violence, no more bread riots occurred in the capital. The events of April 2 did point out that many Richmonders lived in want. When the City Council met a week after the riot, the members' shock and indignation had worn off. Acting through the Overseers of the Poor, an existing charitable agency, the council directed that needy Richmonders receive food and fuel tickets redeemable at two "free markets."

Two months later the council expanded the relief program by ordering two "visitors" into each of twenty districts to determine need and distribute tickets. Still later the council, faced with declining amounts of food and fuel in the "free markets," established a Board of Supplies to coordinate a search in the countryside for food

to be sold at cost in the city. Despite the indifferent success of the board's agent, the city was able to supply food at cost to an average one thousand families per month during the following winter. Eventually the council abandoned the distinction between poor Richmonders and wealthy Richmonders; it ordered the Board of Supplies to secure food "for the city." This exercise in wartime welfare did not prevent some people from being hungry in Richmond. Yet the resourcefulness of the City Council probably prevented many from starving as the pressure of "total war" increased upon the capital.

The sustained strains of home-front war in the Rebel capital severely challenged the hitherto

*And Richmond's Negroes had their place of worship, too, the First African
Baptist Church. It stood just down the street from Monument Church and
had one of the South's largest Negro congregations. Many of them pose here
on Broad Street for a Brady cameraman.* (USAMHI)

conservative city. It would be easy to say that
Richmond's response was often too little too late.
Yet there were no solutions to problems that only
compounded as the military situation deterio-
rated. Richmond confronted wounded soldiers,
Federal prisoners, refugees, crime, inflation,
privation, class conflict, riot, and more. In meeting the challenges of home-front war the city
was ever "becoming," always making some new
sacrifice in order to endure, and never "being,"
in the sense of being able to celebrate some
point at which she had prevailed.

Richmond did become a national capital. A
Prussian visitor probably said it best: "The
moral force of the resistance was also centered
in Richmond, the capital of the rebellion. . . .
The energy of the Confederate resistance that
was typified in Richmond impressed me almost

as much as the great efforts of the army . . . to
hold the field [at Gettysburg] against an overwhelming adversary."

When Major General Thomas "Stonewall"
Jackson died as a result of wounds in May of
1863, they bore his body to Richmond to lie in
state at the Capitol. A crowd estimated as the
largest ever assembled in the city gathered at
the railroad station and followed Jackson's coffin
to Capitol Hill. After the prolonged procession
of three bands, the hearse, and Jackson's rider-
less horse through the city, an observer noted,
"I should think that every person in the city of
Richmond had today buried their nearest and
dearest friend." More than the nerve center of
government and military command, as "moral
force of the resistance" Richmond made a strong
bid for the Confederacy's heart as well.

*The city alms house stood at the northern edge of the capital. It served as a
Confederate hospital during the war until December 1864. Then it became
the temporary quarters of the Virginia Military Institute. This Gardner
image shows graves in the Shockoe Cemetery in the foreground.* (USAMHI)

By 1863 the institutions of the capital were
also national institutions. Religious denomina-
tions printed newspapers, sermons, and tracts in
the city and distributed them throughout the
South. The Medical College of Virginia was the
only medical school in the Confederacy to remain open throughout the war period. And
Richmond's press was one of the most active and
probably the most influential in the South.
During 1863 the Alexandria *Sentinel* moved its
office to Richmond and became the capital's fifth
daily newspaper. The *Sentinel* and the *Enquirer*
were important as quasi organs of the Davis administration; the *Whig* and *Examiner* were
equally important as consistent critics of the
government. The *Dispatch* continued a more
localized focus and pursued a less predictable
policy on national issues. Periodicals also grew

and prospered in the wartime city. The *Southern
Literary Messenger, Southern Illustrated News,*
and *Magnolia, A Southern Home Journal,* especially, attracted wide readership, and *The Southern Punch,* modeled on the London humor
magazine, offered humor of varying quality to
the Confederacy.

Richmond also offered, as the *Whig* reported,
"no lack of resources with which to banish dull
care." The city's theaters attracted the best
entertainers in the South and presented everything from Shakespeare to minstrels. The capital's "official society" led by Varina Davis, the
President's wife, entertained its members, even
in January 1864, with luncheons of "gumbo,
ducks and olives, lettuce salad, chocolate cream,
jelly cake, claret cup, champagne, etc." And "in-
siders" complained of Richmonders' capacity to

*There were other places where the war did not seem to intrude, places like
the tomb of President James Monroe in Hollywood Cemetery. Reekie made
this image on April 15, 1865, the same day that the body of another
President, Abraham Lincoln, was being carried to the embalmers.* (USAMHI)

"swallow scandal with wide open mouths." Less grandiose gatherings were those of the Mosiac Club, whose members, the brightest of the South's intellectuals, gathered whenever one of them fell heir to a quantity of food or drink. Later "starvation parties" came into vogue; host and guests contributed toward musical entertainment and swilled vintage "James River, 1864" for refreshment. No less an authority than General Robert E. Lee encouraged parties in the city for the diversion and relaxation of his troops. And even during the war's last year Mary Chesnut could proclaim from Richmond, "There is life in the old land yet!"

From the beginning, Richmonders were con-cerned, with reason, for the military security of the capital. In the eastern theater of the war, Confederate armies confronted an enemy whose rallying cry was "on to Richmond."

During the spring and summer of 1862 Richmond was the target of Major General George B. McClellan's Peninsular Campaign, and the war reached the suburbs of the city. Richmond's initial response to this peril was a corporate variety of panic. On March 1 President Davis issued a proclamation of martial law in his capital, and Brigadier General John H. Winder became responsible for conducting military rule within a ten-mile radius of the city. He immediately banned the sale of liquor in Richmond, estab-

Richmond was a city playing host to a government at war, and as a result much of the city's normal routine was disrupted and many buildings were converted to wartime purposes. Here the camera views part of the Confederate States Navy Yard at Rocketts, on the James River. The large building in the center is the Quartermaster Department's supply warehouse, one of several buildings in the city devoted to managing supplies for the army. (USAMHI)

lished a system of passports to control movement to and from the city, and began a series of arbitrary political arrests. On April 22 the Confederate Congress voted itself a pay raise and hastily adjourned. All the while McClellan's army moved closer to the city, making ready for what seemed would be a final thrust. And meanwhile in Richmond, Unionist slogans—"Union Men to the Rescue!" and "God Bless the Stars and Stripes!"—appeared in chalk on walls and fences. Elizabeth Van Lew, an old lady who openly proclaimed her Unionist sympathies, prepared a room in her mansion for General McClellan to be her guest.

Although no one could know it at the time, the crisis in Richmond's fate during the spring of 1862 occurred on May 15. With the USS *Monitor* in the van, Union gunboats were steaming up the James to shell the city. Only hastily prepared obstructions and guns at Drewry's Bluff, about seven miles below Richmond, offered any hope of halting the flotilla. At that point, with so much reason to despair, the city seemed to take heart and assert its will. Governor Letcher called a mass meeting at City Hall to organize citizen-soldiers. As the crowd gathered at five in the afternoon, the guns at Drewry's Bluff opened fire on the enemy ships in the river.

Confederate Quartermaster Brigadier General A. R. Lawton was a familiar figure in Richmond and one of the most capable men in the military hierarchy. (MC)

Those assembled realized that if the ships got past the river defenses, the Federals would be able to shell the city at will. Then Mayor Mayo arrived and to the tense crowd shouted defiance at the imminent danger. Mayo vowed that should the occasion arise, some other mayor would have to surrender the city. "So help me God, I'll never do it." Next Letcher took the stump. He said he did not know anything about surrender, but were he given the option of giving up the city or watching it shelled, he would respond, "Shell and be damned." Only later that day did the anxious city learn that Drewry's Bluff had held, that the Union ships were returning downriver, and that the immediate danger was past. And later the genius of Lee emerged to drive McClellan's army from the capital's gates.

Although Federal infantry did not so threaten Richmond again until 1864 and 1865, the city had significant scares in 1862 and 1863 from Union cavalry. During the Chancellorsville Campaign, on May 3, 1863, Richmonders learned that the enemy horsemen were in nearby Hanover County and advancing south toward Richmond. Chaos broke out as bells rang and volunteers hurried out to man the city's fortifications. The commander of Confederate troops in the area announced to a friend that he wished he were dead. The citizen-soldiers were in such a rush to meet the foe that they forgot to carry gunpowder with them for their artillery, and once they remedied that oversight, someone noticed that they had no friction primers with which to fire the weapons. Brigadier General George Stoneman's cavalry came within five miles of the city and turned away. Had they come farther, the 1,500 Federals would have confronted about 900 civilians with impotent artillery.

On March 1, 1864, the *Whig* reported that a column of enemy cavalry had been seen behind Lee's lines, but predicted the Federals would "hardly remain long enough to do much damage." As it happened there were two sizable contingents of Union horses converging upon Richmond. Just after noon that day 3,000 troopers commanded by Brigadier General Hugh Judson Kilpatrick appeared on the northern perimeter of the city; they formed for a charge, but then unaccountably withdrew. A bit later in the afternoon the second body of Federal cavalry threatened the city from the west until driven off by Confederate reserves and volunteers. Richmonders correctly concluded that the two thrusts were designed to be a coordinated attack. But only later did the capital learn the full, frightening details of the Federal plan.

The second Union mounted force rode into an ambush as it attempted to withdraw, and its commander, Colonel Ulric Dahlgren, was among those killed in the fray. On Dahlgren's body were found what appeared to be his orders to his command for the ill-fated mission. The colonel had written that he planned to free the captured Federals on Belle Isle, then cross into the city, "exhorting the released prisoners to destroy and burn the hateful city, and . . . not allow the Rebel leader, Davis, and his traitorous crew to escape." Both Confederates and Federals were horrified at such unchivalric intentions,

There was a city to run as well as a nation, and here at City Hall, on 11th Street, the affairs of Richmond were attended to by a devoted mayor . . . (USAMHI)

and controversy over the authenticity of the "Dahlgren papers" raged long after the event.

In the summer of 1864 General Ulysses S. Grant attempted to pound Lee into submission. That failing, Grant assaulted Petersburg, the small city about twenty miles south of Richmond. Petersburg was important to Richmond as a railroad junction; if Petersburg fell, only one rail line would remain to connect the Confederacy with its capital. Lee's army held Petersburg; Grant settled down to siege—a campaign of attrition against Petersburg, Richmond, and Richmond's army. Lee accepted the siege; he could see no alternative. His army was too weak, numerically and logistically, to fight "those people" (as Lee termed his enemies) in the open, and trenches might keep the odds nearly even until the Federals tired or erred. Earlier, Grant had vowed "to fight it out on this line, if it takes all summer." It did take all summer, and fall, and winter too; Richmond's army remained steadfast to the end, and some of its finest hours came near the close of its life.

Although the fifty miles of trench networks around the capital remained fairly static, battle-line fighting took place daily. When a Confederate strongpoint fell or a portion of the line wavered, reserve troop units composed of industrial laborers and bureaucrats formed and

. . . Joseph Mayo. Early in the war he declared that he would never give up his city to an enemy. In April 1865 he actually went riding out into the countryside looking for the Federals to come and accept the city's surrender and help put out the fires. (VM)

The real seat of power in Richmond, however, was here in the old Brockenbrough house, turned into an executive mansion for President Jefferson Davis. Reekie photographed it on April 12, 1865, just nine days after its former occupant had fled. A few days later, President Lincoln had visited the city and sat in Davis' chair here. (USAMHI)

hurried to reinforce Lee's regulars. Then the work of the industry and government in Richmond ceased for the duration of the emergency, and the Confederacy crumbled a little more. Reliance upon these citizen-soldiers became so frequent that in October 1864, it inspired poetic praise for the "Richmond Reserves":

> Like a beast of the forest, fierce raging
>   with pain,
> The foe in his madness, advances again;
> His eyeballs are glaring, his pulses beat fast,
> While the furies are hastening this effort,
>   his last.
> But the seven-throned queen [Richmond]
>   a calm presence preserves,
> For they've sworn to defend her—the
>   "Richmond Reserves."

However deficient as poetry, the verse displayed an urban consciousness all but unknown three years earlier. And Richmonders who were not poets exhibited a special pride in their city.

On April 1, 1865, the day before Lee evacuated the city, the *Sentinel* offered this thought: "We are very hopeful of the campaign which is opening, and trust that we are to reap a large advantage from the operations evidently near at hand." Not unlike Brussels on the eve of Waterloo, Richmond during the winter of 1864–65 had erupted into a veritable carnival of parties and weddings—*carpe diem*. One resident remembered that people held "not the brilliant and generous festivals of the olden days in Richmond, but joyous and gay assemblages of a hundred young people, who danced as though the music of cannon shells had never replaced that of the old negro fiddler—who chatted and laughed as if there were no tomorrow."

"Tomorrow" came on Sunday, April 2, 1865. Southwest of Petersburg, at Five Forks, the day

*Confederate Vice President Alexander H. Stephens lived here at 12th and
Clay streets, on the corner opposite the Executive Mansion. Though
neighbors, the two executive officers spoke as little as possible.* (USAMHI)

before, Major General George Pickett's division
had been cut off and devoured by the Federals;
the thin line of earth and men at Petersburg
which stood between Richmond and capture
was broken. Lee responded to the situation with
his usual professional competence; he endeav-
ored to save his army by abandoning the now
untenable capital.

Jefferson Davis was at St. Paul's Church when
Lee's telegram arrived from Petersburg. As the
Reverend Charles Minnegerode read the ante-
Communion service, Davis read the sentence of
doom pronounced upon his capital. The President quickly left the church and began the
process of evacuating his government. By the
time Richmond's churches had concluded their
worship, the mass exodus of government officials
from the services had confirmed the worst.

Pandemonium broke out that Sunday afternoon. "The office-holders were . . . making
arrangements to get off. Every car was ordered

to be ready to take them South. . . . The people
were rushing up and down the streets, vehicles
of all kinds were flying about, bearing goods of
all sorts and people of all ages and classes who
could go. . . ." The City Council met to try to
provide protection for private property and to
plan the destruction of liquor supplies in the
city. Meanwhile, the army prepared to destroy
whatever military supplies could not be moved.
Darkness did not slow the frantic activity.

By the early hours of April 3, most of the
military and nearly all of the government officials had left. About three o'clock in the morning a fire began. The blaze probably started as
part of the Confederacy's attempt to destroy
everything that might be of value to the enemy.
The flames engulfed the tobacco warehouses, the
railroad bridges, the arsenal, and soon raged out
of control and burned a large area of the city,
from Capitol Square to the James River. As the
massive fire blazed, rioting began. Several thou-

There were many fine homes in the city, like this, the Van Lew mansion. Its occupant, Elizabeth Van Lew, pretended to be eccentric, earning the sobriquet "Crazy Bet," but she also remained loyal to the Union and sometimes sent information through the lines to the Federals. (USAMHI)

sand people tried to reach the stored rations in the commissary depot before the flames. As a committee appointed by the City Council dumped barrels of whiskey into the streets, rioters drank from the gutters.

The evacuation fire, which smoldered in the debris until late June 1865, was devastating. It consumed more than twenty square blocks and all but destroyed the city's commercial district. Every bank, every saloon, and almost every press in the city was destroyed. Between eight hundred and twelve hundred buildings went up in flames, and damage estimates reached thirty million nineteenth-century dollars.

At dawn on April 3 a Confederate rear guard fired the last remaining bridge over the James and dashed away. Soon thereafter Mayor Mayo, who had sworn never to give up the city, rode out of Richmond to try to find someone to whom to surrender. Eventually he found Union Major General Godfrey Weitzel and made arrangements for the restoration of law and order under an occupation regime. At eight o'clock the Federals entered Richmond and marched through the city to Capitol Square.

A few days later President Abraham Lincoln came to survey his prize. And someone wrote a song to celebrate Richmond's capture. Perhaps more than anything else that song expressed what Richmond had meant to the Confederacy:

Now Richmond has fallen, rebellion is done,
Let all men rejoice for the victory is won!
The city where slavery once dwelt in her pride
Is now in our hands and the rebellion has died.
Now Richmond is taken, they'll harm us no
    more
For treason is crushed and rebellion is o'er.
Our armies have triumphed, the traitors have
    fled.
We've captured their city, secession is dead.

The last hope of the Confederacy perished in the flames of the fallen capital.

*And here on Franklin Street stood the wartime residence of General
Robert E. Lee. The house would become almost as sacred to Virginians as
the executive mansion.* (USAMHI)

*In the environs of the city, war industry bloomed during the war, most
notably here at the Tredegar Iron Works, chief cannon makers for the
Confederacy. Despite a shortage of raw materials, Tredegar was a model of
modern efficiency and production in wartime.* (USAMHI)

These men worked for the Confederate Nitre and Mining Bureau, trying to collect the raw materials for gunpowder and lead and employing a few Negroes in the process. (MC)

The Richmond arsenal manufactured what guns it could with the shortage of materials. (VM)

In this small factory near Hollywood Cemetery, small-arms ammunition was manufactured for the Confederates in the field. (VM)

Mountains of cannon projectiles stood about the arsenal yard, many of them still in place when the Federals took the city on April 3, 1865. (NA)

Besides munitions, Richmond produced flour in abundance, flour that fed the Confederacy's armies. Here are some of the mills in Manchester, across the James from the capital. (USAMHI)

Another view of one of the Richmond mills. (USAMHI)

The capital was rarely in imminent danger before late 1864. Union Colonel Ulric Dahlgren did lead a daring raid on the city on March 2, 1864, but it failed and he was killed in the attempt. His father was Admiral John A. Dahlgren, inventor of the famous Dahlgren gun. For years afterward the controversy raged over whether or not the colonel had instructed his men to kill Jefferson Davis. (P-M)

Brigadier General Walter H. Stevens was in charge of Richmond's defenses, as well as being Lee's chief engineer. He helped supervise the evacuation of the city on the night of April 2–3, 1865, and was one of the last to cross the Mayo bridge over the James before it was put to the torch. (SOUTHERN HISTORICAL COLLECTION, UNIVERSITY OF NORTH CAROLINA, CHAPEL HILL)

Brigadier General Patrick T. Moore was provost in Richmond, and when the dreadful last day came, it was he who ordered government stores burned. The fires spread, and on April 3 the Yankees marched into a . . . (VM)

. . . devastated city. A whole section of Richmond had been razed to the ground. Though rebuilt almost immediately, for decades to come this area would be known as the "Burnt District." (NA)

Whole blocks of warehouses along the James River were destroyed. (NA)

*Levy & Cohen came to record their own views of the ruined city. The large
white building still standing was the old U.S. Customs House, which served
as the Confederate Treasury.* (KA)

*On April 6, with the rubble barely cool, Alexander Gardner made this
panoramic view of the Burnt District, with the state house in the distance.*
(USAMHI, VM)

Yankee horses wait quietly outside the Confederate Treasury, right next to extensive ruins from the fire that was rather selective in its destruction. (USAMHI)

The people of Richmond were soon up and about again in the city, searching among the ruins for surviving belongings, for lost friends and relatives, or just for some remnant of a way of life now suddenly vanished. (USAMHI)

A paper mill that did not survive. (USAMHI)

Part of the mammoth Gallego Flour Mills, totally destroyed. Pictures of their ruins would stand for more than a century as the perfect image of . . . (USAMHI)

. . . the utter destruction of modern war. (USAMHI)

Though water still flowed over the mill wheel, the machinery no longer turned. Like the Confederacy, it had ground to a halt. (USAMHI)

Everything of military value had to be destroyed. The fleeing Rebels set fire to their railroad bridges like this one on the Richmond & Petersburg line. (USAMHI)

Only portions of the line, like this section connecting Belle Isle with Manchester, remained. (USAMHI)

All else was ruin. (USAMHI)

*When the Yankees came, they quickly saved what they could, repaired more,
and got the city working again. Pontoon bridges over the James allowed
traffic to cross once more.* (NA)

City Hall might not bustle for a time, but the Federal soldiers camped across the street ensured that things would be orderly. (USAMHI)

The arsenal yard was a shambles. (USAMHI)

The arsenal itself, shown in this panorama, lay in complete ruins. (USAMHI)

*Camps of laborers, many of them Negroes like these, sprang up to do the
work of rebuilding the railroads.* (KA)

*The canal along the waterfront filled once again, but now with U.S.
Government transports.* (USAMHI)

*And relics of the Confederacy became objects of curiosity for the new rulers
of Richmond. Here, the shot-riddled smokestack of the ironclad* Virginia II.
(MM)

It was a trophy of war now. (USAMHI)

So were scores of pieces of Confederate artillery, lined up at Rocketts for use by the Federals or to be transported to the North. (LC)

Captured guns, still caked with mud from the spring rains, were everywhere.
(NA)

And so was their attendant equipment, like this giant gun sling for carrying pieces of heavy artillery. (LC)

*There were even a few bits of exotica, like the English Whitworth
breech-loading rifle that could fire a solid bolt as far as five miles.* (LC)

*Now the Stars and Stripes flew over Libby Prison, its cells empty of the
human misery that made it infamous.* (USAMHI)

There was a new governor in the governor's mansion, Francis H. Pierpont, who had helped organize the new state of West Virginia and served during the war as "governor" of those Virginia counties under Federal control. Now he took a seat on the porch of his new mansion, ruling the entire state at last. (KA)

The burned bridges over the James were rebuilt. (NA)

The Virginia state house, once Capitol of the Confederacy, despite a few broken window panes, went back to the work of housing a state legislature only. Mathew Brady stands fifth from the right on the porch. (USAMHI)

Crowds milled about the Washington monument in Capitol Square once more, where Reekie photographed both Federal soldiers and recently paroled Confederates on April 14, 1865. (USAMHI)

Yankee officers like Major General E. O. C. Ord could pose with his wife and daughter on the porch of the Confederate executive mansion. (USAMHI)

And Old Glory waved at last over a burned and battered but surviving Richmond. In a remarkably short time the city would rebuild, moving with the reunited nation into a new era. (NA)

An End at Last

LOUIS MANARIN

When blood and bravery and indomitable will could do no more,
the Southern banners were furled

"AFTER FOUR YEARS of arduous service, marked by unsurpassed courage and fortitude, the Army of Northern Virginia has been compelled to yield . . ." Thus began General Robert E. Lee's farewell address to his army. The decision to yield had not come easy. Only after it became obvious that it would be useless to go on did Lee agree to surrender those who had remained steadfast to the end.

When the end came, it was not unexpected. The Confederate ranks had been thinned by battle, attrition, and the realization that will and determination were not enough. The valiant defense of the Petersburg line, the battle at Sayler's Creek southwest of Richmond, the retreat to the west, and the running attacks of Major General Philip Sheridan's cavalry had taken their toll in dead, wounded, captured, and missing. Many of the last had taken the opportunity to slip away in the confusion of battle and the retreat march.

The night sky on April 8, 1865, presented Lee's men with visible evidence of the military situation. They had been fighting rearguard and flank attacks, but now the sky reflected the red glow of campfires to the east, south, and west. The Federal army had succeeded in moving past the Rebel left flank and across the route of re-

treat. Only to the north was there an absence of the red glow. Lee's army was almost surrounded.

As the troops bedded down, there was an uneasiness. The army was stretched out and vulnerable to the hit-and-run attacks of the Federal cavalry. Out of the night the blue-clad troopers would swoop down and do their damage and then retire under the cover of darkness. Brigadier General Lindsay Walker's artillerists had successfully repulsed one lightning Federal strike, but when Brigadier General G. A. Custer's troopers struck a second time, about nine o'clock in the evening, they captured twenty-four pieces of artillery. The silence from Walker's camp told the Confederates what had happened.

Lee met with Lieutenant General James Longstreet, Major General John Gordon, and Major General Fitz Lee during the evening of April 8 and informed them of the correspondence he had had with Union General U. S. Grant. After reading Grant's letter of April 7 calling for the surrender of the Army of Northern Virginia, Longstreet had counseled his commander with the words "Not yet." In response to Lee's reply asking for clarification on terms, Grant had called for surrender of the

*Petersburg theirs, jubilant Federal soldiers caper on the ramparts of Fort
Sedgwick, raising their hats and pointing off toward the now silent
Confederate lines.* (LC)

army under conditions stating that the men
would be on parole until properly exchanged.
Surrender was the last option for Lee, and as
long as he could, he would keep his army in the
field. He proposed to meet with Grant to discuss
the restoration of peace, not to negotiate a surrender. He had not received a reply at the time
of his meeting with his generals on the evening
of April 8. After discussing their options, they
agreed that one more effort would be made to
break through toward Lynchburg. If they could
make it through, the army would turn southward. The plan called for the cavalry under
Fitz Lee, supported by the II Corps under Gordon, to drive the Federals back in front, wheel to
the left and hold the enemy while the army
moved behind their screen.

When the sun came up on Palm Sunday morning, April 9, 1865, Gordon's men, numbering
about 1,600, were in position a half mile west of
Appomattox Court House. On his right, Gordon
saw that Fitz Lee's 2,400 troopers extended his
line. As darkness turned to light, the Federal
earthworks became visible across the field. If
Federal cavalry defended them, then Gordon
and Fitz Lee felt they could force them back. If
the Federal infantry was up, then the end was at
hand.

Major General Bryan Grimes, the fiery North
Carolinian, asked to lead the attack and Gordon
told him to advance all three divisions. The
Federal troopers behind the earthworks gave
way as Gordon's men pressed forward and captured two pieces of artillery. Wheeling to the

*It was the Federal victory on April 1, 1865, at Five Forks, southwest of
Petersburg, that forced General R. E. Lee at last to evacuate that city and
Richmond. Here Rebel prisoners captured in the fight line up on their way
to the rear.* (USAMHI)

left, the jubilant gray-clad infantry opened the
road to Lynchburg. Within an hour, Fitz Lee, on
Gordon's right flank, reported the presence of
Federal infantry. Major General Edward Ord,
with three Union divisions, had marched his
men all day and night and had arrived "barely in
time." Gordon sent for reinforcements, but
Longstreet was being pressured and expected an
attack momentarily on the rear guard. Union
regiments appeared on Gordon's right and rear,
and Federal cavalry began to demonstrate on his
left flank as if to drive a wedge between the Confederate forces. Within three hours the situation
had changed from a glimmer of light to darkness.

When he received reports from his commanders, Lee decided to meet with Grant between
Longstreet's and Major General George Meade's
lines. A truce was ordered and Longstreet was

told to inform Gordon. Upon receipt of the
order, Gordon directed an officer to ride out
under a white flag to inform Ord of the truce.
The officer returned with Custer who demanded
immediate and unconditional surrender in the
name of General Sheridan. Refusing to recognize
Custer's authority, Gordon declined to surrender. Custer demanded to see Longstreet and
Gordon sent him to the rear under escort. When
Custer repeated his demand to Longstreet, "Old
Pete" also refused to recognize him and ordered
him to leave. In the meantime, Gordon had
given the word to Fitz Lee, and Lee pulled
Brigadier General Thomas Rosser's, Brigadier
General Thomas Munford's, and the greater part
of his cavalry command out of the action to escape the surrender. Recognizing General Sheridan coming through the lines, Gordon rode out

And now the Yankees lay pontoon bridges over the James River for the march into Richmond, occupied at last. A Russell view showing some of the Manchester mills, across the river from the capital. (USAMHI)

to meet him. Gordon showed him Lee's truce order and both men agreed to a cease-fire until they received word from their commanders.

Grant notified Lee that he could not discuss terms of peace but that he hoped no more blood would be shed. Lee then wrote and asked Grant for a meeting to discuss terms of surrender. Meanwhile, Lee met with Meade, and a truce was declared on that part of the line. Lee then returned through Longstreet's lines to await word from Grant. On the edge of an apple orchard, he stretched out on a pile of fence rails covered with a blanket. Little was said. Officers came up to discuss the situation with members of his staff and Longstreet came to meet with his commander. Lee was worried about the terms. It had been a hard fought struggle and his men had given their all. Now, he was faced with having to admit defeat. Word was passing through his army. Men cried out in rage for one more fight. Tears came to the eyes of many when they received word that the army was going to be sur-

rendered. Others breathed a sigh of relief that it was over. Artillerists on the move were told to turn in to the nearest field and park their guns. Some units had made it through to Lynchburg before the end came, but those that remained did not like the idea of surrendering the powder they had been forced to save.

A little after noon on April 9, a Federal courier rode up to the Confederate camp to accompany Lee to the meeting with Grant. Colonel Orville E. Babcock delivered Grant's reply to Lee's letter. Grant agreed to meet and asked Lee to pick the place. Lee would not delegate the responsibility of arranging the surrender. He asked Colonel Walter Taylor, his adjutant general, to accompany him, but that officer asked to be spared the unpleasant task on the grounds that he had been on two long rides that morning. Lieutenant Colonel Charles Marshall of Lee's staff mounted his horse as did Sergeant G. W. Tucker, who had been at Lieutenant General A. P. Hill's side when he was

*Major General Godfrey Weitzel is the general who first takes over the city,
sending out a telegram that announced on April 3, "We entered Richmond."
He stands, boots crossed, on the left of the steps, along with his staff.* (VM)

mortally wounded before Petersburg. Lee, Marshall, and Tucker, accompanied by Babcock, rode toward Appomattox Court House. Marshall was sent forward to find a suitable place to hold the meeting. Tucker was sent with him.

As they rode into the small village, Marshall met Wilmer McLean. This gentleman had lived about a mile from Manassas Junction. After witnessing the battle there in 1861, McLean moved to Appomattox to escape the war. Marshall told him of his mission and McLean showed him an old dilapidated unfurnished house. When Marshall informed him that it was not adequate, McLean offered his home as a meeting place. Marshall sent Tucker back to tell Lee and Babcock while he went into the house

to select a room. When they arrived, Lee and Babcock joined Marshall in the parlor. Babcock stationed an orderly outside to direct General Grant.

About a half hour later, Grant rode up. Babcock opened the door and Grant entered the room alone. The two generals shook hands, exchanged greetings, and sat down. After whispered conversation with Grant, Babcock left the room and returned with a number of Federal officers. Among the group were Generals Sheridan and Ord, Brigadier General Horace Porter, Colonel Adam Badeau, and Lieutenant Colonel Ely Parker. They formed a semicircle behind Grant.

After some pleasantries with Grant about ser-

Immediately Yankee ships like the Unadilla *start the work of clearing the James of obstructions and "torpedoes," opening it to traffic.* (KA)

vice together in the Mexican War, Lee broached the subject of surrender terms. Grant outlined his thoughts calling for the surrender of all equipment and supplies. The men would be paroled not to take up arms until properly exchanged. Lee acknowledged acceptance and Grant put the terms in writing. Lee reviewed them and when Grant asked if he had any suggestions, Lee did mention that the terms did not provide for the horses owned by the men in the ranks. Pointing out that it did provide for the officers, Grant replied that he would not change the terms but he would instruct his officers to allow any man who claimed to own a horse or mule to keep it for farming.

Grant instructed that his letter be copied and Lee directed Marshall to draft a reply. While the writing was being completed, Grant introduced his officers to Lee. It was not a pleasant experi-

ence for Lee, and as soon as the formalities were over, he brought up the matter of Federal prisoners. Grant agreed to accept them. When Lee requested that a train from Lynchburg be allowed to pass so he could supply his men with provisions, it was learned that the train had been captured by Sheridan the night before. Grant offered to send Lee food, and after discussion as to the amount, he directed that 25,000 rations be sent to Lee's men.

Lee made some changes in Marshall's draft of the letter accepting the surrender terms. Borrowing a piece of paper, Marshall copied the letter and Lee signed it. Marshall sealed the letter and presented it to Colonel Parker who gave him Grant's surrender terms letter. The exchange of letters formally completed the surrender of the Army of Northern Virginia. Before leaving, Lee asked that Meade be notified of the surrender to

*And quickly the traffic commenced. General U. S. Grant's headquarters boat,
the* River Queen, *can now ply the waters of the James. Aboard this boat the
abortive Hampton Roads Peace Conference had taken place back in February
1865. President Lincoln and Grant met aboard the vessel for conferences in
March, and on April 4 it brought the President to Richmond for a tour of
the captured city.* (USAMHI)

avoid any possible flare-up of fighting. He also
requested that the two armies be kept separate
for the time being. Grant agreed and dispatched
men to notify Meade. It was close to 4 P.M. when
Lee and Grant shook hands again, and Lee
bowed to the other officers and left the room. On
the porch, he called for his horse, and as he
mounted, Grant came down the steps. The
Union general removed his hat and his subordinates followed. Lee acknowledged their
gesture by raising his hat. Without a word, he
turned Traveller and rode out of the yard.

Lee knew that Grant had given favorable
surrender terms. What could have been a hu-
miliating experience was made more bearable
by the genuine courtesy and respect displayed on
both sides. As he rode into his lines toward his
camp at the apple orchard, Lee's veterans began
crowding around asking if the army had been

surrendered. With tears in his eyes, he told them
that it had been. Expressions of anger, frustration, and sorrow came from the men. Upon Lee's
arrival at the camp, he notified Colonel T. M. R.
Talcott, commanding the Engineers, that the
rations would be coming in. Lee then walked
away to be by himself. He paced up and down
to relieve the pressures pent up inside of him.
His solitude was interrupted by visiting Federal
officers who wanted to meet him. After receiving
a letter from Grant appointing commissioners to
arrange the details of the surrender, Lee
mounted Traveller to return to his own headquarters. Along the road he was met by more
men from his army. The word of the surrender
had passed quickly and the road was lined on
both sides. Officers on horseback stood behind
the lines. When he arrived at his headquarters,
others were waiting to see him, to talk to him,

Lincoln transferred to the USS Malvern *for part of the journey to Richmond, entertained by its flag commander . . .* (USAMHI)

. . . Rear Admiral David D. Porter. Porter here wears crape in mourning for the President, who lay dead barely more than a week after his visit. (USAMHI)

Soon the visitors flooded the docks at City Point and Richmond both.
Members of Major General George Meade's family crowd the deck of this
steamer at City Point, anxious to see the general and to view the scenes of
conquest. (P-M)

to shake his hand. That evening, while seated around the campfire, Lee instructed Marshall to draft a farewell address to the army.

The next day, April 10, Lee dispatched orders to his subordinate commanders to prepare final reports on the last campaign. When he found that Marshall had not prepared the draft of the farewell address, he told him to go into his ambulance where he would not be disturbed. Longstreet, Gordon, and Brigadier General William N. Pendleton were appointed by Lee as commissioners to draft the surrender procedures. Grant had appointed Major Generals John Gibbon, Charles Griffin, and Wesley Merritt. These men met in the McLean house the same day to make arrangements for the formal

surrender, the transfer of public property, private horses, and mules, and the lease of transportation to officers. It was also agreed that the terms would embrace all men within a twenty-five-mile radius of the courthouse and units that were operating with the army on April 8, except those that were over twenty miles from Appomattox on the ninth. Each parole was to be signed by the soldier's commander or his staff officer, not by the Federal provost marshal. The signed parole was sufficient for passage through Federal lines. By a separate order, Grant authorized free travel on Federal transports and military railroads.

During the morning of April 10, Grant had attempted to ride over to meet with Lee but

But though the enemy capital had fallen, the war was not over. It could never be over so long as this wily and elusive adversary remained at large. Another Julian Vannerson portrait of Robert E. Lee gave little hint that the man behind this peaceful aspect was a champion war. (VM)

But now he was on the run. As he evacuated Richmond, he took with him what he could and destroyed what he could not. Within days Reekie photographed wreckage left behind. (USAMHI)

was stopped by Confederate pickets. When he heard of this, Lee mounted Traveller and rode out to meet his former adversary. The two men greeted each other by lifting their hats. Grant expressed a desire to prevent further bloodshed and suggested that if the other Confederate armies would surrender then peace would come. He felt that Lee could use his influence and prestige to bring this about, but Lee felt it was not his decision but President Jefferson Davis'. After about a half hour, the two men parted. On his way back to camp, Lee met General Meade. The two conversed and then rode back to Lee's headquarters.

When Marshall finished his draft of the farewell address, Lee reviewed it. He struck out one paragraph that he felt was too harsh and changed some of the words. The address was then copied

and given to Lee for his signature. Once signed, copies of General Order No. 9 were made, signed by Lee, and distributed to his subordinate commanders. They had it transmitted to the men in the ranks. Copies were made by officers and men and brought to Lee for his signature.

The next day, April 11, the campaign reports came into Lee's headquarters from his subordinate commanders, and he began to prepare his own final report. Muster rolls were made out for all Confederate units and copies were forwarded to both headquarters. A total of 28,231 men of all arms of the service were reported. The paroles, which had to be printed, were received. Formal surrender of the artillery and cavalry occurred on this day. Union Major General John W. Turner's division, of the Army of the James, witnessed the transfer of equipment and

Meade was after the fleeing Confederates, Meade and his generals. Shown here a few weeks later, they are, from the left, Brevet Brigadier General George Macy, provost; Brevet Major General A. S. Webb, chief of staff; Major General Andrew A. Humphreys, commanding the II Corps; Major General Charles Griffin, commanding the V Corps; Meade; Major General John G. Parke, commanding the IX Corps; Brevet Major General Henry J. Hunt, chief of artillery. The brigadier at right is unidentified. (USAMHI)

animals as the members of Confederate artillery units left their guns parked for the last time. Those who claimed horses or mules were allowed to keep them. Upon receipt of their paroles, they said good-bye to comrades and began the trek home. The remaining Confederate cavalry of Major General W. H. F. "Rooney" Lee's division laid down their swords and firearms before Major General Ranald Mackenzie's troopers. With their paroles in hand, they rode off, not to take up arms until properly exchanged.

The Confederate commissioners had asked that the infantry be allowed to stack arms, cartridge boxes, and flags in their camps, but Grant would not consent. The surrender could not be

a symbolic gesture of walking away from the instruments of war. It had to be an act of relinquishing equipment and flags and the act had to be witnessed. Declining to give up their battle flags, some units tore them up and distributed pieces to the members. Some flags were smuggled out by men who refused to surrender and slipped away during the night. Some were secreted under the clothing of men who took part in the final ceremony.

On the morning of April 12, the Confederate infantry prepared to carry out the final act. The units formed in ranks, with officers and flags in position. General John Gordon's command started down the ridge first. As the Confederate column came up the hill, Brigadier General

It was Major General Philip Sheridan who brought on the Confederate disaster at Five Forks, and thereafter his cavalry dogged the retreating Rebels all along their route. Then, on April 6, he and part of Meade's infantry caught them at Sayler's Creek. (USAMHI)

Joshua L. Chamberlain, commanding the Federal division, gave orders for the bugler to sound carry arms, the marching salute. Gordon responded by saluting Chamberlain and ordering his men to carry arms. Victor saluted vanquished and they returned the honor. Gordon's men marched beyond the Federal column and halted. The ranks were dressed and the order was given to fix bayonets. The command to stack arms came next, and the men moved across the road and stacked their arms. Cartridge boxes were hung from the muskets and battle flags were rolled up and laid on the stacks.

The units re-formed in the road and marched past the courthouse and halted. Here they broke ranks, shook hands, and bade each other farewell as the other units moved through the cordon to stack arms. Some men returned to camp, but most of them turned toward home. Men from the same area usually left in small groups under command of the ranking officer. They carried with them the news that the Army of Northern Virginia had been surrendered. Lee officially notified President Davis of this in his report of April 12, and although he did not witness the surrender, Lee remained on the field until the act was completed. With his own parole in hand he turned his face toward Richmond, and with members of his staff he started the long journey back.

In fact, on April 10 news of Lee's surrender reached Davis at Danville, in southern Virginia, where he had paused on his flight from Richmond, and late that day he left by rail for Greensboro, North Carolina. The Confederate cavalry and artillery units that had escaped before the army was surrendered made their way to Lynchburg, in the west, where, after consulting the Confederate Secretary of War John C. Breckinridge, they disbanded. Some units made their way south intent on joining General Joe Johnston in North Carolina, while others struck out for home. As word of Lee's surrender crossed the mountains and men from his army brought the word, other units began to dissolve or disband. Major General Lunsford Lomax's command, operating between Lynchburg and Danville began to disintegrate as the Virginia units left the ranks. Word of Lee's surrender caused Colonel William Nelson to disband his artillery battalion at Pittsylvania Court House and to distribute the horses among the men. The Federal cavalry entered Lynchburg on April 13 and on April 15 General Lomax and Brigadier General William L. Jackson disbanded their commands at Buchanan, in the Shenandoah Valley. Federal Major General Winfield Scott Hancock extended Grant's terms to all soldiers of the Army of Northern Virginia in the valley if they would come in and receive their paroles. At Millwood, on April 21, Colonel John Singleton Mosby disbanded his Rangers. Effective resistance was at an end in Virginia by the end of the month.

Meanwhile, at Greensboro, President Davis

It was terrible. Nearly one third of Lee's army was captured, including Brigadier General Seth Barton. (USAMHI)

Also taken was Brigadier General Montgomery D. Corse. The Yankees simply overwhelmed them. (USAMHI)

met with Generals Johnston and P. G. T. Beauregard and his Cabinet on April 12. Johnston's army was at Hillsborough while Major General William T. Sherman's was preparing to enter Raleigh. Johnston recommended negotiation but Davis felt that it would only result in surrender. Outvoted, Davis agreed to authorize Johnston to meet with Sherman. While they were discussing conditions in North Carolina, the last major city of the Confederacy fell. Mobile, Alabama, was occupied by Union troops under Major General E. R. S. Canby. Confederate forces under Major General D. H. Maury had evacuated the night before toward Meridian, Mississippi, with hopes of joining Johnston's army in North Carolina.

Sherman's men occupied Raleigh on April 13 and pressed on to Durham Station the next day. On the fourteenth Johnston communicated with Sherman and sought a temporary suspension of

hostilities pending discussions of peace. After negotiations as to time and place, they agreed to meet on April 17 on the road between Durham Station and Hillsborough. Sherman left Raleigh by train for Durham Station, and there he met Brigadier General Hugh Kilpatrick who provided a Union cavalry escort. As Sherman's party set out with a cavalryman in the lead carrying a flag of truce, Johnston and Lieutenant General Wade Hampton were moving toward Durham Station with an escort. Hampton's orderly carried the flag of truce.

When the two groups met, Johnston and Sherman shook hands and introduced their aides. Johnston noted that he had passed a small farmhouse, so he and Sherman rode back down the road to James Bennett's log farmhouse. Lucy Bennett met them at the door, and after granting their request to use the house, she retired with her four children to one of the outbuild-

The next day Major General Thomas Rosser attempted to hold the vital railroad crossing of the Appomattox River at High Bridge, west of Petersburg. A desperate little fight ensued. (VM)

Brigadier General James Dearing engaged Federal Brigadier General Theodore Read in a pistol duel that left Read dead and Dearing dying, the last Confederate general to die of wounds in battle. (USAMHI)

ings. The two men closed the door to the one-room house and discussed amnesty and surrender terms in private. Unable to reach a decision on all points, they agreed to meet again the next day. On the eighteenth Confederate Secretary of War Breckinridge joined the discussion and it was then that Sherman drew up a memorandum of agreement.

In their discussion the three men went beyond the original intent of the meeting and considered terms for a general armistice, dealing with reconstruction policies that were not in fact within Sherman's authority to establish. Sherman believed he was expressing President Lincoln's wishes in his terms. But Lincoln was dead, murdered on April 14, and Andrew Johnson now sat in the White House.

The agreement did put an end to the fighting,

even though the other terms would be rejected by the Federal authorities. With the exception of Major General James H. Wilson's Union cavalry raids in Georgia and Alabama and Major General George Stoneman's in western North Carolina, most of the remaining engagements east of the Mississippi were minor skirmishes. Jefferson Davis moved to Charlotte where he approved Johnston's agreement with Sherman. Unknown to Davis at the time, Sherman was being informed that the agreement had been disapproved by Washington and he was directed to resume active campaigning within forty-eight hours if Johnston did not surrender.

At Johnston's request, Sherman met with him again at the Bennett place on April 26. By the terms of the agreement of that day, Johnston's

High Bridge and the nearby wagon road bridge were supposed to be burned by the Confederates once they had crossed over them. (USAMHI)

army was to be mustered at Greensboro and there the ordnance supplies were to be turned in and the men were to be paroled. Brigadier General John M. Schofield, who was to be Federal departmental commander, agreed to six supplemental terms when Johnston objected to the general terms. He assured Johnston that there would be sufficient transportation, that each brigade could keep one seventh of their arms until they reached their state capital, that both officers and enlisted men could retain their private property, that troops from Texas and Arkansas were to be provided water transportation, and that all naval forces within the limits of Johnston's command were also included. The men were to be supplied with ten days' rations

so they would not have to live off the countryside. The agreement, signed by Johnston and Schofield, brought an official end to hostilities in North Carolina.

Johnston announced the termination of hostilities to the governors of the Confederate states and the Confederate Army. When word was received that the Army had been surrendered, men began leaving. Major General Joseph Wheeler vowed he would not surrender and he left with those of his command who would follow him to attempt to find President Davis. Wade Hampton, who was not personally with Johnston's army at the time, declared that he was not included in the surrender and would not stay. When his cavalrymen left, he rode after them and ordered

However, Colonel T. M. R. Talcott of Lee's staff was unable to get the fires set in time, and the Yankees rushed the bridge and put them out. Everything for Lee was going awry now. (VM)

After Sayler's Creek, Lee was in danger of having more generals than privates. On April 7 Brigadier General Henry A. Wise joined him. Former Virginia governor and a brother-in-law of the General Meade now dogging them, Wise led a battered division out of the trap at Sayler's Creek. When Lee teased him, saying he could be shot for what he said about a superior officer who ran away, Wise replied "Shot! I wish you would shoot me. If you don't, some Yankee probably will within twenty-four hours." (USAMHI)

them to return. While they did so, he rode to join President Davis. For those units remaining with the Army, muster rolls were prepared and paroles were issued. Those units at Bush Hill, Randolph County, were paroled on June 29 and each man received $1.25 in silver as final pay. This was part of the approximately $38,000 in Confederate Treasury silver that Johnston ordered to be distributed equally to officers and men. Those units at Greensboro were paroled on May 1 and 2, and on the latter day, Johnston's farewell address, General Order No. 22, was read to the troops.

Meanwhile, those units that had remained in northeastern North Carolina had been isolated. Some simply disbanded when they received word of Lee's surrender or of the first Johnston-

Sherman agreement. Brigadier General Laurence S. Baker withdrew his force from Weldon on April 13. When he heard of Lee's surrender, he decided to disband his force and to make an attempt to join Johnston's army with those who would follow. Efforts to penetrate beyond the Union scouting parties and pickets failed, so he sent word to the Union commander at Raleigh that he would surrender his force under the first

The next day, April 8, Lee hoped to find provisions for his starving army awaiting him here at Appomattox Station. He found nothing. (LC)

Johnston-Sherman agreement. His offer to surrender was accepted and his men were paroled at Bunn's House, Nash County, on April 20, 1865.

Other units refused to surrender and simply took their arms and went home. One section of Company C, 13th Battalion North Carolina Light Artillery had been on detached service with the Army of Northern Virginia and had made it to Lynchburg before Lee's surrender. Instead of disbanding, they made their way south and joined the other section of the company attached to Johnston's army near Greensboro. When word of Johnston's surrender came, the men of the first section, fearing they would be covered by its terms and thus not properly exchanged, left camp and were not reported on the company's final muster roll.

As Johnston's army began disbanding after April 26, Lieutenant General Richard Taylor and Canby formulated surrender terms on May 2 based on the Appomattox agreement. Two days later, at Citronelle, Alabama, General Taylor surrendered the forces in the Department of Alabama, Mississippi, and East Louisiana. Major General Sam Jones, commanding at Tallahassee, Florida, surrendered the forces under his command on May 10, the day President Davis was captured near Irwinville, Georgia.

Small groups continued to surrender east of the Mississippi, but because the main forces in that area had surrendered, President Johnson proclaimed "armed resistance . . . virtually at an end." West of the Mississippi, Brigadier General M. Jeff Thompson surrendered at Chalk Bluff, Arkansas, on May 11. He, too, agreed to

Now the generals who had lost their commands begin to find their way into his lines. Major General Bushrod Johnson lost his, or so he thought, at Sayler's Creek. His men fought their way out under Wise. (USAMHI)

Brigadier General William P. Roberts, the youngest general in the Confederacy, was only twenty-three and lost his command at Five Forks. Lee had no more men to give him at Appomattox. (USAMHI)

the Appomattox terms. The last remaining Confederate army in the field was under General E. Kirby Smith. The Army of Trans-Mississippi was surrendered under Appomattox-type terms agreed to during a meeting at New Orleans on May 26. At that meeting Lieutenant General S. B. Buckner represented General Kirby Smith and Major General Peter J. Osterhaus represented General Canby. When General Kirby Smith approved the agreement on June 2, the army was surrendered. Except for some troops under Brigadier General Jo Shelby, who refused to accept the surrender terms and led his men into Mexico, Confederate military resistance was at an end.

On the high seas, the CSS *Shenandoah* continued to attack Union whaling vessels until word was received on August 2 that the war was over. Lieutenant James Waddell, commanding the *Shenandoah* set sail for Liverpool, England, where he surrendered his ship to British authorities on November 6, 1865. It was not until April 2, 1866, that President Johnson proclaimed the insurrection at an end in Georgia, South Carolina, Virginia, North Carolina, Tennessee, Alabama, Louisiana, Arkansas, Mississippi, and Florida. On August 20, 1866, he extended his proclamation to include Texas, the last of the Secessionist states. The terms set down by Grant and Lee had set the tone for those to come. They were magnanimous, not harsh, but firm. They acknowledged respect for the vanquished and the need to begin jointly the rebuilding of the Union.

Lee was trapped. Desperately he allowed Major General Bryan Grimes to make a last attack on the morning of April 9. He could not cut his way out, and that left no alternative but for Lee to meet Grant to discuss terms of surrender. (USAMHI)

By April 9 the last avenue of escape for Lee was cut off, largely thanks to the swiftness of one of Sheridan's best division commanders, Brigadier General George A. Custer. He would never again experience the glory he knew at Appomattox. Eleven years later he would die looking for it at Little Big Horn. (USAMHI)

They met here, in the Wilmer McLean house, in Appomattox Court House.
Walking up these steps . . . (LC)

. . . accompanied by his military secretary,
Lieutenant Colonel Charles Marshall . . .
(TULANE UNIVERSITY, NEW ORLEANS)

. . . Lee entered this parlor. A postwar image shows the now bare room
where Lee and Grant met to make peace. For the Army of Northern
Virginia, four years of arduous service were done. (NA)

Grant detailed a few of his most trusted generals to meet with Lee's lieutenants to work out the formalities of surrender. Major General Charles Griffin was one. (USAMHI)

The gallant cavalryman Major General Wesley Merritt was another. For him the Civil War was only the beginning of a brilliant career that went on for thirty-five more years and included service in the Spanish-American War. (CWTI)

On April 12, 1865, when the Confederate infantrymen formally marched up and stacked their arms for the last time, Grant detailed Brigadier General Joseph J. Bartlett to receive them. With that symbolic act, the war in Virginia was done. (P-M)

The collapse was everywhere. Down in North Carolina, Major General William T. Sherman finally brought Confederate General Joseph E. Johnston and his army to bay near Durham Station. In this modest home, the Bennett place, Johnston and Sherman met to arrange the surrender of yet another Confederate army. (LC)

Johnston's army was a shadow. Regiments had been so depleted that men like this private from the 33d Tennessee were members of units composed of five and six regiments combined and still understrength. (HERB PECK, JR.)

*The generals in North Carolina were as battered as the army. Brigadier
General Laurence S. Baker could hardly wear his uniform for all the wounds
he bore, and still he was on active service.* (VM)

Out in Mississippi the story was the same. Near Vicksburg the Federals set up a special camp for the exchange of prisoners, realizing that the war was all but over. Here in April 1865 a photographer caught what was probably one of the very last such meetings as Confederate officers confer under flag of truce with their Yankee counterparts. (VITOLO-RINHART GALLERIES, NEW YORK CITY)

Officers without commands, like Brigadier General William R. Peck, simply came into Federal lines to take their parole. A mammoth six feet six inches tall, Peck made quite a catch. (STEVE MULLINAX)

Everywhere the signs of impending Union occupation sprang up. In Huntsville, Alabama, Brigadier General Emerson Opdycke established his headquarters in this house, obviously there to stay for a while. (USAMHI)

Nearby Major General David Stanley set up his IV Corps headquarters.
(USAMHI)

There was no one in Alabama to stop them. On May 4,the last Confederate army east of the Mississippi surrendered to Major General E. R. S. Canby near Mobile. (USAMHI)

The last army was that of Lieutenant General Richard Taylor, son of President Zachary Taylor and brother-in-law of Jefferson Davis. (DAM, LSU)

Here at the Baton Rouge, Louisiana, arsenal, the artillery of Taylor's army sits, row upon row, after the surrender. (DAM, LSU)

The havoc and destruction continued even after Taylor's surrender. On May 25 some twenty tons of Confederate powder exploded in a warehouse in Mobile, leveling a fair-sized area and doing $5 million in damage. (USAMHI)

The only substantial Confederate force left in the field was the Trans-Mississippi, and on May 26 it too succumbed. Colonel Thomas P. Ochiltree of Texas could affect a brigadier's uniform that he was not entitled to wear, but all his protestations of inevitable victory could not affect the outcome of the war for his army. (MC)

Perhaps realizing that they were the end of an era, the last organized army to surrender, the ranking officers of the Trans-Mississippi met to preserve their portrait for posterity in one of the most remarkable Confederate photographs in existence. Seated second from the left is the army commander, General Edmund Kirby Smith. Seated to his right, is Brigadier General Henry W. Allen, forced to use a cane after a wound suffered at Shiloh, now governor of Confederate Louisiana. He helped Smith negotiate the surrender terms. Seated at Smith's immediate left is his chief of staff, Brigadier General William R. Boggs. The identity of the remaining officers is unknown, but they are presumably members of Smith's staff. The presence of Allen makes it probable that this image was made at the time the surrender negotiations were under way. If so, it is the last image made of Confederate generals on active service. (CONFEDERATE MUSEUM, NEW ORLEANS)

Even as the armies were surrendering, the Federals were reclaiming the South. Charleston fell to them back in February 1865, and now Yankee soldiers filled the streets of the former seedbed of secession. The Post Office was put back in business. (JAMES G. HEAVILIN)

And the grounds of the Charleston Arsenal once more held Union guns— Parrott rifles used in the siege of Charleston—mixed with captured Confederate cannon. Flags and bunting draped from the trees reveal that this image was probably made on April 14, the fourth anniversary of the fall of Fort Sumter. (NYHS)

Dignitaries flocked to Charleston on that day for the special ceremonies. For their edification, they could view row upon row of cannon and ammunition. (CHS)

But above all they could go out to Fort Sumter. The Federal fleet in the harbor sent its most colorful flags up the halyards to celebrate the day. (LC)

And old and ailing Major General Robert Anderson, now retired, who had lowered the Stars and Stripes on April 14, 1861, was there. (USAMHI)

After the speeches and ceremony Anderson raised on the Fort Sumter flagpole the very same Stars and Stripes that he had taken down four years before. With the war now all but done, all that remained was the ceremony and the symbolism, working to give some meaning to all that had happened. (T. SCOTT SANDERS)

Yet the final surrender would not come for months. Lieutenant James I. Waddell, commanding the Confederate commerce raider Shenandoah, *did not learn of the surrenders until August. And on November 6, 1865, seven months after Lee surrendered and almost six months after Smith, Waddell gave up his ship to British authorities in Liverpool. That, at last, was an end to it.* (MC)

The guns at last were silent, never to speak again. (ÑA)

*And at his home in Richmond, on April 16, 1865, General Robert E. Lee
posed for his portrait for the last time in the uniform he had ennobled.
Mathew Brady importuned him to pose, and in the end the general
consented. For all the wear that the years and the cares have inflicted, there
is still in his eyes the look of a man who may have been worn down to defeat
but who was never beaten. Already he is on his way to becoming an immortal
hero to all Americans.* (NA)

*But for a few, even the admission of defeat is too much. Old Edmund Ruffin
of Virginia, the fire-eating Secessionist who fired one of the first shots at Fort
Sumter in 1861, who hailed John Brown's raid on Harpers Ferry in 1859
because it would bring on secession, and who loathed all things Northern
and Yankee, refused to yield. On June 17, 1865, after everyone had
surrendered, Ruffin wrote in his diary: "And now . . . with what will be near
to my latest breath, I hereby repeat . . . my unmitigated hatred to Yankee
rule—to all political, social, & business connection with Yankees, & to the
perfidious, malignant, & vile Yankee race." Then he put a rifle muzzle in his
mouth and pulled the trigger. Having fired one of the war's first shots, he
fired as well one of its last. (VM)*

The "Late Unpleasantness"

WILLIAM C. DAVIS

The war done, there was peace to wage, and battles anew
with the hatreds remaining, and challenges ahead for a nation reuniting

IT WAS ALL BUT DONE, the long unimaginable nightmare over. General Robert E. Lee's once seemingly invincible Army of Northern Virginia was reduced to a shadow and surrendered on the grassy roadside of Appomattox. In North Carolina the South's other major eastern army was at bay and its commander, General Joseph E. Johnston, was suggesting to his antagonist Major General William T. Sherman that they meet to explore the possibilities of peace. Mobile, the Confederacy's last great city, had fallen. The flag of the Union flew once more over the unrecognizable ruins of Fort Sumter, where the whole dreadful business began. The small Southern armies farther west still held out, but the avenues of escape open to them were dwindling. The Confederate government was in flight after the fall of Richmond, and to more and more of its soldiers the awful truth became evident that there was nothing left to keep fighting for. It was all over.

But like the dying moments of a robust man worn down by illness, there could still be a last, sudden outburst, some final surge of desperate energy before death. The Civil War would not quietly die in its sleep. There was a final act of bitter, blinding, senseless hate to perform, and

who better to stage it than an actor. For months John Wilkes Booth, nationally famed player, sometime oil speculator, inveterate rakehell with the ladies of Washington and New York, had been planning his greatest performance. He would never take up arms to defend the South he so loudly espoused, but late in 1864 he devised a theatrical scheme to kidnap President Lincoln and spirit him away to the Confederacy as hostage for the release of Confederate prisoners held in the North—even for Southern independence itself. How much of the plan sprang from genuine patriotism and how much came from the simple egotistical impulse of a born posturer may never be known. What is certain is that repeated attempts were foiled through accident or ineptitude. Then came Lee's surrender and the symbolic end of the war. All else would be anticlimax, and now Booth's plan seemed pointless. But rather than abandon his schemes, he simply gave their goal a new and more sinister direction. Now Lincoln must die, not to save the Confederacy but in vengeance for having conquered it.

Booth chose a theater for his stage, of course, and the April 14, 1865, evening performance at Ford's Theatre of *Our American Cousin*. The

In the midst of jubilation came terror, a last act of hate to poison the peace.
Here, in the theater of John T. Ford, on the evening of April 14, 1865,
President Lincoln came to see a play. (LC)

Lincolns were to attend. The dreadful act of that night is engraved indelibly upon every American consciousness. At about 10:20 P.M. actor Harry Hawk down on the stage delivered one of the most amusing lines of the farce, calling an actress a "sockdologizing old mantrap!" There was an outburst of laughter in the theater. Perhaps Lincoln, sitting in a box to the right of the stage, laughed as well. Ironically, the four letters at the end of that line, "trap," formed the last human syllable he would ever hear. At that very instant he was himself sitting in a trap. As Hawk delivered the line, Booth stepped silently into the box, unseen, directly behind the President. He held a small derringer pistol in front of him, its muzzle no more than six inches from the back of Lincoln's head. Before the laughter died down, he pulled the trigger.

A round bullet, an ounce or more of lead, burst from the muzzle and struck Lincoln an

The President and his wife sat in the box at the right, their guests in the one at the left. A portrait of George Washington and a United States Treasury guard flag decorated the railing. (USAMHI)

inch or two behind his left ear. Starting to flatten as it pounded its way through his skull, driving bits of hair and tissue and bone before it, the missile entered the brain, shock waves from the impact sending fractures racing around both sides of the skull. Already Lincoln's head was virtually destroyed. Meanwhile the bullet careered onward through the cerebellum, causing Lincoln to raise his right arm convulsively, though by then the deadly lead had continued in its path, destroying the million and more instinctive and learned reflexes that had made

But actor John Wilkes Booth staged a different play that night. When he leaped from that railing to the stage in his last dramatic performance, he left behind him confusion and shock in the box, and a bullet in Lincoln's brain. (LC)

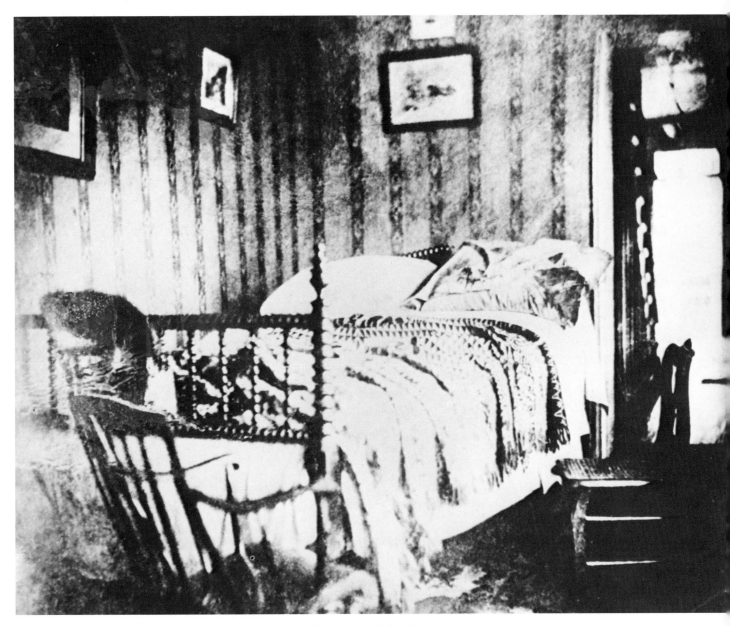

*Across the street, to the Peterson rooming house, they carried the President,
and into this back room. Here, all through the night, he labored for breath,
unconscious. Here at 7:22 A.M., April 15, he died. Within minutes after the
body was carried out, photographer Julius Ulke brought his camera into the
still undisturbed room. Here he made at least two images that would remain
lost for nearly a century. They showed the bed in which the President died,
the coverlet that left his bare feet protruding as they laid the long and lanky
Kentuckian diagonally on the mattress. And they showed the pillow soaked
with Lincoln's blood as it oozed from his head wound. From humble
beginnings he had come, and so he went, in a humble rooming house. Yet it
was no place for the death of a President. (LO)*

The White House went silent in shock, and the Union prepared for a long mourning. (USAMHI)

Lincoln a good rail-splitter and a miserable dancer.

The cerebellum was largely a ruin when the bullet smashed into the hypothalamus and thalamus, probably destroying all of Lincoln's senses except smell. Here, too, lay all the seats of ancient instincts for flight from danger, but now it was too late to fly. Finally the fatal ball plunged on into the forepart of the cerebral cortex, erasing as it went untold memories—the faint recollections of his beloved mother, the truth of his supposed love for Ann Rutledge, the pain of the loss of two of his sons, and the incalculable burden of leading his nation through war to the peace that lay at hand. Finally Booth's messenger of hate halted its path somewhere behind the right eye. The President was unconscious. Out of pure physical reflex, the body would struggle on, holding to life until the next morning. Carried from Ford's Theatre to a rooming house belonging to one William Peterson

across 10th Street, it would ooze blood onto pillows and gasp at breath for several hours. But all that had made Lincoln what he was had died before the laughter trailed away from Hawk's portentous last word, "mantrap."

The North lurched into mourning, a grief more prolonged than any in its history. So great a tragedy coming in train with so great a triumph almost unnerved many Americans, even some in the South. The public outpouring of lamentation from pulpit and press was staggering. Lincoln's body literally went on tour for funerals in New York, Philadelphia, Baltimore, and elsewhere. For twenty days the casket traveled before at last it came to rest in Springfield, Illinois, the city he had moved to as a young man.

Back in Washington, Ford's Theatre was closed and the Peterson house across the street became a tourist attraction. A Massachusetts soldier, Charles Nightingale, returning from the war, visited the place and stepped into the room

The funeral parade up Pennsylvania Avenue in Washington, D.C., began the formal outpouring of grief. A wing of the Capitol appears in the right distance. (USAMHI)

where Lincoln died. Neatly placed on the simple bedstead he saw "the bloody pillow upon which the nation's martyr passed from time to eternity." Nightingale, as so many others, could not but be moved. "I shall never forget my feelings as I stood there gazing with feverish excitement upon that blood-stained pillow," he wrote a few days later. "They were of awe and madness, indescribable, deep."

For two weeks after the murder the dark days continued. The manhunt for Booth and his accomplices spread throughout the nation. Some who had been his confederates in the kidnapping scheme were quietly arrested. So was Mary Surratt, mother of one of the plotters and keeper of a Washington boardinghouse where kidnapping —and some said murder—plans were hatched. Finally, on April 26, Booth was cornered in a

shed near the Rappahannock River in Virginia. Refusing to surrender himself, he fell to a bullet fired in the dark, perhaps from one of his pursuers, perhaps from his own gun. He died shortly after dawn, the same day that General Johnston surrendered at last to General Sherman in North Carolina and the war east of the Alleghenies came virtually to an end. The next day, as if to add a final terrible coda to the most doleful fortnight in living memory, the steamer *Sultana*, loaded with 2,000 or more Union soldiers, most of them recently released prisoners who had survived Confederate prison camps and were going home from the war, exploded on the Mississippi as she steamed north of Memphis. At least 1,200 died and perhaps hundreds more that were unaccounted for. It was up to that time the worst single marine disaster in history,

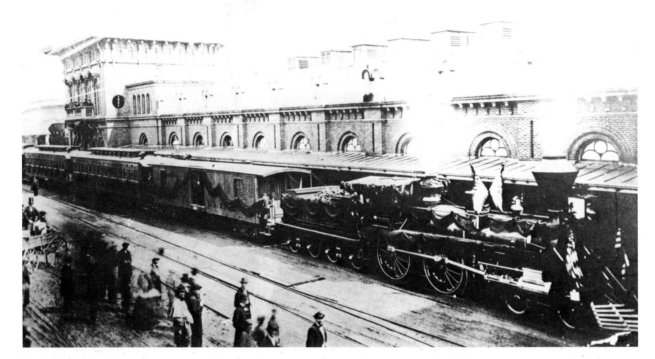

And then the funeral train began its long journey, bringing Lincoln's remains to a host of cities in the North so that the people could pay their final respects to the man who led them from war to peace. When the train arrived at Harrisburg, Pennsylvania, on April 22, a local photographer came out to record this previously unpublished image of the engine and cars at the depot. (EDWARD STEERS, JR.)

and once more, so recently euphoric over victory, the North was plunged into gloom and mourning.

The Union badly needed something to cheer it from its despair. After all, it had won the war, preserved itself, put down rebellion, ended slavery, and—some claimed—prevented the death of democracy for all time. There were a million heroes in blue to honor for their services before they took discharge, and Washington decided to stage a mammoth celebration both to do the Union veterans justice and to lift the nation from its grief. A Grand Review was scheduled for May 23–24, 1865.

The first day the noble old Army of the Po-

tomac marched from the Capitol down Pennsylvania Avenue and past the White House. This was the aristocrat of Federal armies, marching smartly, well dressed, tempered by repeated defeats and vindicated by final victory. All the memories of the Seven Days, of Second Manassas and Antietam and Fredericksburg, of humiliation at Chancellorsville and revenge at Gettysburg, filed past the stands as rank upon rank of blue marched out of time and into posterity. The next day came Sherman's armies from North Carolina, Westerners mostly, roughly dressed, rawboned, ill-disciplined, lackluster on parade, yet bringing with them the greatest string of victories of any army on the continent.

City Hall in New York City, on April 24, is thronged with people eager for a last look at the kindly visage of Father Abraham. (INTERNATIONAL MUSEUM OF PHOTOGRAPHY AT GEORGE EASTMAN HOUSE, ROCHESTER, N.Y.)

Two days later the last remaining Confederate army surrendered in Louisiana, and it was all done.

To be sure, there were still a few Confederate holdouts, not least the remnant of the Rich-mond government. Having fled their burning capital, President Jefferson Davis and his Cabinet hopped from place to place, establishing temporary capitals as they tried to stay ahead of their pursuers and rally their remaining soldiers.

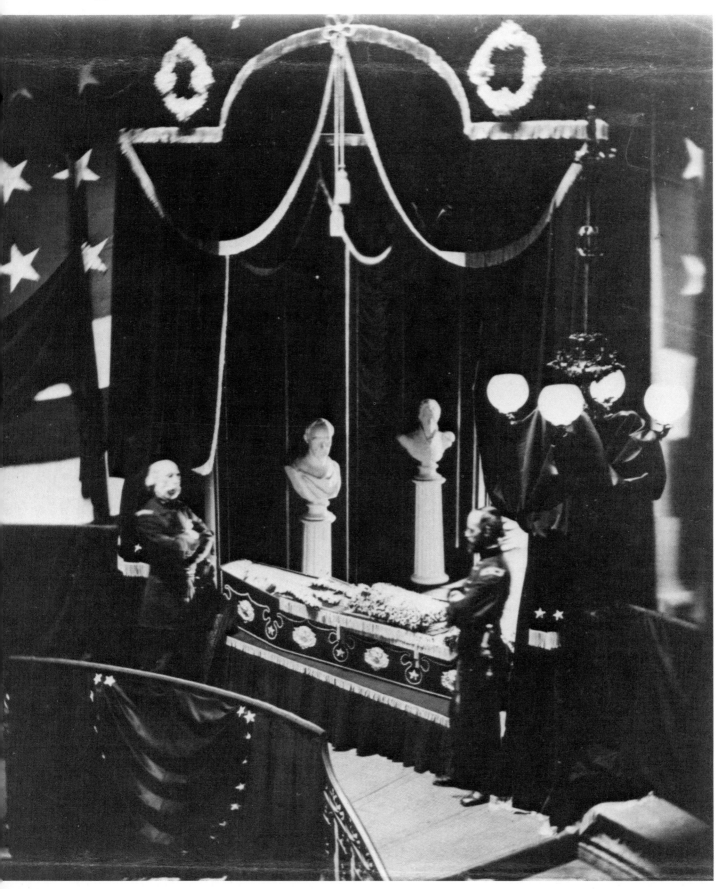

They reached North Carolina only in time to consult with Johnston while he asked Sherman for terms, and then the flight continued. Along the way, members of his Cabinet who had stood by him for years one by one dropped out of the party to make their own separate peace with the victors, until by May 4, at Washington, Georgia, there were none remaining but his Secretary of War, John C. Breckinridge, and his Postmaster General, John H. Reagan. While Breckinridge set out to lead their pursuers on a false trail, Davis left to make a last bid to escape the country. But near Irwinville, Georgia, on May 10, the President's party was surprised by Federal troops and captured without struggle. Of all the high officers of the government, only Breckinridge and Secretary of State Judah P. Benjamin finally escaped to safety.

Retribution was inevitable, yet slow in coming and on a lesser scale than for any other civil conflict in human memory. The first to feel it would be those involved in the President's murder. In June 1865, in a long and controversial trial, eight defendants, including Mrs. Surratt and the Maryland doctor Samuel Mudd who treated Booth during his flight, were put on the dock charged with conspiracy to assassinate Lincoln. Though all probably had knowledge of or involvement in the kidnapping schemes, it is still uncertain which if any of them had foreknowledge of Booth's eleventh-hour decision to kill the President. In the end, four who could not be directly connected with the assassination were sentenced to long prison terms. Four others, including Mary Surratt, were sentenced to the gallows. Their hangings on July 7 drew international attention, more because of the execution of a woman than for any other reason.

And for a time the executions seemed to satisfy much of the North's need for vengeance against the South. Indeed, incredible as it seems after four years of the costliest and bloodiest war yet fought in the hemisphere, only one Confederate would actually be brought to trial and charged with crimes. Major Henry Wirz, the hapless and admittedly unsympathetic commandant of the infamous Confederate prison camp near Andersonville, Georgia, was accused of willfully torturing and starving, even murdering, defenseless Union prisoners under his command. No one will ever completely sift truth from fancy in his story, though it is probable that he was no worse and no better than any other unfortunate Southern officer assigned to oversee tens of thousands of captured Federals packed into cramped quarters with too little food and almost no sanitation. But Andersonville had become in the North a symbol of Rebel cruelty and barbarism on an emotional scale so great that a scapegoat was inevitable—some small taste of Southern blood to balance the scale against the deaths from starvation and disease of thousands of Union men. On November 10, 1865, Wirz went to the scaffold, in relative terms probably an innocent man. Yet, ironically, he was symbolic of the incredible tolerance and magnanimity of the victors, for—however unjust—his would be the only execution of an enemy soldier for war crimes, a restraint unparalleled in the history of civil conflict.

Perhaps there was little time for retribution because the men of both armies, North and South, were too busy returning home to find what remained of the life they had left four years before. It was a staggering problem. In 1865 the Union had just over 1,000,000 men

This is what they saw. The only known image of Lincoln in death was made as he lay here in City Hall, flanked by his honor guards, Rear Admiral Charles Davis on the left and Brevet Brigadier General Edward D. Townsend on the right. Jeremiah Gurney, Jr., made the image, which shows Lincoln's face dimly visible in the open casket and, resting on top of the coffin, the flowered initials "AL." Secretary of War Edwin M. Stanton objected to the photograph because he found it macabre and ordered it suppressed and the negative destroyed, but this one print survived, to be discovered again in 1952. (ILLINOIS STATE HISTORICAL LIBRARY, SPRINGFIELD)

Albany, New York, hung with crape, awaits the arrival of the funeral train.
(ALBANY INSTITUTE OF HISTORY AND ART)

under arms, spread literally from Atlantic to Pacific, Maine to Texas. Just the transportation needed to get Massachusetts men home from Texas and Hoosiers back from Virginia, taxed every resource of rail and water. The Union armies could not be disbanded all at once, either. First, new recruits would be released. Then men in hospitals, then men whose enlistments expired earliest. The disbanding and discharge was already under way in the East before the last Confederate army in the West had yet surrendered. And when the soldiers were finally mustered out, they were sent home with money in their pockets, some $270,000,000 of it.

How different it was for the defeated Confederates, and yet it could have been far worse. Following the magnanimous course of Grant at Appomattox, there were no punishments or recriminations when the other Southern armies capitulated. Men and officers were made only to take their paroles, surrender their arms, and go home. Federal supply trains were opened to their

*And back in Springfield, Illinois, Lincoln's home is draped in black in
preparation for the last of the funeral ceremonies before he is laid to rest.*
(CHICAGO PUBLIC LIBRARY)

former foes, men who claimed to own horses
were allowed to take them, and the still-proud
Confederates were simply permitted to find their
way home. The few who refused either to take
parole or admit defeat fled to the hills, intent
upon continuing the war in partisan fashion, but
they were few indeed, accomplished nothing, and
either abandoned their efforts or, as in Missouri,
abandoned their patriotic pretensions and
simply became brigands.

For weeks following the surrenders, the roads
of the South were filled with passing Confederates, ragged men, often in tears, occasionally
stopping to ask food or water and to pass the
news of the surrenders. Grant and Sherman ar-

ranged some transportation for those who lived
far to the West, but most of them walked, sometimes for weeks, before they found their homes.
A New York journalist in the South watched
the exodus, and could not conceal that he was
"daily touched to the heart by seeing these poor
homesick boys and exhausted men wandering
about in threadbare uniforms, with scanty outfit
of slender haversack and blanket roll hung over
their shoulders, seeking the nearest route home."

The receptions that met the men in blue and
gray when they found their homes were as different as the flags they had fought for. Throughout
the North there was jubilation, a joy that could
not entirely be stilled even by the Lincoln

tragedy. As regiment after regiment came marching home, great cities and tiny courthouse towns bedecked themselves with bunting and flags to give their boys a cheering welcome. One last time the hardened veterans marched in parade down their home streets. Many stood in rank for a final photograph, to be reproduced by the score and treasured for years to come. Officers and men, equals once more, shook hands, slapped backs, laughed, and more often wept, as they said farewell not only to their war service, but also to the most exciting days of their lives. The conflict lay behind them now, and so, with it, they left much of the best of their youth.

There was joy in the South as well, of a different kind. The war was lost and no one could be joyful about that, but at last it was over and the men were coming home. Everyone could take some comfort at least from that. But there were no parades in Richmond or New Orleans. The regiments arrived in bits and pieces, not as whole units, and the men quietly went to their homes, or what remained of them. In a region worn and starved to gauntness by the past four years, there was little enough for survival, much less for lavish receptions. Many Confederates found their homes fallen to ruin from neglect or destroyed by Northern raiders or Southern vandals. The families they had left in 1861 had often been forced to flee as refugees, often moving hundreds of miles to stay ahead of the enemy. Cut off from contact for months, some soldiers would have to spend more months, even years, trying to find the loved ones left behind.

Yet in at least one way, soldiers of both the Union and Confederacy were the same. They could take comfort from the fact that they had lived to go home again. So many others did not. Hundreds of thousands lay buried in the soil of Tennessee and Virginia and Pennsylvania and so many other places. Many had been hastily interred after battle. Even more had succumbed to accidents and disease. Tens of thousands on both sides had died in prisons. As quickly as possible, families on both sides began the often heartbreaking and frustrating work of trying to find the remains of their sons and husbands, to bring them home. It was a great silent exodus, wagons and trains and steamers carrying a veritable host of mute, moldering passengers, whose bodies were making a final journey that their spirits had made long before.

In the defeated and impoverished South, there was neither money nor inclination to establish formal cemeteries for the Confederate dead, beyond those already dictated by circumstance near the battlefields. But in the North, even before the end of the war, a movement began for the creation of national military cemeteries to honor the fallen brave. Lincoln had spoken at the dedication of one in Gettysburg, Pennsylvania, on November 19, 1863. Others were established at Alexandria, Virginia; at Vicksburg, Mississippi; and most notably at Arlington, Virginia. Here on the southern bank of the Potomac, on grounds that once were part of the estate of Robert E. Lee, one of the most beautiful cemeteries in the nation was established shortly before war's end. Lee would never return here again, but thousands who died fighting him would rest beneath his land.

Just as they memorialized their dead, so did the men of the Union begin almost immediately to memorialize what they had done. Well before the war ceased, local officials at Gettysburg and Antietam and elsewhere began envisioning parks, lands at the battlefields to be set aside to preserve the memory of what had occurred there. And by 1864 there were even a few markers and monuments starting to sprout on the landscape, all of them Northern. In the winter of 1864–65 men of Brigadier General William Gamble's brigade built two red sandstone pyramids on the field near Manassas, Virginia, each commemorating the men in blue who fell in the battles of First and Second Bull Run. On June 10, 1865, with the war done, several hundred soldiers and dignitaries came to formally dedicate the monuments, the first of hundreds of such scenes in the years to come.

Confederates, too, joined in the drive to preserve the memory of what they had tried to achieve, though understandably in a region depressed by the war, the immediate impetus was more economic than historical. At Petersburg, Virginia, within months after Lee's surrender, an enterprising former Confederate was operating probably the first battlefield museum in the country, charging twenty-five cents for visitors to view relics of the great Battle of the Crater.

Meanwhile, the rest of the Union will not rest until justice is done to Lincoln's murderer and his accomplices. When all the accused are apprehended, they will stand trial before this military commission, posing here in Mathew Brady's Washington studio. They are, from the left, Colonel Charles H. Tompkins; Major General David Hunter, president of the commission; Major General August Kautz; Brevet Brigadier General James Ekin; Major General Lew Wallace; John A. Bingham; Brigadier General Albion Howe; Brigadier General Thomas M. Harris; Judge Advocate General Joseph Holt; Brigadier General Robert S. Foster; Colonel Henry L. Burnett; and Colonel D. R. Clendenin. (NA)

A quarter could be a lot of money in a stricken region. Every resource in the South had been stretched to exhaustion by the war, and those not used up by the Confederates themselves had most likely been destroyed or damaged by the invading Federals. Transportation was at a standstill. Rolling stock and tracks had either been ruined from lack of maintenance or parts taken up and melted to make cannon, or wrecked by raiders. There were virtually no sound river steamers to get waterborne commerce moving again. The telegraph lines were down, and there was little good news for them to carry in any case. While some regions were almost untouched by the war, others had seen their fields ravaged by overplanting and the demands of feeding armies, and their cities ruined by bombardment, razed by fires, or turned squalid from overcrowding by refugees. At war's end Southerners were not only largely a displaced people; the South was almost a displaced region. Lee and the other most sensible Confederate leaders knew this without having to look and offered the wisest counsel they could. Go home, they told their men, go home quietly, without bitterness, and go to work rebuilding. Accept the verdict of the war and put it behind.

The most prominent Confederate of them

Their verdict reached on June 30, 1865, the commission sent four conspirators to the gallows. Here on July 7, in the yard of the Old Penitentiary in Washington, D.C., they mounted the scaffold. They sat down while Brigadier General John Hartranft read aloud their sentences and the order for execution. He stands beneath the umbrella in the center of the group, paper in his hand. Seated at the far right is George Atzerodt, charged with attempting to murder Vice President Andrew Johnson. Immediately next to him sits David Herold, who had fled with Booth and helped in his foiled escape attempt. Sitting just behind the center post is Lewis Paine, who tried to assassinate Secretary of State William Seward; just visible on his head is a straw hat that he had playfully snatched from the head of a bystander before he mounted the steps. Seated at far left is Mrs. Mary Surratt, who kept the boardinghouse where the conspirators met. (LC)

Now they stand, their hands and legs being bound and the nooses put in place. Chief executioner Christopher Rath is personally placing Paine's noose. Everyone grudgingly admired the courage of the young man. "I want you to die quick," Rath was saying to Paine. "You know best," replied the condemned. (LC)

all would never accept the outcome of the conflict. Yet as the postwar era began, Jefferson Davis was awaiting a verdict of his own. He and several other Confederate politicians who had held office in the old Union, were under indictment for treason, which should hardly have been a surprise. In most other nations of the nineteenth-century world, they would have been stood against a wall and shot. But here a peculiar mix of tolerance, exhaustion, and uncertainty produced an entirely different sort of denouement for the leaders of the rebellion. Of them all, only Davis would come close to trial, and in even his case it would become evident that the Union government did not really know what to do.

The trap is sprung and justice is done. (LC)

As the bodies still dangle from their ropes, the boxes for their burial are stacked beneath them as the crowd starts to melt away. The gallows will be sawed into souvenirs. (LC)

At first Washington officials believed—or wanted to believe—that Davis and his leaders had been involved in the Lincoln murder. Indeed, there is some evidence that prosecutors may even have tried to persuade deponents at the assassination trial to perjure themselves to implicate Davis, but the attempt failed. For two years Davis was kept a prisoner at Fort Monroe, Virginia, but the Federal authorities would never bring him before a jury. By 1867 friends had arranged for his release on bail, and passions had cooled to the point that the government actually believed that trying Davis for treason could be an embarrassment. He would certainly be convicted if tried, and then what should they do with him? The law prescribed execution, but that would only enrage the South, thus far rather docile in defeat, and probably cause controversy with European nations that had entertained some sympathy with the Confederacy. In the end the Federal authorities simply let the case lapse, and Davis remained a free man, bitter and unwilling to the end to admit defeat. The few other imprisoned leaders went free as well. It was a remarkably bloodless aftermath to the bloodiest war in American history.

Yet the South was not to pass from war to peace without paying some price, gentle though it may have been compared to that paid by other defeated peoples. Reconstruction of loyal state governments had already begun under Lincoln as Southern territory came once more under Federal control. "We must extinguish our resentment if we expect harmony and Union," Lincoln had told his Cabinet the very day he was shot. Emissaries including General U. S. Grant traveled through the South to gauge the temper of the people, and most concluded with Grant that Southerners accepted the verdict of the war and wanted to rejoin the Union as quickly as possible.

For nearly two years there was surprisingly little interference in Southern affairs, as white Southerners once more elected men of their own kind to their legislatures and tried to send them to Congress. But during that time it became increasingly evident that an old pattern was reemerging. The same men who had led the South before the war were in charge once again and attempting to act as if the war had not happened. Once again they were claiming for their states the right to decide in matters in which the Republican majority in Congress believed Congress' right was paramount. Worse, though the slaves had all been freed, Southern states were enacting "Black Codes" which in effect returned them to a kind of servitude by enormously restricting their freedoms. In April and June 1866, when it came time to debate the civil rights act and the Fourteenth Amendment to the Constitution, which, among other things, guaranteed the vote to Negroes, the South balked, and the radical wing of the Republicans, who had always favored stern treatment of the former Confederate states, decided that the South had not learned its lesson. Triumphant in Congress, the Radical Republicans succeeded in instituting for the next decade a plan of "reconstruction," the excesses of which have been exaggerated in the ensuing century but which nevertheless did visit upon the Southern mind and spirit a wound never yet erased.

The day of the "carpetbagger" had come— the Yankee opportunist went South to profit from cheap land and labor while native Southerners barely survived. There is truth to some of the carpetbagger legend, though the reverse of the coin is that these entrepreneurs brought with them an influx of capital and energy which played a strong role in reviving the Southern economy.

Lincoln's death leaves a new President in his stead. Andrew Johnson of Tennessee, Lincoln's second Vice President, a man who will try to follow in Father Abraham's steps, without much success. (USAMHI)

Republicans went South, and some Southerners joined with them—the "scalawags"—to run the Reconstruction state governments. Most Southern states at one time or another after the war fell under Republican rule. Often it was good, honest government, but in some few celebrated cases it was corrupt and abusive. Despite the long-held myth that the former slaves came to control several states, the fact is that in only one state, South Carolina, did Negro representatives hold a majority and that for only a single term in one house. There were no Negro governors, nor were the great mass of freed slaves a serious social threat to their former masters. Nevertheless, so fearful were Southerners of their former chattels, that groups like the Knights

There is more tragedy to come even when the fighting is stopped. With thousands of Federal prisoners being freed from Confederate prison camps, steamers like the Sultana *were brimmed with passengers as they transported men up the Mississippi from Vicksburg to the North. On April 27, just the day after this image of the ship was made, her boiler exploded in midstream north of Memphis and the vessel went down in the darkness. With over 2,000 men aboard, she took nearly three fourths of them down with her. It was the worst ship disaster in the nation's history.* (LC)

of the White Camellia, the White Brotherhood, and of course the Ku Klux Klan arose to intimidate the Negroes and preserve white supremacy. Even prominent Confederate leaders condemned the violence and lawlessness of these vigilante groups, though their rise is hardly surprising. Having just suffered the humiliation of being the first and only Americans ever defeated in a war—and Southerners had always prided themselves on their military prowess—they were in its aftermath faced simultaneously with economic collapse, social and political revolution, and the sudden appearance in their midst, as free

men, of millions of Negroes who had every reason to despise Southern whites. The white Southerners were in their way every bit as terrified as the Negroes they sought to intimidate.

Of course, there were many—perhaps as many as 10,000—who simply refused to take part in the South's travail, or who felt they dare not. Beginning with the flight of some of the Cabinet members and generals in 1865 and continuing on through the late 1860s, thousands of Southerners abandoned the country to go into exile, fearful of indictments against them, unwilling to live again under Yankee rule or bent on starting

While the military surrenders were taking place in early April, there was a small band of Confederates trying to flee the country—President Jefferson Davis and his Cabinet. (LC)

Brigadier General Henry H. Walker commanded the Confederate troops in the Danville, Virginia, area, and Davis ordered him to go to North Carolina and join General Joseph E. Johnston's army, not knowing that even then Johnston was preparing to sue for terms. (VM)

One by one the officers and Cabinet members with Davis dropped along the wayside, to attempt their own individual escape or else to surrender and take their chances. Vice President Alexander H. Stephens simply went home and awaited his arrest, accepting it calmly. (CM)

new lives elsewhere. By far the majority of them went to Mexico where whole colonies of ex-patriates were founded. Many of the generals took service there with the Emperor Maximilian, while their families tried to carve out new lives in the revolution-torn country. It did not work, however, and within a few years most of them had returned to the South.

Similar colonies were set up in Brazil and in other South and Central American countries. A small band of ex-Confederates dwelled in Havana for years after the war, and many more went to Europe. Judah P. Benjamin, Davis' Secretary of State, remained in England for the rest of his life, becoming a successful barrister and Queen's Counsel. Major General William

W. Loring left the United States in 1869 and entered the service of the Khedive of Egypt, ironically serving in the same army as some adventuring ex-Union officers. And many, like the escaped Breckinridge, simply wandered abroad until the indictments against them were lifted, anxious simply to return home and start their lives anew. Breckinridge himself went from Cuba to Canada to Europe and back to Niagara, Canada, once more, patiently looking across the border to the United States and longing for the day of his return. He and the thousands of others may have been Confederates for four years, but they had been Americans a lot longer, and very few would not return to their homes eventually.

In the United States Southerners looked to many things to help them rebuild their personal and sectional fortunes. Recognizing the utter destruction of their transportation systems in the

General Braxton Bragg, on the other hand, stayed with the presidential party almost to the end, acting as Davis' chief military adviser. An unpublished portrait made probably by the Montgomery, Alabama, photographer A. C. McIntyre in 1862. (CM)

In the end the last Cabinet officer standing by Davis was his Secretary of War, John C. Breckinridge, also a major general. He commanded the escort as the fleeing President moved through the Carolinas and into Georgia. (USAMHI)

war and needing to modernize and rebuild in order to once more get their crops to market, a boom wave of railroad building commenced throughout the South, often financed by Northern entrepreneurs. To lend a cachet of authority to the enterprises, a host of former Confederate military luminaries became active or figurehead officers of the new lines. Joseph E. Johnston, Nathan B. Forrest, Breckinridge, P. G. T. Beauregard, and many more became railroad presidents, and most took an active role in leading the struggle to rebuild. When states like Louisiana instituted lotteries to rebuild their treasuries, men like Beauregard and feisty old Major General Jubal A. Early supervised them. And scores of former Confederates entered the life insurance business as several new firms were capitalized to sell policies and raise investment

funds for rebuilding. Of course the old Confederates could not stay out of politics either. Though they had to take a loyalty oath and those who had been under indictment had to formally apply for restoration of their rights of citizenship, in a short time their voices were once more heard in state legislatures and the halls of Congress. No longer did they have the power to cripple or halt the national government as before, but in alliance with Northern Democrats and others tiring of Radical Republican rule, they finally came back to the point where in the disputed 1876 presidential election, they controlled the deciding electoral votes. Thus they made their bargain. Republican Rutherford B. Hayes, with fewer popular votes than his Democratic rival, Samuel J. Tilden, would be President, but Reconstruction would end. With Federal soldiers withdrawn from the South and control of civil

*Here in Abbeville, South Carolina, in the home of Armisted Burt, Davis
held his last council of war. He wanted to continue the war; Breckinridge
and the others told him it was over.* (USAMHI)

affairs once more entirely in the hands of Southerners, the final political vestiges of war and
defeat were removed. Now it remained to heal
the emotional wounds.

The old Union—the states of the North—
was not idle in the decade after the war. It continued to grow in power and prosperity, virtually forcing the rest of the world to take notice
of the infant Yankee giant come to adulthood in
the family of nations. All the industrial world
had watched the war, and now it saw the mani-
festations of a newly confident, even belligerent,
United States rising to its potential. Yankee
trade expanded throughout the globe and virtually dominated its own hemisphere. The bright

new and mighty squadrons of American warships
cruised the world's seas, demonstrating Union
naval power and modernity. American influence
in the affairs of other nations began to be felt,
and her old friend and older adversary Great
Britain was once again made to feel the sting of
defeat by her Yankee cousin. Already fearful
that the cocky and powerful Americans would
renew the age-old drive to wrest Canada from
her, Britain was forced to submit to international
arbitration in 1872 over the *Alabama* claims,
American demands for millions of dollars in
reparations for the damage done to Union shipping by Confederate raiders fitted out in British
ports. The British paid their penalties manfully,

Finally, near Irwinville, Georgia, the pursuing Federals closed in and captured Davis. Lieutenant Colonel Benjamin Pritchard led his 4th Michigan Cavalry against Davis' camp and thereby won himself a brevet rank of brigadier. Pritchard sits third from the left. (DUDLEY H. PRITCHARD)

and the long Anglo-American friendship, though often strained, would continue.

If as a result of the war the Union became a world power, so, too, did the conflict ensure its grasp on territory already claimed as its own. The years of fighting had a profound impact upon the settlement of the great expanse of unsettled, uncharted West. A few campaigns, even a few small battles, had been fought for control of the hundreds of thousands of miles of plains and mountains. The Indians could hardly profit from the great war taking place in the East. At best it gave them a brief rest from the inevitable push to dispossess them. Yet even before the war ended, the massive migration of whites began, and directly as a result of the conflict. Besides the soldiers who came West and besides the civilians and camp followers who inevitably clustered

about the army camps, there came also thousands of men who had little choice. No one knows how many deserted from both armies during the war, but very few of them could be expected to go home to probable capture and certain disgrace. They went West instead. Hardly the most desirable of settlers, they almost ensured that the next few years would be lawless and wild in a land of men without creed. And when the end of the war left thousands more too accustomed to the practice of raiding and near-lawless adventuring to quit, it was inevitable that they, too, should go West. As a result the so-called Wild West was the direct offspring of the Civil War, and not unnaturally it would fall also to veterans of the war to go to the new settlements to preserve law and order. The James brothers had been Confederate guerrillas. "Wild Bill" Hickok

The President and his band were brought to Macon, Georgia, where photographer A. J. Riddle made this May 13, 1865, image of the ambulance and wagon which carried Davis and his party. Pritchard's troopers fill the street in front of Major General James Wilson's Federal headquarters. Prison awaited Davis, though he would never be tried or convicted of treason. (USAMHI)

had served the Union. For them and many more the days of the Old West were little more than a continuation of the adventure of the war.

For every bully boy and bravo who crossed the plains, however, thousands of other more peaceable settlers came, tired of the East, ruined by the war, or simply anxious for something better than what they had. These are the people who "won" the West, not from the Indians or the bandits but from the land itself. Southerners and Northerners alike made the trek, and it went far toward reconciliation that they built towns and counties and states together. All that land out there just waiting gave them something to fight for in common, something to help rebuild the fraternal bonds that war had severed. Were it not for the West, reconciliation might have taken far longer than it did.

Of course, time would be the greatest healer of them all. As the years passed and the soldiers got older and gentler, so too did the passions. By the end of the century nostalgia and forgiving memory had already erased much of the bad, covering what remained in a patina of romance and myth. Veterans of both sides banded together in fraternal organizations—the mighty Grand Army of the Republic, the proud United Confederate Veterans. Intended originally as political action groups, they came in time to look more toward the care of the aging veterans, the infirm, those disabled by the war. Around the country, North and South, homes for the indigent and helpless veterans appeared. In annual conventions, the old generals and leaders came forth again and again to talk to their comrades of past glories and present patriotism. Through

Some were more fortunate than Davis. Secretary of War Breckinridge did successfully escape in a hair-raising adventure through Florida and across the Gulf Stream that saw him dodging Federal patrols, turning pirate, and nearly perishing in a storm at sea. The month-long ordeal showed in his face when, a few days after reaching Cuba, he sat for this photograph, probably by Charles D. Fredericks' Havana studio. (WILLIAM C. DAVIS)

the dim, teary-eyed vision of the old fading soldiers, the memories grew less and less distinct, and all the more treasured.

In time they all had to go, to follow in death all those uncountable legions already departed on the nation's battlefields. Ironically, of the great men, Lee was the first to depart. The war killed him as surely as if a bullet had struck him down. He lived only until 1870, when he was only sixty-four, a symbol of peaceful acceptance of the war's verdict, a champion of reconciliation. Grateful and tolerant to the last, he threatened one of his professors at Washington College with dismissal if the man ever spoke

disrespectfully of General Grant in his presence. The mourning was universal throughout the South and even in the North at the great warrior's passing, noble to the very end.

His old adversary Grant outlived him by fifteen years, with a nobility that, in its way, matched that of Lee. Lifted in 1872 to the highest office in the gift of the American people for his victory, Grant the President endured scandal and disgrace and financial disaster, to end his days still universally admired as a simple, honest soldier. His heroic struggle in his last days to complete his memoirs and provide for his family touched men everywhere. He beat the cancer that killed him only by days, leaving behind one of the finest memoirs ever written by a soldier and an example of courage which even his former enemies admired.

Of course there were those who held their bitterness to the end. Jefferson Davis would never admit defeat, never accept the war's lessons. To the last of his days he sought to win with his pen what his sword had lost. Though they never loved him as they did Lee, still his people admired and respected their old President. When he died in 1889, the last of the great political leaders of the war, even the North was respectful.

But the people were always the more touched by the generals and soldiers, the men who really fought the war, and they were the ones who seemed more readily able to forgive and forget. Nothing could be more touching than the last days of the archrivals Sherman and Johnston. They had not met prior to the war. Their acquaintance began at First Bull Run. They met again in the Vicksburg Campaign and then all across Georgia on the road to Atlanta. In the war's last days they faced each other in the Carolinas until finally Johnston surrendered. Thereafter the two became cordial friends, in the manner of thousands of others, and when the great Sherman finally passed away in 1891, his old friend and enemy Johnston was there as an honorary pallbearer, standing bareheaded in the pouring rain. A friend admonished the old Confederate to put his hat on, but he would not. If the positions had been reversed, he said, and Sherman were standing there mourning a dead Johnston, the Federal would not have put his hat

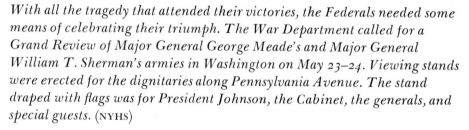

With all the tragedy that attended their victories, the Federals needed some means of celebrating their triumph. The War Department called for a Grand Review of Major General George Meade's and Major General William T. Sherman's armies in Washington on May 23–24. Viewing stands were erected for the dignitaries along Pennsylvania Avenue. The stand draped with flags was for President Johnson, the Cabinet, the generals, and special guests. (NYHS)

on. And so the old Confederate took cold and was dead of pneumonia within weeks.

More and more the remaining vestiges of the old war reminded Americans of their common bonds and virtues rather than their onetime controversies. Grand reunions of veterans blue and gray were held to celebrate the anniversaries of dates once held terrible. At Gettysburg in 1913 and again in 1938, mammoth reunions paid for by the nation brought thousands of old soldiers forth once more to walk the field of battle where some had fought and relive the old times. All across the country national military parks were established to memorialize what both sides stood and fought for. In time they all came to realize that it had been a very American war, exemplifying, North and South, all of the best and worst in themselves as Americans.

And throughout it all, from Appomattox on, for generations forward, down to the last living veteran, the constant companion of the Civil War experience, the camera, was there recording the passing of an era. Like America itself, the photographers after the war moved on, to the West, out into the world. They, like their nation, had given their youth, their best years, to the epic struggle of North and South. But they were not finished by that war. They and their craft would move ahead while their achievement made it possible for future generations always to look back.

They were all timeless men in their way, preserved in the images for all time. They had lived the spirit of their era, of an age now gone by but which can never die, thanks to them. They were all men, now long dead, who will yet live forever.

Crowds gathered early all along the route, anxious to cheer the brave men who had delivered the Union and put down the Rebellion. (USAMHI)

They were not disappointed. In the most magnificent parade the capital had ever seen, thousands upon thousands of blue-clad soldiers marched from the Capitol down Pennsylvania Avenue toward the Executive Mansion. Captain A. J. Russell took his camera into the Capitol dome to record this outstanding view of one brigade marching down the avenue. (USAMHI)

At the other end of the street, near Willard's Hotel at right, Alexander Gardner or an assistant made scene after scene of the passing heroes. An unidentified major general lifts his hat in salute before his command passes by. (USAMHI)

The first infantry to pass in review on May 23 was the IX Corps of Major General John Parke. The general and his staff ride at the front. (USAMHI)

Major General A. A. Humphreys and his II Corps soon followed, Humphreys a blur of motion in the lead. (USAMHI)

THE PUBLIC SCHOOLS OF WASHINGTON WELCOME THE HEROES OF THE REPUBLIC. HONOR TO THE BRAVE—*so read one of hundreds of signs that greeted the soldiers. This one is on the Capitol building, as crowds of men, ladies, and school children line the street. In the background, the building's columns are still wrapped in mourning for the dead Lincoln.* (USAMHI)

Hour after hour the soldiers and their wagons and cannon passed along the street, marching to the beat of their drums and the sound of the special march composed for the occasion. (NYHS)

The flag flew at half staff, but it and all the crape could not dampen the spirits of this two-day orgy of patriotism and celebration. (USAMHI)

Every new regiment marching down Capitol Hill did so to resounding cheers from the men and boys and the ladies waving their handkerchiefs. (P-M)

Johnny was at last marching home again. (P-M)

Sometimes the enthusiastic bystanders walked out into the avenue itself to get a closer look. (USAMHI)

The dignitaries, meanwhile, sat patiently through the endless hours of passing troops. (NYHS)

*The victories of the armies were printed on the bunting hanging from the roof of the reviewing stand—*SPOTSYLVANIA, ANTIETAM, CHATTANOÓGA, *and more. In this image made on the second day of the review, as Sherman's army passes by, General Meade sits at the far right of the central part of the stand. Next to him, holding a newspaper, is General Sherman. Secretary of the Navy Gideon Welles sits in the center of the group, just to the left of a bouquet of flowers, and at the far left of the advanced gallery Secretary of War Stanton turns his head to talk with an unseen Lieutenant General U. S. Grant.* (KA)

On this second day, Major General Henry W. Slocum rode at the head of his Army of Georgia. (USAMHI)

Soon Major General John A. Logan followed, behind him the Army of the Tennessee stretching back to the horizon. (USAMHI)

Brigadier General Jefferson C. Davis led the XIV Corps, his horse a mere blur in the image, along with what appears to have been a bystander running across the street. (USAMHI)

Then came the XX Corps, as the endless procession lasted on through the day. (USAMHI)

*With their marching done, the officers of the armies gathered before the
camera of Alexander Gardner for a final group portrait, the last time they
would all be together. General Sherman sits here in the center, with the
generals and other members of his staff.* (LC)

*General Grant stands at the center with his staff, including Lieutenant
Colonel Ely S. Parker, seated second from the left, a Seneca Indian who
served as Grant's military secretary. It was he who transcribed Grant's terms
to Lee at Appomattox. Brevet Major General John Rawlins, Grant's chief of
staff, sits on Grant's immediate left, and Adjutant General Seth Williams sits
on the other side of Grant.* (AIG)

General Meade and his staff sit for Gardner, Meade in the center. Artillery chief Major General Henry Hunt sits at Meade's immediate right. (MHS)

Then it was time to celebrate around the Union. Philadelphia dresses itself up to receive its sons once more. (FREE LIBRARY OF PHILADELPHIA)

The generals, too, went home, though not all of them for good. Galena, Illinois, decorated one of its main streets for the return of a man who was once one of its most obscure citizens, Lieutenant General U. S. Grant. GENERAL: THE "SIDE-WALK" IS BUILT *reads the banner, perhaps referring to some bit of civic progress while Grant was busy with the war.* (CARL H. JOHNSON, JR.)

An Ohio regiment lines up for the last muster in Cleveland, a glad time, yet not without sorrow. Most of these young Americans would never again experience anything to compare with their days at war. (LC)

On July 26, 1865, the 23d Ohio was mustered out of service, and its officers met here at the monument they had already erected to the regiment in Cleveland after its service at Antietam, Maryland, in 1862. It is perhaps the first—certainly one of the first—regimental monuments erected, and it marks as well the rise to prominence of two future American Presidents from the regiment. Brigadier General Rutherford B. Hayes, once colonel of the 23d Ohio, stands immediately left of the monument, his head just visible above the shoulder of the man in front of him. And the officer standing second to the right from the marker is probably Major William McKinley. Few regiments could claim such distinguished alumni. (USAMHI)

*There were those who would never go home. Now that the battlefields were
silent, the work of removing the hastily buried dead and reinterring them
could begin in earnest. It was an odious and difficult task.* (USAMHI)

*But it was worth the effort, and quickly the nation gave its honored dead a
fitting resting place. Here is a soldiers' cemetery in Alexandria, Virginia.
Many of the dead could not be identified; only numbers appear on their
grave markers.* (USAMHI)

At Arlington National Cemetery, on grounds that were once the property of Robert E. Lee's family, thousands more were laid to rest. Ironically, Privates J. Kelly and J. Richards, beneath the two stones at front center, both died on their country's birthday, July 4, 1864. (USAMHI)

And the work of marking and memorializing the battlefields began, with Bull Run (Manassas) being fittingly the first. On June 10, 1865, William Morris Smith made this image of the ceremonies dedicating the battle monument on Henry House Hill. (LC)

*There were speeches to listen to, and this crowd is reasonably attentive.
Standing hands on hips at the right is Major General Samuel P. Heintzelman,
who fought in the battle here at Bull Run in 1861. Next to him, arms folded,
is Major General Montgomery C. Meigs, quartermaster general of the Union
armies, and next to him, at his left, is Brigadier General Alexander B. Dyer.*
(AIG)

*And here the generals and bystanders stand for the camera, beneath the
plaque that offers the monument "IN MEMORY OF THE PATRIOTS." (NA)*

Elsewhere in Virginia, the survivors of a shattered Confederacy will have to wait awhile before they can erect their monuments. They are even hard put just now to care adequately for their dead. Here in Richmond's Hollywood Cemetery, in April 1865, the mounds of earth testify to fresh burials, and the rude headboards testify to the utter inability to provide more than the barest ceremony for these fallen men. That would change in time. (LC)

There were difficult years ahead for the South. Happily, there were few reprisals against individuals as a result of the war. Champ Ferguson of Tennessee would suffer one of them, however. Guilty of murdering several white and Negro Federal soldiers in 1864, he was tried in Nashville in the summer of 1865. This portrait was made the day before his hanging. (HP)

Only one Confederate officer was brought to trial for "war crimes," Major Henry Wirz, the commander of the infamous prison camp at Andersonville, Georgia. Despite his probable lack of intent in bringing about the deaths of thousands of Union prisoners, the horrors of Andersonville had to be avenged. On November 10, 1865, reporters gather in Washington, D.C., to witness Wirz's execution. (LC)

Alexander Gardner brought his camera to capture the scene as, with the Capitol dome in the background, the trap is released and Wirz plummets to his death. (LC)

As his lifeless body swings at the end of the rope, the dead of Andersonville are revenged. (LC)

Jefferson Davis was indicted for treason in May 1866, but no trial was forthcoming. These were the jurymen before whom he was to be tried, yet the trial never came. In 1867, after exactly two years in prison, Davis was released on bail. (VM)

For a time, elections were left once more in the hands of Southerners, but more and more Northern Republicans would come to enlist the new votes of the freed slaves to win office. Actual rule by the carpetbaggers was greatly exaggerated by ex-Confederates, but it did happen. The number of Federal uniforms in this Baton Rouge, Louisiana, electioneering wagon, speaks to the support given one candidate by the Northern conquerors. (DAM, LSU)

Then came the occupation of the South by Federal troops and the years of Reconstruction. A regiment of Union troops in Memphis, Tennessee, in June 1865. (HP)

With the South divided into military districts, Federal generals were sent to administer them. Here in Atlanta, in 1868, General Meade sits (center right) on the porch of his residence as district commander. (P-M)

The former Confederates fought back however they could, in the legislative halls and in out-of-the-way places by night, seeking to intimidate both the Negroes and the whites who collaborated with them. They rode out of the darkness dressed in frightening robes and hoods. (LO)

In time the disorganized raiders formed more formal secret societies, the most notorious coming to be called the Ku Klux Klan. Here, on December 20, 1871, one of their members who had been captured and turned state's evidence poses in his regalia at Holly Springs, Mississippi. (HP)

The great Confederate cavalry chieftain Lieutenant General Nathan B. Forrest for a time served as Grand Wizard of the Klan, but around 1868 ordered it disbanded when he perceived that it was leading only to ineffective violence. (DAM, LSU)

Other former Confederates tried in different ways to survive Reconstruction and rebuild themselves as well. General P. G. T. Beauregard was proud enough of his service as late as 1872 to be still autographing his wartime portrait. He and other generals looked to railroading to bring the South into the industrial age. (VM)

Some, like Wade Hampton, once a great cavalryman, fought in the political arena to combat Reconstruction. Hampton became governor of South Carolina in 1876, was reelected in 1878, and then served two terms as a U.S. senator. (CM)

Thousands who could not face life in a defeated South emigrated to other countries, most notably Mexico. The family of Major General Sterling Price suffered a shipwreck on its way to Mexico in 1865. They pose here with other survivors, Mrs. Price seated at the center. (MISSOURI HISTORICAL SOCIETY, ST. LOUIS)

Awaiting them in Mexico in 1865 were some of the generals who had exiled themselves rather than surrender. Standing left is Major General John B. Magruder and next to him is Brigadier General William P. Hardeman. Seated from the left are Major Generals Cadmus Wilcox, Sterling Price, and Thomas C. Hindman. All would eventually return to the United States when the Mexican colonization attempt failed. (NA)

Others went to Canada. Here, standing at the far left, is the Confederacy's last Secretary of War, Major General John C. Breckinridge, posing with his family in front of Niagara Falls in 1867. Still under indictment for treason, Breckinridge did not dare return to the United States, though he wanted to desperately. The best he could do was come here to Canada to live, so he could look across the Niagara River and see the country from which he was self-exiled. In 1869 he finally returned after amnesty was declared by President Johnson. (WCD)

President of the Fenians was Colonel John O'Mahony of the 40th New York. (WG)

Meanwhile, the Confederates' old adversaries were spreading out and leaving the country, though for other reasons. Irishmen like Brigadier General Thomas Sweeny, born in County Cork, began to look to Canada as a place to attack England so as to force her to free their native Ireland. Sweeny and other so-called Fenians invaded Canada in 1866, but the whole movement failed comically. (THOMAS SWEENEY)

The Union itself was expanding, looking to stretch its influence beyond its borders. The shipbuilding begun during the war continued. War vessels like the USS Ammonoosuc, *a cruiser here under construction at the Boston Navy Yard in 1864, would be completed after the war to join one of the most modern fleets in the world.* (MM)

The mighty USS Madawaska, *largest commissioned vessel in the Navy, was renamed* Tennessee *in 1869 and made flagship of the Adriatic and North Atlantic Squadron.* (USAMHI)

Here at Rio de Janeiro, Brazil, the USS Guerriere, *flagship of the South
Atlantic Squadron, sits at anchor.* (USAMHI)

The powerful USS Kearsarge *cruised the Pacific, stopping here in Sydney,
Australia, in 1869.* (NHC)

And the powerful monitor USS Miantonomoh *was sent on a major European tour in 1866–67, to learn what she could of naval facilities there and to impress Europeans with the new naval might of the United States. She certainly did the latter. "The wolf is in our fold," lamented the London* Times. *She appears here at Málaga, Spain, early in 1867.* (NHC)

So much did the Union now feel its muscle that it took Great Britain to task in 1869 for serving as outfitting agent for Confederate ships like the raider Alabama. In the deliberations over claims for damage done to Union shipping by that vessel and other raiders, these Yankee commissioners . . . (WG)

. . . negotiated in 1872 with these British leaders for the eventual payment of $15 million to the United States. (WG)

The Yankees were moving West, too, expanding their influence in their own continent. Here at Fort Sanders, Wyoming, in 1866, there was a notable gathering of luminaries. Former Major General Grenville M. Dodge stands at far left; he had now left the Army and was building the Union Pacific Railroad. Second to the right from Dodge is Major General Philip Sheridan, and second to the right from him is Major General John Gibbon; both Sheridan and Gibbon were now facing hostile Indians on the Plains.

Wearing a white hat and leaning on the fence to the right of Gibbon is Lieutenant General U. S. Grant, now commanding general of the Army, and the man in white vest standing in the very center of the photo is Major General William T. Sherman. Standing at far right is Major General John A. Rawlins, and next to him is Colonel Adam Badeau. The white-bearded man in cape and top hat is Brevet Major General William S. Harney, now retired. They were all on a tour of inspection of the route of the Union Pacific.
(GENE PANTANO)

For other former Union generals the years after the war were less exciting,
less active. Major General Ambrose Burnside sits at center, with Major
General Robert Anderson seated at the right. It is 1865 and Burnside would
go on into industry and politics. Anderson would be dead in 1871, worn out
by the war. (VITOLO-RINHART GALLERIES, NEW YORK CITY)

Some tried to profit as best they could from their
war experiences. The actress Pauline Cushman
made a shabby career of sorts by appearing in her
uniform and telling the story of her dramatically
unsuccessful days as a Federal spy. (NYHS)

But for many of the other veterans, there was nothing left but a lifetime on public or private charity. This New Jersey soldier gave a lot for his country. (WILLIAM C. MC KENNA)

The nation tried to do what it could in return, and indeed few war veterans were ever cared for better than the Union's boys in blue. Here in the National Home for Disabled Volunteer Soldiers in Dayton, Ohio, an excellent library was provided for the soldiers' entertainment. An 1876 image by the Mote Brothers. (RJY)

Gradually the old leaders grew older. Age is marking Generals Heintzelman and Sheridan as they sit here, second and third from the left. And Admiral David Farragut is weighted with years as well as gold braid. Gradually they will die away. Farragut will be the first of this group to go, in 1870.
(CHICAGO PUBLIC LIBRARY)

And his once proud warship the USS Hartford *will, like Farragut, grow old. In 1876 she came to Philadelphia for the great Centennial Exposition.* (P-M)

Other veteran ships like the USS Idaho *will simply be laid up in the navy yards, with nothing left to do.* (NHC)

For the once proud monitors USS Shawnee *and USS* Wassuc *the same fate lay ahead, to be tied up at the Boston Navy Yard with nothing to look forward to but salvage for scrap.* (CHS)

Even the USS Miantonomoh, *after its world cruise, would wind up at a slip on the Charles River next to the two monitors.* (NHC)

*As the years went on, the colors faded and the old Confederate leaders slowly
began to wane and disappear. Here at White Sulphur Springs, Virginia, in
the 1870s, General Joseph E. Johnston stands to the right, with family and
friends. Major General Jeremy Gilmer stands on the opposite side of the
trunk; at far left of the picture stands Brigadier General John S. Preston;
and the man seated at right is Major General George Washington Custis Lee,
son of . . . (VM)*

. . . General Robert E. Lee. Photographer A. H. Plecker of Lynchburg captured this image of Lee and Traveller during the summer of 1866. The general was aging rapidly. (AIG)

*By 1869, when he sat for this unpublished Brady portrait, Lee was just
sixty-two and had barely a year to live.* (WCD)

In October 1870 the great general was dead. On October 14 this procession carried his remains from his residence in Lexington, Virginia, to the chapel of Washington College, of which he had been president since 1865.
(WASHINGTON AND LEE UNIVERSITY, LEXINGTON, VIRGINIA)

The next day the funeral services were held in the chapel, while the crowds outside gathered to pay their respects. Gray-clad cadets of the Virginia Military Institute at Lexington stand in the center. For Virginia and the South it is a farewell to their most memorable era, and to their greatest national hero. (WASHINGTON AND LEE UNIVERSITY)

There are more heroes left to die. On July 22, 1885, with two clouded terms as President and four years as one of the greatest generals of his age behind him, U. S. Grant is dying of cancer in a cottage at Mount McGregor, New York. He had just finished the heroic task of writing his memoirs against the most immutable deadline of all, his own death. (CHAPMAN R. GRANT)

The next day the general's chair was empty, draped in black. Another era ended.
(CHAPMAN R. GRANT)

"Little Aleck" Stephens, troublesome Vice President of the Confederacy, lived until 1883, unrepentant to the last, and uncompromising. (WA)

For Jefferson Davis, there was at least the small satisfaction of outliving all of the other major leaders of the war—Lincoln, Grant, Lee. Here he stands on the steps of his home Beauvoir in Mississippi. (TU)

He devoted the last years of his life to writing his history of the Confederacy, trying to win with the pen what he had lost by the sword. He, too, never fully admitted defeat or error and never entirely forgave his old foes. (CONFEDERATE RELIC ROOM AND MUSEUM, COLUMBIA, SOUTH CAROLINA)

Here in this study at Beauvoir Davis began the work of creating his version of the Lost Cause myth. Here he wrote his Rise and Fall of the Confederate Government, *his personal apologia and the first in the unending stream of works by former Confederates designed to prove that even if the South did not win the war, it should have done so. The echoes that began in this modest, book-lined room are sounding still. (LC)*

But he, too, had to answer the final call. In 1889, in New Orleans, the Confederacy's one and only President lay dead, and with him went much of the history and the enduring myth of the Lost Cause. (CONFEDERATE RELIC ROOM AND MUSEUM)

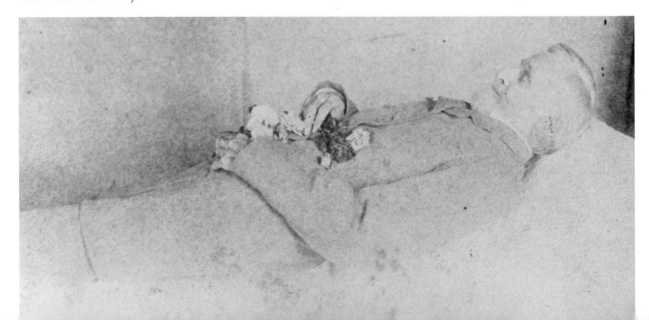

In 1876 trees and grass grew on the heights overlooking Fredericksburg, Virginia, where in 1862 they sprouted only guns. An image by Edward L. Wilson & W. Irving Adams. (DUKE UNIVERSITY LIBRARY, DURHAM, NORTH CAROLINA)

At Gettysburg, Pennsylvania, greatest battlefield of them all, the soldiers were laying cornerstones for monuments as early as July 4, 1865, when the 50th Pennsylvania Infantry gathered here for a dedication. At the end of that month they were mustered out of service. (OAKLAND MUSEUM, OAKLAND, CALIFORNIA)

As the years went on, the monuments and markers multiplied. By the 1880s Little Round Top already bristled with them. Gettysburg was on its way to becoming the best-marked battlefield in the world. (USAMHI)

The soldiers came back after the war to establish homes like this Gettysburg house, as orphanages for the children left behind by men who fell for the cause. Grant himself stands second from the right in this 1867 image. The Soldiers' Orphans Home at Gettysburg operated until 1887. (LC)

*Enterprising Southerners beat out their old adversaries in realizing the
tourist potential of the battlefields. It was late in 1865 when a Virginian
opened a small museum here at the Crater at Petersburg.* (TU)

*The Crater became a popular tourist attraction, each visitor paying
twenty-five cents to view the artifacts and look at the great hole made by the
Yankee mine in July 1864, during the siege. When this image was made in
1867, visitors were a daily occurrence.* (LEE A. WALLACE, JR.)

*For all of them, the men and generals and photographers and the people who
stayed at home and waited, it had been the most momentous experience of
their lives. Never again would they and their country endure such a trial,
and emerge so ennobled. They had lived the last days of American innocence.*
(KA)

The old soldiers themselves got older, the memories fading along with the old animosities. The veterans gathered in reunions, North and South, and even the once-maligned Negro soldiers were often welcome. Old Jefferson Shields was Confederate Major General Stonewall Jackson's wartime cook and now a frequent visitor at Stonewall Brigade reunions. This image was made around 1905, forty years after the war ended. (LEONARD L. TIMMONS)

As the parades went on year after year, there were fewer and fewer of the old heroes to fill the wagons. Here in 1913, fifty years after Gettysburg and Vicksburg, the old gentlemen are looking ever closer to the grave. (LEONARD L. TIMMONS)

Many of the soldiers had gone to war as beardless boys; they emerged as men, in a modern nation bright with promise for the future. Behind them now lay the hatreds, the blood . . . (HP)

. . . and the memories. (NA)

Abbreviations

AIG	Americana Image Gallery, Gettysburg, Pa.
CHS	Chicago Historical Society, Chicago, Ill.
CM	Confederate Museum, New Orleans, La.
CWTI	Civil War Times Illustrated Collection, Harrisburg, Pa.
DAM, LSU	Department of Archives and Manuscripts, Louisiana State University, Baton Rouge
HP	Herb Peck, Jr.
KA	Kean Archives, Philadelphia, Pa.
LC	Library of Congress, Washington, D.C.
LO	Lloyd Ostendorf Collection
MC	Museum of the Confederacy, Richmond, Va.
MHS	Minnesota Historical Society, St. Paul, Minn.
MJH	Michael J. Hammerson
MM	Mariners Museum, Newport News, Va.
NA	National Archives, Washington, D.C.
NHC	Naval Historical Center, Washington, D.C.
NYHS	New-York Historical Society, New York City
P-M	War Library and Museum, MOLLUS-Pennsylvania, Philadelphia
RJY	Robert J. Younger
SCL	South Caroliniana Library, University of South Carolina, Columbia
SHC	Southern Historical Collection, University of North Carolina, Chapel Hill
TU	Tulane University, New Orleans, La.
USAMHI	U.S. Army Military History Institute, Carlisle Barracks, Pa.
VM	Valentine Museum, Richmond, Va.
VHS	Vermont Historical Society, Montpelier
WA	William Albaugh Collection
WCD	William C. Davis
WG	William Gladstone Collection
WRHS	Western Reserve Historical Society, Cleveland, Ohio

The Contributors

RUSSELL F. WEIGLEY is one of America's most distinguished military historians. For over twenty years a professor at Temple University, in Philadelphia, he is the author of *Quartermaster General of the Union Army*, a biography of General Montgomery C. Meigs, *History of the United States Army*, and *Eisenhower's Lieutenants: The Campaign of France and Germany, 1944–1945,* among many other distinguished works.

CHARLES R. HABERLEIN, JR., has spent the past seventeen years as Photographic Curator and Historian at the Naval Historical Center in Washington, D.C., the nation's finest collection of naval illustrations. A contributor of articles to several publications in the field of naval history, he has also been of inestimable assistance with naval matters in the production of this series of volumes.

JOHN G. BARRETT has spent three decades on the faculty of the Virginia Military Institute at Lexington, is a Guggenheim Fellow, and is the author of several acclaimed Civil War books, including *Sherman's March Through the Carolinas; The Civil War in North Carolina; Letters of a New Market Cadet,* which he edited with Robert K. Turner, Jr.; and *North Carolina Civil War Documentary.*

RICHARD J. SOMMERS is one of the foremost authorities on the military aspects of the Civil War and has long been a contributor of articles to magazines and journals concerned with the period. He is

in addition the author of the acclaimed *Richmond Redeemed: The Siege at Petersburg* (1981), the winner of the first Bell I. Wiley Prize for distinguished research and writing in the field of the Civil War. He is currently Archivist at the U.S. Army Military History Institute, Carlisle Barracks, Pennsylvania.

EMORY M. THOMAS is professor of history at the University of Georgia and the author of a series of distinguished works in the Civil War field, including *The Confederate Nation; The Confederacy as a Revolutionary Experience;* and *The American War and Peace, 1860–1877.* He is the acknowledged authority on Richmond in the war and authored *The Confederate State of Richmond.* He is also a contributor to a previous volume in this series.

LOUIS MANARIN has long been associated with research and writing on the Confederacy and the Civil War. State archivist at the Virginia State Library in Richmond, he is the author of *Richmond Volunteers* and *The Bloody Sixth,* as well as editor of such works as *The Wartime Papers of R. E. Lee.* Among his most lasting contributions to Civil War scholarship is his editorship of the three-volume *North Carolina Troops 1861–1864: A Roster,* probably the finest work of its kind for any of the Confederate states.

WILLIAM C. DAVIS, who conceived and edited *The Image of War* series, is the author or editor of some fifteen books on the Civil War, including *Breckinridge: Statesman, Soldier, Symbol; The Orphan Brigade; Battle at Bull Run;* and a three-volume general narrative of the war titled *The Imperiled Union, 1861–1865.* For many years editor and publisher of *Civil War Times Illustrated* and other historical magazines, he currently devotes full time to his writing.

Index

This index covers all six volumes of *The Image of War 1861–1865*. **Roman numerals in boldface** indicate the volume to which reference is made. **Arabic boldface numbers** denote photographs of the subject mentioned. Commonly known abbreviations are used for frequently repeated terms—e.g., HQ for headquarters, POWs for prisoners of war, RR for railroad.

Conestoga, USS, **II**—260, **312**, **V**—**354**, 355
"Confederate coffee," **II**—175
Confederate Congress, **I**—167, 205, **II**—49, 277, 406; **IV**—134, 231, 243, 307, 361, **VI**—285, 293; move to Richmond, **I**—167, **VI**—280
Confederate Engineer Bureau, **IV**—190
Confederate Medical Department, **IV**—231, 243, 272
Confederate Navy, **I**—219, 220; Bureau of Ordnance and Hydrography, **II**—61; free blacks in, **IV**—362; officers as POWs, **IV**—**412**, **413**, 415; Rocketts Yard, **VI**—**293**, 318; ship-building program, **I**—221, 223–24, 232, **II**—49–50, 59–62, **80–85**, 265, 267, **IV**—134–37; warships bought in Europe, **I**—224, **II**—49, **IV**—134–35, 143–44, 148–49, 151, 159, 162, **V**—99, **VI**—388. *See also* Blockade runners; Commerce raiders; Naval operations; Navy Department (CSA)
Confederate Nitre and Mining Bureau, **III**—342, **VI**—300
Confederate States of America: created, **I**—27, **68**, **VI**—277; early high war spirit, **III**—332, 336, 338, 346, **VI**—282; later demoralization, **III**—349–50, **V**—71, **VI**—186; Richmond as capital of, **I**—167–68, **VI**—280–83, 290–91, 292–93
Confederate States Naval Academy, **I**—219, 238
Confederate States War Department, **I**—178, **II**—149, **III**—349, **VI**—286
Confederate Treasury, **VI**—**305**, 308, 340
Congaree River, **VI**—154, **174**
Congress, USS, **II**—50, **III**—111, 140, 141
Congress Hall (Philadelphia State House), **I**—15
Connecticut regiments: 1st Artillery, camp, **I**—146; 1st Heavy Artillery, **II**—47, 181–82, 224, **III**—264; 1st Heavy Artillery siege train, **II**—20; 3rd, **I**—195; 13th, Baton Rouge cemetery of, **IV**—132; 23rd, **IV**—449
Connor, James S., **II**—157
Connor, Patrick E., **V**—392
Conrad, the, **IV**—146
Conscription, **I**—364, 369, 395
Conspirators, Lincoln assassination, **VI**—**373**, 382; executions, **VI**—373, **378–81**; trial commission, **VI**—377, 378. *See also* Booth, John Wilkes
Constitution, USS, **I**—218, 222, 223, 232
Constitutional Union Party, **I**—24
Construction Corps. *See* U.S. Military Railroad Construction Corps
Continental Army, **II**—11
Continental Guard, **III**—377
Continental Iron Works, **II**—55, **74**
"Contraband" blacks, **II**—133, 309, **III**—201, 212–16, 372; Baton Rouge HQ of, **II**—**309**; Beaufort hospitals for, **II**—95, **III**—372; flocking to Union army, **III**—212, 215–18, 232, **VI**—130; origin of word, **III**—201
Contract laborers, importation of, **I**—369
Convalescent camps, **IV**—**265–66**

Cook, George S., **I**—10, 83, 90, 91, 348, 410, 413, **446**, **III**—207, **IV**—201, 202, 203, **VI**—10, 11
Cook, Philip, **V**—**232**, **VI**—**255**
Cooke, John R., **III**—**95**, 96
Cooke, Philip St. George, **II**—121, **IV**—304
Cook's galley, camp, **II**—**104**
Cooley, Samuel A., **I**—6, 11, 412, **442–44**, **452–53**, **II**—86, **87–88**, 246, **III**—219, 223, **IV**—15, 187, 198, 207, **V**—10, 144, **VI**—10, 45, 159; Beaufort gallery of, **I**—**443**, **II**—86, **87–88**; portfolio of photographs, **II**—**87–99**
Coonskin Tower (at Vicksburg), **IV**—**49**
Cooper, James H., **VI**—209
Cooper, Samuel, **V**—320
Cooper Iron Works (Cartersville, Ga.), **V**—**256**
Cooper River, **IV**—166
Cooper Union (New York City), **IV**—266
Coosaw Ferry (to Port Royal Island), **I**—251
Coppens, Gaston, **I**—345, **II**—168
Copperheads, **I**—395, 398
Corcoran, Michael, **I**—193, 213, **II**—223
Corcoran Legion (164th New York), **VI**—210
Cordes, Henry, **V**—291
"Corduroy" roads, **II**—185
Corinth, Miss., **I**—268–69, 270, 271, 275, 276, 319, **320–21**, 322–26, **327–28**, 412, **432**, **II**—263, **IV**—13; Dodge HQ in, **III**—**353**; fall of, **II**—272
Cornwallis, Lord Charles, **II**—11, 36, 46
"Cornwallis' Cave," **II**—**46**, 47
Corps d'Afrique, **III**—210–11, **238**
Corps hospitals, **IV**—238, 241
Corse, John M., **V**—**280**
Corse, Montgomery D., **VI**—**337**
Cosby, George B., **I**—298, **IV**—52
Cosmopolitan Company, **IV**—367
Cotton, **I**—36, 366, **II**—107, 109, **III**—203, 214, 227, 235; blockade running of, **III**—113–14; confiscations, **IV**—66, **V**—15, 150; Red River Campaign booty, **V**—346, 347, 350, 353; slave labor, **I**—34, 36–37, **III**—336; trade, **I**—33, **III**—335–36
Cotton gin, **I**—34, 37
Couch, Darius N., **III**—69, 74–75, 82, 304
Courts-martial, **II**—200, 251, **IV**—242–43
Covington, Ga., **VI**—148
Covington, USS, **V**—353, **375**
Cox, Jacob D., **V**—32–33, 34, **255**, 256
Cox's Landing, Va., POW exchange at, **IV**—**425**
C. P. Williams, USS, **II**—**282**
Crampton's Gap, Md., **III**—18, 19
Crane, Charles H., **IV**—251
Crater, Battle of the, **VI**—192, **240**, 241, **242**, 243–44; museum, **VI**—376, **445**
Craven, John J., **IV**—243
Craven, T.A.M., **VI**—90
Crawford, Samuel W., **I**—91, 92, 95, 106, 121, **II**—**364**, **III**—387, 388, 423
Crawford, Uriah, **V**—259
Creek Indians, **V**—391
Crews, Charles C., **IV**—331
Cricket, USS, **V**—352

"Crime Against Kansas" (Sumner), **I**—17, 41
Crimean War, **I**—347, 410, **IV**—232, 245, **VI**—10, 20, 22
Crittenden, George B., **I**—267, **290**
Crittenden, John J., **I**—25, 290
Crittenden, R. D., **IV**—414
Crittenden, Thomas L., **V**—17, 18, 21, 33
Crittenden Compromise, **I**—25
Croaton Sound, **III**—115, 117
Crocker, Marcellus, **IV**—42
Crockett, David, **I**—284
Crook, George, **I**—73, **IV**—336, 345, **V**—303–4, **309**, 315
Cross, Edward, **III**—387, 420
Cross Keys, Battle of, **II**—334–35, **344**, 345, 346
Croucher, J. H., **IV**—9
"Crowd poisoning," **IV**—245
Crow's Nest signal tower, **VI**—**222**, **236**, 237
Crow Valley, **V**—241
Crump, Billy, **II**—216
Cuba, **III**—132, 173, **IV**—160; Southern exiles in, **VI**—386, **391**
Cuba, the. *See Lady Sterling*
Cub Run, Va., **I**—172, 205
Culpeper, Va., **II**—350, 352, **III**—217, **342–44**, 352, 381, 383, **IV**—309; Army of the Potomac at (1864), **V**—173, **176**, 180; Meade HQ at, **III**—352, **383**, **IV**—**92–93**; railroad depot at, **II**—**351**, 438
Culpeper Court House, **II**—113, **365**, **III**—66; Confederate POWs at, **II**—365
Culpeper Mine Road, **V**—175
Culp's Hill fight (Battle of Gettysburg), **III**—386, 388, 389, **424–25**, 428
Cumberland, Md., **IV**—345; railroad-canal junction at, **II**—414
Cumberland, USS, **I**—223, **II**—50, **III**—102, 110, 120, 140, **VI**—89, 107
Cumberland & Pennsylvania RR, **II**—414
Cumberland Coal & Iron Co. yard, **VI**—49
Cumberland Gap, Tenn., **I**—276, **V**—19; Federal capture of, **V**—19, 27
Cumberland Landing, Va., **II**—116, **III**—215; Army of the Potomac at, **II**—**120–25**
Cumberland River, **I**—267–68, 291, **IV**—312, **V**—38; fortified bridge on, **II**—411
Cumberland Sound, **V**—106
Cumming, Kate, **III**—349
Cummings, A. Boyd, **IV**—64
Cummings' farm (near Petersburg), **VI**—184
Cummings Point, S.C., **IV**—166, 170, 172, 176
Curtin, Andrew, **I**—376
Curtis, Edward, **IV**—251
Curtis, Samuel, **V**—378, **414**, 415
Cushing, Alonzo, **III**—168, 392
Cushing, William B., **II**—81, **III**—159, 160, **167**, 168
Cushman, Pauline, **I**—407, **VI**—431
Custer, George Armstrong, **II**—152, **III**—62, 440, **IV**—309, 311, 313, **323**,

Hardee, William J. (*cont'd*)
  Campaign, **V**—240, 243, 248, 249, 252,
  289; in Carolinas Campaign,
  VI—158–59; at Savannah, **VI**—149–50
Hardee's Tactics, **I**—127, 340
Hardeman, William P., **V**—439, **VI**—423
Hardin, Martin D., **III**—255
Harding, William, **IV**—357
Harding Pike, **V**—38
Hardtack, **II**—175, **202**, **208**, 209, 211,
  IV—279
Hard Times, La., **IV**—19
Harewood Hospital (Washington, D.C.),
  IV—248, 260; mess room, **IV**—264
Harney, William S., **VI**—430
Harper, R. H., **III**—124
Harper House (Slocum HQ), **VI**—178
Harpers Ferry, Va., **I**—44–45, **II**—322,
  332–34, 340, 360, **III**—16, 18, 19–20,
  21, **26**, 27, 34, **IV**—282, 290, **V**—303,
  304–5; destruction of 1862, **II**—334,
  III—19–20; Jefferson Rock, **I**—428;
  John Brown's raid at, **I**—22, 44–48,
  II—340, **VI**—362; U.S. Arsenal ruins
  at, **I**—424, **II**—333, **V**—304
Harper's Weekly, **I**—346, 411, **II**—105,
  187, **III**—127, **IV**—24, 118
Harriet Lane, USS, **I**—223, **III**—110
Harris, D. B., **IV**—170, **190**
Harris, Mathias, **I**—80
Harris, Nathaniel H., **VI**—196, **263**
Harris, Thomas M., **VI**—377
Harrisburg, Pa., **III**—13, 382; Lincoln
  funeral train at, **VI**—370
Harris farm (at Spotsylvania), **V**—181,
  187
Harrison, Benjamin, **VI**—177
Harrison, Napoleon B., **II**—282
Harrisonburg, Va., **II**—327, 328, 334
Harrison's Landing, Va., **II**—119, 121,
  122–23, 172, 348, 392
Harrodsburg, Ky., **I**—276
Harrolson, John, **III**—341
Harrow, William, **III**—47
Hart, O. H., **IV**—286
Hartford, USS, **I**—225, 272, **II**—268–69,
  284–86, 311, **313**, **IV**—60, 64, **VI**—86,
  88–90, **91–92**, 94, **101–2**, 103, **120**,
  434
Hartranft, John, **VI**—195, **378**
Hartsuff, George L., **III**—34
Hatch, John P., **II**—343, **IV**—176, **227**,
  229
Hatcher's Run, Va., **III**—212, **VI**—188,
  194, 195, 252, 257–58
Hathaway's Wharf, San Francisco,
  V—398
Hatteras. *See* Cape Hatteras
Hatteras, USS, **IV**—142
Hatteras Inlet ("The Swash"), **III**—110,
  115, 117, 129
Haupt, Herman, **II**—401, 405, 406, 412,
  415, 416, 417, 418, 420, 433, 442,
  III—322, **326**, **IV**—11, 12, **VI**—20–21;
  bridge designs of, **II**—421–32
Havana, Cuba, **III**—132, **V**—160;
  Federal patrol of, **III**—173; Southern
  exiles in, **VI**—386, **391**
Hawes, Richard C., **I**—275
Hawk, Harry, **VI**—364, 368
Hawkins, John P., **II**—195
Hawkins, Rush, **III**—18, 99

Hawkins farm ("Orange Turnpike),
  V—190
Hawkins's Zouaves, **III**—18, **99**. *See
  also* 9th New York
Hawks, Wells J., **II**—323
Haw's Shop, Va., **V**—185
Hay, John, **II**—290
Hayes, Rutherford B., **II**—216, **V**—334,
  VI—408; 1876 election, **VI**—387
Hayes (E.) & Co. ambulance wagon,
  VI—84
Hayne, Paul Hamilton, **III**—339
Haynes' Bluff (Yazoo River), Federal
  landing at, **IV**—19, 28
Haynsworth, George E., **I**—80
Hays, Alexander, **III**—390, **434**, **V**—189
Hays, Harry T., **III**—389, **V**—202
Hazel Grove, Va., **III**—301–4
Hazel River, **II**—367, **IV**—280; pontoon
  bridge, **IV**—107
Hazel Run, **III**—71
Hazen, William B., **VI**—149–50
Head, Truman ("California Joe"),
  IV—97
Head of the Passes, **II**—264, 266, 268;
  naval battle at, **II**—257–58
Hébert, Paul O., **V**—432
Hecksher, John G., **II**—236
Heffelfinger, Jacob, **IV**—109
Heiman, Adolphus, **I**—298
Heintzelman, Samuel P., **I**—192, 204,
  214, 418, **II**—17, 117, 143, **III**—285; at
  Second Bull Run, **II**—351, 353, 354,
  359, **388**; after the war, **VI**—411, **433**
Helena, Ark., **V**—415
Helm, Ben Hardin, **V**—20, **28**
Helm, W. W., **IV**—414
Hendershot, Robert H., **V**—237
Henderson, the, **I**—280
Henry, E. E., **V**—12, 340, 422
Henry, Judith, **I**—200, **II**—386
Henry, Patrick, **VI**—288
Henry Hill, Va.: Civil War monument,
  VI—410–11; in First Bull Run,
  I—196–97, 199, **200**, 201; in Second
  Bull Run, **II**—360, 381
Henry House, **I**—172, **II**—360; ruins,
  I—200, **II**—386
Henry's repeating carbine, **VI**—64–65
Herbert, Arthur, **VI**—262
Herold, David, **VI**—378–81
Herrick, H. J., **I**—32
Herron, Francis J., **IV**—48, **V**—417
Hesler, Alexander, **I**—64
Hesseltine, Col. and Mrs. Francis,
  II—281
Heth, Henry, **III**—383, 384, 390, **393**,
  396, 397, **V**—**237**, **V**—194
Hewitt, John Hill, **III**—341
Hiawassee bridge blockhouse, **II**—410
Hibernian Hall (Charleston, S.C.),
  IV—219
Hickok, William ("Wild Bill"), **V**—383,
  VI—389
Hicks, David, **V**—205
Higginson, Thomas Wentworth,
  III—209, 210
High Bridge, Va., **VI**—338, **339**, 340
Hill, Ambrose Powell, **I**—74, **II**—158,
  III—301, 310, **397**, **V**—174, 175, 183,
  VI—191, **263**, 327; death of, **VI**—196,
  263; at Gettysburg, **III**—381, 383,

385, 388, 394, 397, 401, 404, 432; at
  Harpers Ferry, **III**—20, 34–35; at
  Mechanicsville and Gaines's Mill,
  II—119, 120, 122, 158, 159; at Second
  Bull Run, **II**—349, 350, 358, 359, 385
Hill, Daniel Harvey, **II**—11, 37, 48,
  III—16, 17, 343, **V**—17, **28**, **VI**—169;
  at Antietam, **III**—24, 27, 30, 32, 33;
  at South Mountain, **III**—18, 19, 20–21
Hill, James J., **I**—370
Hillsboro Pike, **V**—38, 39
Hillsborough, N.C., **VI**—337
Hilton Head, S.C., **I**—255–58, 261, 412,
  II—86, **100–11**, 196, **III**—243,
  IV—167, 382, **V**—10, 101; Commissary
  Store House, **I**—444; Drayton's
  plantation, **III**—206; Elliott planta-
  tion, **IV**—283; Federal capture of,
  IV—167, **V**—103; Fellows HQ at,
  I—108–9; graves, **I**—262, **II**—110;
  Hunter's HQ at, **II**—99; "Merchant
  Row," **IV**—168; ordnance yard,
  II—101, **IV**—208; Pope plantation at,
  I—35; Port Royal House, **IV**—169;
  "Robbers Row," **I**—442; Seabrook
  plantation at, **II**—107–10; Sherman
  (T. W.) HQ at, **II**—239; signal sta-
  tions, **II**—101–2; slaughterhouse,
  VI—46; 3rd New Hampshire at,
  I—441, **II**—103–7; war supplies at,
  II—99–101, **VI**—15; wharf at, **I**—255,
  II—100; workshops and barracks,
  I—260. *See also* Bay Point, S.C.; Fort
  Walker
Hindman, Thomas C., **V**—17, 415, 416,
  417, **VI**—423
Hippisley, H. M., **II**—28
Hitchcock, Ethan Allen, **IV**—401, **429**
H. L. Hunley, the, **V**—150
Hodges (Brady assistant), **I**—423
Hodgson, Joseph, **III**—341
Hoffman, Henry, **II**—178
Hoffman, William H., **IV**—397–99, 400,
  401, 402, **406**, 411, 415–17, 444
Hoffman's Battalion, **IV**—400, **416**
Hoke, Robert F., **III**—327, **VI**—179, 180
Holiday celebrations, soldiers', **II**—192,
  252–54, **IV**—264
Hollins, George N., **I**—234, **II**—257, 258,
  259, 260, 267
Hollow Tree Gap, Tenn., **V**—41
Holly Springs, Miss., **I**—361, **IV**—20,
  VI—420
Holmes, Oliver Wendell, Jr., **V**—309
Holmes, Silas, **I**—423
Holmes, Theophilus H., **V**—441
Holston River, **V**—76, **77–79**, 81; rail-
  road bridge, **IV**—354, **V**—75
Holt, Joseph, **I**—50, **VI**—377
Homecomings, **I**—212, **388–90**, **VI**—145,
  375–76, **406–8**
Honey Springs, Okla., **III**—211
Hood, John Bell, **II**—390, **III**—9, 27,
  35, **43**, **90**, 338, 415, **IV**—339, **V**—20,
  83, 240, **266**, **VI**—17; Atlanta Cam-
  paign, **V**—240, 243, 244, 248–52,
  266–67, 274; at Gettysburg, **III**—387,
  415; invasion of Tennessee (1864),
  V—30–41, 83, 84, 89, 93, 95–98,
  VI—148, 151; Johnston replaced by,
  V—247–48, 266
Hooker, Joseph ("Fighting Joe"),

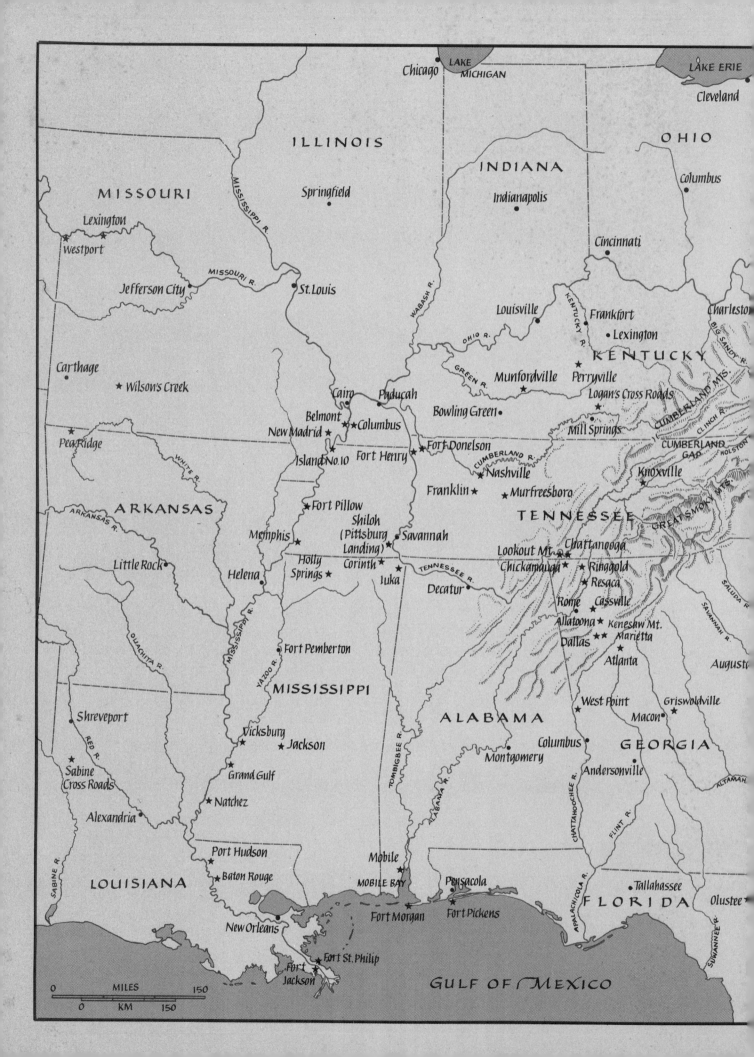